THE BATTLE FOR KHE SANH

By

Captain Moyers S. Shore II, USMC

PCN 19000411000

HISTORY AND MUSEUMS DIVISION

HEADQUARTERS, U. S. MARINE CORPS

WASHINGTON, D. C.

Printed 1969

Reprinted 1977

CHINA

NORTH
VIETNAM

LAOS

*GULF
OF
TONKIN*

17°   17°

★KHE SANH

THAILAND

ICTZ

IICTZ

SOUTH
VIETNAM

CAMBODIA

*GULF
OF
SIAM*

↑
N

IIICTZ

SEA

IVCTZ

SOUTH   *CHINA*

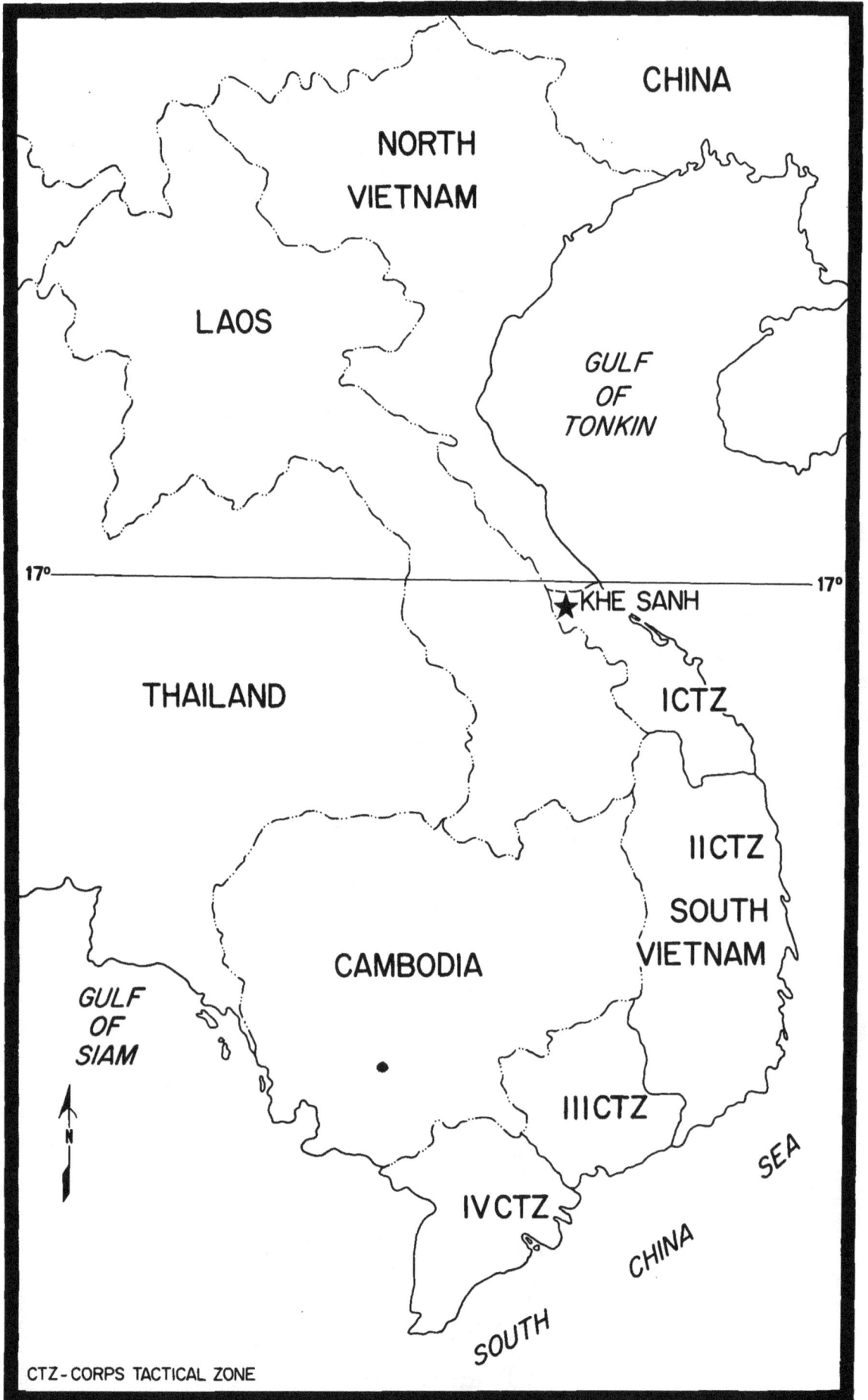

CTZ-CORPS TACTICAL ZONE

K.W.White

SOUTHEAST ASIA

Oblique aerial photograph of the Khe Sanh Combat Base

(United Press International Photo by Kyoichi Sawada)

PROLOGUE

It is with pleasure that the Marine Corps presents this account of the Battle for Khe Sanh which stands as one of the most crucial and bitterly contested struggles in the Vietnam War. Throughout the existence of our Corps, thousands of men have been called upon to further the cause of freedom on scores of battlefields around the globe. At Khe Sanh, a new generation of Marines, aided by their gallant U. S. Army, Navy, Air Force, and South Vietnamese counterparts, admirably upheld this tradition and wrote a thrilling new chapter in the history of armed conflict.

The two senior U. S. commanders in Vietnam who supervised the defense--General William C. Westmoreland, USA, and Lieutenant General Robert E. Cushman, Jr., USMC--have contributed immeasurably to the production of this work and have also provided their astute summaries of the operation which appear in the following pages. I heartily endorse their statements as well as the approach and conclusions of this history.

In addition, I am grateful to the individuals and agencies of all the Services who have provided valuable assistance through written comments and personal interviews which are reflected in the text. In particular, I wish to extend our appreciation to Mr. David D. Duncan, a veteran combat photographer who has graciously consented to our use of the brilliant pictures he took during an eight-day visit to the combat base. These truly professional shots graphically depict the face of the siege and enhance the narrative.

The sum total of these contributions, I feel, is an objective, readable account of this important battle which honors the valiant American and South Vietnamese troops who held Khe Sanh. I can think of no more fitting tribute to these men--both living and dead--than to simply relate the events as they happened. This, then, is their story.

L. F. CHAPMAN, JR.
General, U.S. Marine Corps
Commandant of the Marine Corps

REVIEWED AND APPROVED 28 May 1969

FOREWORD

As the commander of the United States Military Assistance Command, Vietnam, during the battle of Khe Sanh, I welcome publication by the U. S. Marine Corps of this historical study. The Marines' heroic defense of the Khe Sanh area against numerically superior North Vietnamese forces stands out among the many battles fought to defend the Republic of Vietnam against Communist aggression.

The enemy's primary objective of his 1968 TET Offensive was to seize power in South Vietnam by creating a general uprising and causing the defection of major elements of the Armed Forces of the Republic of Vietnam. In conjunction with this, the enemy apparently expected to seize by military action large portions of the northern two provinces lying just south of the Demilitarized Zone and there to set up a "liberation government." The virtually unpopulated Khe Sanh Plateau, which lay astride the enemy's principal avenue of approach from his large base areas in Laos, was obviously an initial objective of the North Vietnamese Army. Its seizure would have created a serious threat to our forces defending the northern area and would have cleared the way for the enemy's advance to Quang Tri City and the heavily populated coastal region. There is also little doubt that the enemy hoped at Khe Sanh to attain a climactic victory, such as he had done in 1954 at Dien Bien Phu, in the expectation that this would produce a psychological shock and erode American morale.

My subordinate commanders and I were particularly sensitive to heavy fighting in the populated areas, since this would result in substantial destruction to the towns and villages and cause unnecessary suffering by the civilian population. We wanted to avoid this situation to the greatest extent possible by denying the enemy freedom of movement through the Khe Sanh area and into the coastal region. At that time we did not have sufficient troops, helicopters, or logistical support in the northern provinces to accomplish this entirely through mobile operations, and competing requirements for troops and resources did not permit immediate reinforcement from other areas of South Vietnam. The situation was further complicated by long periods of fog and low cloud ceilings during January, February, and March, which made helicopter operations difficult and hazardous.

To maintain our presence on the Khe Sanh Plateau, our only choice at the time was to secure the airstrip we had built on the plateau since this facility was essential as the forward terminus of our supply line. From here we could maintain our military presence in the area and, through the use of our firepower, make it costly for large enemy forces to advance while we awaited the end of the bad weather of the northeast monsoon and constituted the forces and logistics necessary to strike out on offensive operations.

Another factor favoring the decision to hold Khe Sanh was the enemy's determination to take it. Our defense of the area would tie down large numbers of North Vietnamese troops which otherwise could move against the vulnerable populated areas whose security was the heart of the Vietnamese pacification program. Our decision to defend also held the prospect of causing the enemy to concentrate his force and thereby provide us a singular opportunity to bring our firepower to bear on him with minimum restrictions. Had we withdrawn to fight the enemy's force of over two divisions in the heavily populated coastal area, the use of our firepower would have been severely restricted because of our precautionary measures to avoid civilian casualties and minimize damage to civilian property.

Based on my decision to hold the Khe Sanh Plateau, Lieutenant General Cushman's and Lieutenant General Lam's first task was to reinforce the area with sufficient strength to prevent the enemy from overrunning it, but at the same time to commit no more force than could be supplied by air. While the battle of Khe Sanh was being fought, emphasis was placed on the buildup in the northern provinces of the necessary troops, helicopters, and logistic support for mobile offensive operations to open Highway 9 and move onto the plateau when the weather cleared at the end of March.

This report provides a detailed and graphic account of events as they unfolded. It centers about the 26th Marine Regiment, the main defenders of the Khe Sanh area, who tenaciously and magnificently held off the enemy during the two-and-one-half-month siege. Yet the battle of Khe Sanh was an inter-Service and international operation. Consequently, appropriate coverage is given to the contributions of the U. S. Army, Navy, and Air Force, and to South Vietnamese regular and irregular military units, all of whom contributed to the defense of the area and to the destruction of the enemy. As Marine artillery from within the fortified positions pounded the enemy, Army

artillery located to the east provided heavy, long-range fire
support. Fighter aircraft from the Marines, Air Force, and
Navy provided continuous close air support, while B-52 bombers
of the Strategic Air Command dealt decisive blows around-the-
clock to enemy forces within striking distance of our positions
and against enemy supply areas. Further, Marine and Air Force
airlift together with Army parachute riggers logistically sustained the defenders during the siege despite heavy enemy
antiaircraft fire.

In early April, when the weather cleared and the troop and
logistic buildup was completed, a combined force of U. S. Army
U. S. Marine, and Republic of Vietnam units, coordinated by the
U. S. Army's 1st Cavalry Division (Airmobile), maneuvered to
link up with the 26th Marines and rout the remaining enemy
elements. Meanwhile, U. S. Marine Corps engineers expe-
ditiously opened Highway 9 to the plateau. The crushing defeat suffered by the North Vietnamese Army during the siege
cost the Communists untold casualties, shattered two of their
best divisions, and frustrated their dream of a second Dien
Bien Phu.

The battle of Khe Sanh is but one facet of the long and
complicated war in South Vietnam. It is one in which the
aggressive nature of North Vietnam, the resolute determination
of our fighting forces, and the local defeat of the armed enemy
can all be clearly seen.

W. C. WESTMORELAND
General, United States Army

PREFACE

In the extreme northwestern corner of South Vietnam there stands a monument to the free world. Unlike those which commemorate the victories of past wars, this one was not built on marble or bronze but the sacrifies of men who fought and died at a remote outpost to halt the spread of Communism. This is the story of those men--the defenders of Khe Sanh--and the epic 77-day struggle which not only denied the North Vietnamese Army a much needed victory but reaffirmed to the world the intention of the United States to hold the line in Southeast Asia. In addition to having been a contest of men and machines, this was the test of a nation's will.

As a history, this work is not intended to prove any point, but rather to record objectively the series of events which came to be called the Battle of Khe Sanh. These events spanned a period from April 1967 to April 1968. The rationale for the buildup along the Demilitarized Zone and the commitment to hold the small garrison is presented as a logical extension of the three-pronged strategy then employed throughout I Corps and the rest of South Vietnam; this balanced campaign included pacification programs, counterguerrilla activity, and large unit offensive sweeps. Although isolated, the Khe Sanh Combat Base was a vital link in the northern defenses which screened the Allied counterinsurgency efforts in the densely populated coastal plains from invasion by regular divisions from North Vietnam. P obstructing this attempted invasion, American and South Vie amese forces at Khe Sanh provided a shield for their contemporaries who were waging a war for the hearts and minds of the people in the cities, villages, and hamlets farther to the south. In the process, a reinforced regiment--the 26th Marines--supported by massive firepower provided by the Marine and Navy air arms, the U. S. Air Force and Marine and Army artillery, defended this base and mangled two crack North Vietnamese Army divisions, further illustrating to Hanoi the futility of its war of aggression.

Later, after the encirclement was broken and additional U.S. forces became available, the Allies were able to shift emphasis from the fixed defense to fast-moving offensive operations to control this vital area astride the enemy's invasion route. In these operations, our troops thrust out to strike the enemy whenever he appeared in this critical region. This shift in tactics in the spring of 1968 was made possible by favorable weather, the buildup of troops, helicopters, and logistics that had taken place during the winter of 1967-68. An additional factor was the construction of a secure forward base across the mountains to the east of Khe Sanh, from which these operations could be supported. The Khe Sanh Combat Base then lost the importance it had earlier and was dismantled after its supplies were drawn down, since it was no longer needed. The strategy of containing the North Vietnamese Army along the border remained the same; but revised tactics were now possible.

But in 1967 and early 1968, neither troops nor helicopters, logistics nor the forward base were available to support the more aggressive tactics. The enemy lunged into the area in force, and he had to be stopped. The KSCB with its airstrip was the pivotal point in the area from which Allied firepower could be directed and which the enemy could not ignore. It was here that the 26th Marines made their stand.

This study also provides insight into the mechanics of the battle from the highest echelon of command to the smallest unit. In addition, appropriate coverage is provided to the supporting arms and the mammoth logistics effort which spelled the difference between victory and defeat. While this is basically a story about Marines, it notes the valiant contributions of U. S. Army, Navy, and Air Force personnel, as well as the South Vietnamese.

The account is based on records of the U. S. Marine Corps, selected records of other Services, and appropriate published works. The comments of and interviews with key participants have been incorporated into the text. Although this monograph has been cleared for publication by the Department of Defense, most of the documents cited retain a security classification.

R. E. CUSHMAN, JR.
Lieutenant General, U. S. Marine Corps
Commanding General, III Marine Amphibious Force

TABLE OF CONTENTS

The Battle for Khe Sanh

by

Captain Moyers S. Shore II, USMC

INTRODUCTION

"Attention to Colors." The order having been given,
Captain William H. Dabney, a product of the Virginia Military
Institute, snapped to attention, faced the jerry-rigged flag-
pole, and saluted, as did every other man in Company I, 3d
Battalion, 26th Marines. The ceremony might well have been at
any one of a hundred military installations around the world
except for a few glaring irregularities. The parade ground was
a battle-scarred hilltop to the west of Khe Sanh and the men
in the formation stood half submerged in trenches or foxholes.
Instead of crisply starched utilities, razor sharp creases, and
gleaming brass, these Marines sported scraggly beards, ragged
trousers, and rotted helmet liner straps. The only man in the
company who could play a bugle, Second Lieutenant Owen S.
Matthews, lifted the pock-marked instrument to his lips and
spat out a choppy version of "To the Colors" while two enlisted
men raced to the RC-292 radio antenna which served as the flag-
pole and gingerly attached the Stars and Stripes. As the mast
with its shredded banner came upright, the Marines could hear
the ominous "thunk," "thunk," "thunk," to the southwest of their
position which meant that North Vietnamese 120mm mortar rounds
had left their tubes. They also knew that in 21 seconds those
"thunks" would be replaced by much louder, closer sounds but no
one budged until Old Glory waved high over the hill.

When Lieutenant Matthews sharply cut off the last note of
his piece, Company I disappeared; men dropped into trenches,
dived headlong into foxholes, or scrambled into bunkers. The
area which moments before had been bristling with humanity was
suddenly a ghost town. Seconds later explosions walked across
the hilltop spewing black smoke, dirt, and debris into the air.
Rocks, splinters, and spent shell fragments rained on the
flattened Marines but, as usual, no one was hurt. As quickly
as the attack came, it was over. While the smoke lazily drifted
away, a much smaller banner rose from the Marines' positions.
A pole adorned with a pair of red, silk panties--Maggie's Drawers

1

--was waved back and forth above one trenchline to inform the enemy that he had missed again. A few men stood up and jeered or cursed at the distant gunners; others simply saluted with an appropriate obscene gesture. The daily flag-raising ceremony on Hill 881 South was over.

This episode was just one obscure incident which coupled with hundreds of others made up the battle for Khe Sanh. The ceremony carried with it no particular political overtones but was intended solely as an open show of defiance toward the Communists as well as a morale booster for the troops. The jaunty courage, quiet determination, and macabre humor of the men on Hill 881S exemplified the spirit of the U. S. and South Vietnamese defenders who not only defied the enemy but, in a classic 77-day struggle, destroyed him. At the same time, the fighting around the isolated combat base touched off a passionate controversy in the United States and the battle, therefore, warrants close scrutiny. For proper prospective, however, one first needs to have a basic understanding of the series of events which thrust Khe Sanh into the limelight. In effect, the destiny of the combatants was unknowingly determined almost three years earlier at a place called Red Beach near Da Nang.

PART I

BACKGROUND

When the lead elements of the 9th Marine Expeditionary
Brigade,commanded by Brigadier General Frederick J. Karch,
slogged ashore at Da Nang on 8 March 1965, Communist political
and military aspirations in South Vietnam received a severe
jolt. The buildup of organized American combat units had begun. In May 1965, the 9th MEB was succeeded by the III Marine
Amphibious Force (III MAF) which was comprised of the 3d Marine
Division, the 1st Marine Aircraft Wing, and, within a year,
the 1st Marine Division. The Commanding General, III MAF was
given responsibility for U. S. operations in I Corps Tactical
Zone which incorporated the five northern provinces and, on 5
June 1965, Major General Lewis W. Walt assumed that role. (See
Map 1). Major units of the U. S. Army moved into other portions
of South Vietnam and the entire American effort came under the
control of the Commander, U. S. Military Assistance Command,
Vietnam (ComUSMACV), General William C. Westmoreland.(1)

The Marines, in conjunction with the Army of the Republic
of Vietnam (ARVN), set about to wrest control of the populace
in I Corps from the Viet Cong and help reassert the authority
of the central government. The Allies launched an aggressive
campaign designed to root out the enemy's source of strength--
the local guerrilla. Allied battalion- and regimental-sized
units screened this effort by seeking out and engaging Viet Cong
main forces and North Vietnamese Army (NVA) elements. Smaller
Marine and ARVN units went after the isolated guerrilla bands
which preyed on the Vietnamese peasants. Thousands of fire
team-, squad-, and platoon-sized actions took a heavy toll of
the enemy and the Viet Cong were gradually pushed out of the
populated areas. Whenever a village or hamlet was secured,
civic action teams moved in to fill the vacuum and began the
long, tedious process of erasing the effects of prolonged
Communist domination. Progress was slow. Within a year, however, the area under Government security had grown to more than
1,600 square miles and encompassed nearly half a million people.
As government influence extended deeper into the countryside,
the security, health, economic well-being, and educational
prospects of the peasants were constantly improved. There was
an ever increasing number of enemy defectors and intelligence
reports from, heretofore, unsympathetic villagers. By mid-1966,

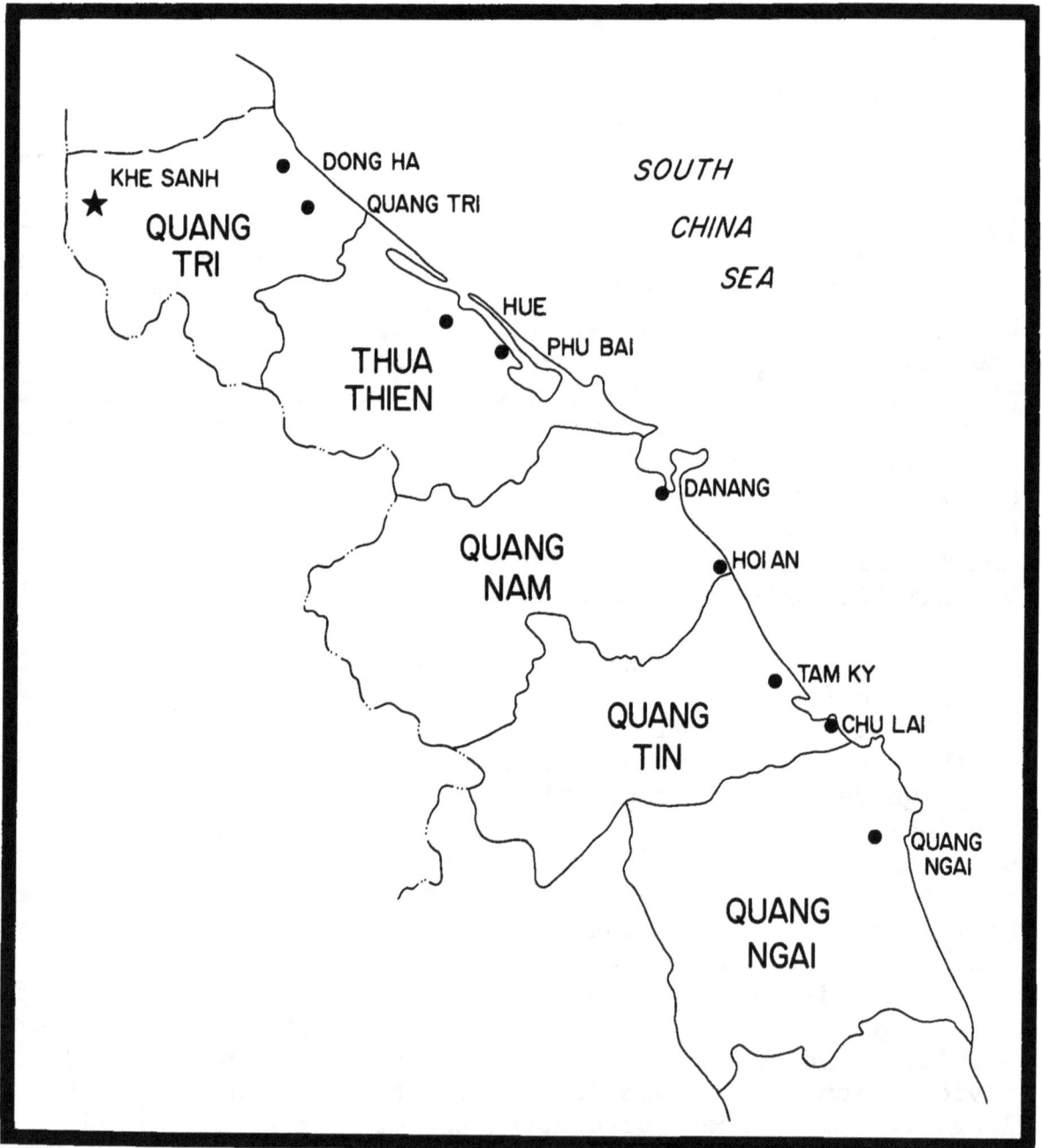

KHE SANH

DONG HA
QUANG TRI

QUANG
TRI

SOUTH

CHINA

SEA

THUA
THIEN

HUE

PHU BAI

DANANG

QUANG
NAM

HOI AN

TAM KY

QUANG
TIN

CHU LAI

QUANG
NGAI

QUANG
NGAI

MAPI

K.W.White

I CORPS TACTICAL ZONE

Allied military operations and pacification programs were slowly but seriously eroding the enemy's elaborate infrastructure and his hold over the people.(2)

It soon became apparent to the leaders in the North that, unless they took some bold action, ten years of preparation and their master plan for conquest of South Vietnam would go down the drain. From the Communists' standpoint, the crucial matter was not the volume of casualties they sustained, but the survival of the guerrilla infrastructure in South Vietnam. In spite of their disregard for human life, the North Vietnamese did not wish to counter the American military steamroller in the populated coastal plain of I Corps. There, the relatively open terrain favored the overwhelming power of the Marines' supporting arms. The enemy troops would have extended supply lines, their movement could be more easily detected, and they would be further away from sanctuaries in Laos and North Vietnam. In addition, when the propaganda-conscious NVA suffered a defeat, it would be witnessed by the local populace and thus shatter the myth of Communist invincibility.

If the Marines could not be smashed, and the Communists had tried several times, they had to be diverted or thinned out. The answer to the enemy's dilemma lay along the 17th Parallel. Gradually, they massed large troop concentrations within the Demilitarized Zone (DMZ), in Laos, and in the southern panhandle of North Vietnam; in short, they were opening a new front. Nguyen Van Mai, a high Communist official in Phnom Penh, Cambodia, predicted: "We will entice the Americans closer to the North Vietnamese border and...bleed them without mercy." That remained to be seen.(3)

In response to the enemy buildup along the DMZ throughout the summer and fall of 1966, General Walt shifted Marine units further north. The 3d Marine Division Headquarters moved from Da Nang to Phu Bai, and a Division Forward Command Post (CP) continued to Dong Ha so that it could respond rapidly to developments along the DMZ. In turn the 1st Marine Division Headquarters moved from Chu Lai to Da Nang and took control of operations in central and southern I Corps. For specific, short-term operations, the division commanders frequently delegated authority to a task force headquarters. The task force was a semipermanent organization composed of temporarily assigned units under one commander, usually a general officer. Because of the fluid, fast-moving type of warfare peculiar to Vietnam, the individual battalion became a key element and went where it was needed the most. It might operate under a task force headquarters or a regiment other than its own parent unit. For example, it would not be uncommon for the 2d Battalion, 9th Marines to be attached to the 3d Marines while the 2d Battalion, 3d Marines was a part of another command. Commitments were met with units that were the most readily available at the time.(4)

With the buildup of American troops in Quang Tri province, there logically followed the buildup of installations. Dong Ha was the largest since it served as the brain and nervous system of the entire area. Eight miles to the southwest was Camp J. J. Carroll, a large artillery base. The Marine units there were reinforced by several batteries of U. S. Army 175mm guns which had the capability of firing into North Vietnam. Located at the base of a jagged mountain ten miles west of Camp Carroll was another artillery base--the Rockpile. This facility also had 175mm guns and extended the range of American artillery support almost to the Laotian border. In addition, the Marines built a series of strongpoints paralleling and just south of the DMZ. Gio Linh and Con Thien were the two largest sites. (See Map 2).

During the remainder of 1966 and in the first quarter of 1967, the intensity of fighting in the eastern DMZ area increased. Each time the enemy troops made a foray across the DMZ, the Marines met and defeated them. By 31 March 1967, the NVA had lost 3,492 confirmed killed in action (KIA) in the northern operations while the Marines had suffered 541 killed. For the Communists, it appeared that direct assaults across the DMZ were proving too costly--even by their standards.(5)

The Khe Sanh Plateau, in western Quang Tri Province, provided the NVA with an excellent alternative. The late Doctor Bernard B. Fall compared the whole of Vietnam to "two rice baskets on opposite ends of a carrying pole." Such being the case, Khe Sanh is located at the pole's fulcrum in the heart of the rugged Annamite Range. Studded with piedmont-type hills, this area provides a natural infiltration route. Most of the mountain trails are hidden by tree canopies up to 60 feet in height, dense elephant grass, and bamboo thickets. Concealment from reconnaissance aircraft is good, and the heavy jungle undergrowth limits ground observation to five meters in most places. Dong Tri Mountain (1,015 meters high), the highest peak in the region, along with Hill 861 and Hills 881 North and South dominate the two main avenues of approach.(*) One of these,

---

(*) The number indicates the height of the hill in meters.

6

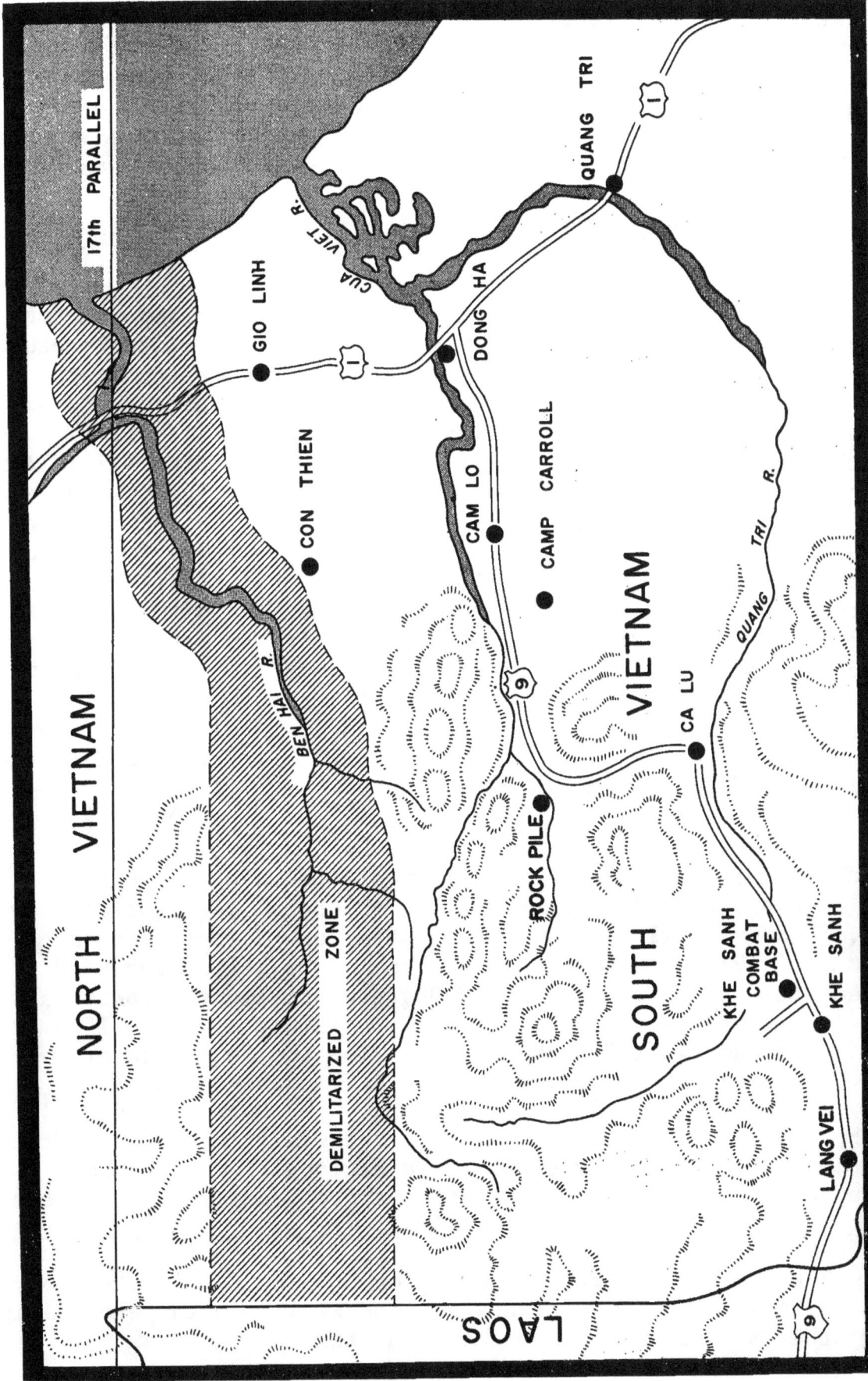

NORTHERN QUANG TRI PROVINCE

E.L. WILSON

MAP 2

7

the western access, runs along Route 9 from the Laotian border, through the village of Lang Vei to Khe Sanh. The other is a small valley to the northwest, formed by the Rao Quan River, which runs between Dong Tri Mountain and Hill 861. (See Map 3). Another key terrain feature is Hill 558 which is located squarely in the center of the northwestern approach. The only stumbling block to the NVA in early 1967 was a handful of Marines, U. S. Army Special Forces advisors, and South Vietnamese irregulars. (6) (See Map 3).

The "Green Berets" were the first American troops in the area when, in August 1962, they established a Civilian Irregular Defense Group (CIDG) at the same site which later became the Khe Sanh Combat Base (KSCB). The first Marine unit of any size to visit the area was the 1st Battalion, 1st Marines (1/1) which, in April 1966, was participating in Operation VIRGINIA. In early October 1966, the 1st Battalion, 3d Marines, which was taking part in Operation PRAIRIE, moved into the base and the CIDG camp was relocated near Lang Vei, 9,000 meters to the southwest where it continued surveillance and counterinfiltration operations. The battalion remained at Khe Sanh with no significant contacts until February 1967 when it was replaced by a single company, E/2/9.(*) In mid-March 1967, Company E became engaged in a heavy action near Hill 861 and Company B, 1/9 moved in to reinforce. After a successful conclusion of the operation, E/2/9 returned to Phu Bai, and B/1/9 remained as the resident defense company.

The KSCB sat atop a plateau in the shadow of Dong Tri Mountain and overlooked a tributary of the Quang Tri River. The base had a small dirt airstrip, which had been surfaced by a U. S. Navy Mobile Construction Battalion (Seabees) in the summer of 1966; the field could accommodate helicopters and fixed-wing transport aircraft. Organic artillery support was provided by Battery F, 2/12 (105mm), reinforced by two 155mm howitzers and two 4.2-inch mortars. The Khe Sanh area of operations was also within range of the 175mm guns of the U. S. Army's 2d Battalion, 94th Artillery at Camp Carroll and the Rockpile. In addition to B/1/9 and the CIDG, there was a Marine Combined Action Company (CAC) and a Regional Forces company located in the village of Khe Sanh, approximately 3,500 meters

---

(*) The designation E/2/9 stands for Company E, 2d Battalion, 9th Marines. This type of designation will be used perodically for other Marine units throughout the text.

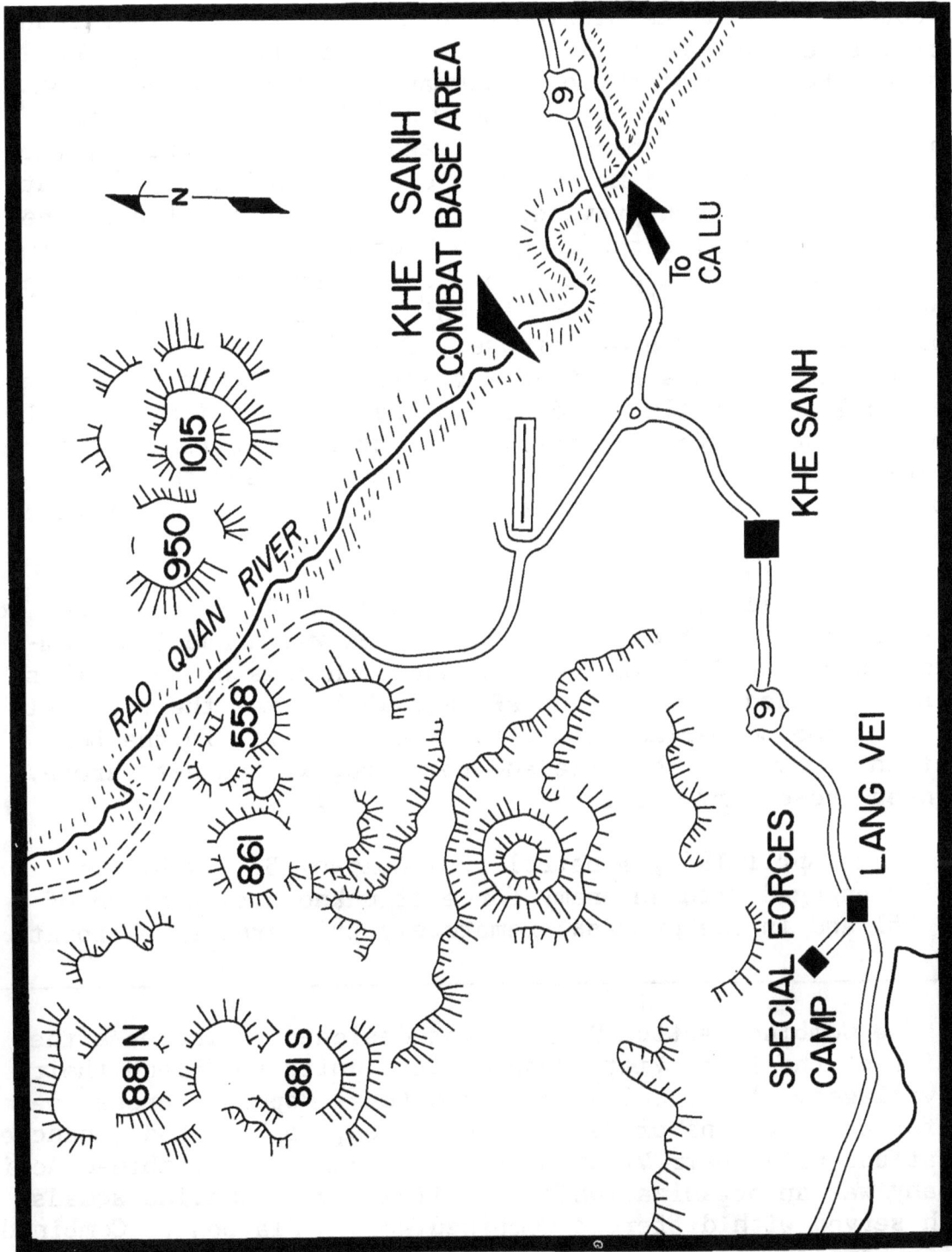

KHE SANH VALLEY

MAP3

9

south of the base.(*)

All these units sat astride the northwest-southeast axis of Route 9 and had the mission of denying the NVA a year-round route into eastern Quang Tri Province. The garrison at Khe Sanh and the adjacent outposts commanded the approaches from the west which led to Dong Ha and Quang Tri City. Had this strategic plateau not been in the hands of the Americans, the North Vietnamese would have had an unobstructed invasion route into the two northern provinces and could have outflanked the Allied forces holding the line south of the DMZ. At that time, the Americans did not possess the helicopter resources, troop strength, or logistical bases in this northern area to adopt a completely mobile type of defense. Therefore, the troops at the KSCB maintained a relatively static defense with emphasis on patrolling, artillery and air interdiction, and occasional reconnaissance in force operations to stifle infiltration through the Khe Sanh Plateau. In the event a major enemy threat developed, General Walt could rapidly reinforce the combat base by air.(7)

On 20 April 1967, the combat assets at KSCB were passed to the operational control of the 3d Marines which had just commenced Operation PRAIRIE IV. The Khe Sanh area of operations was not included as a part of PRAIRIE IV but was the responsibility of the 3d Marines since that regiment was in the best position to oversee the base and reinforce if the need arose. The need arose very soon.(8)

On 24 April 1967, a patrol from Company B, 1/9 became heavily engaged with an enemy force of unknown size north of Hill 861 and in the process prematurely triggered an elaborate

---

(*) The Combined Action Program was designed to increase the ability of the local Vietnamese militia units to defend their own villages. These units, referred to as Popular Forces, were reinforced by groups of Marines who lived, worked, and conducted operations with their Vietnamese counterparts. A Combined Action Company was an organization controlling several Marine squads which served with different Combined Action Platoons. Combined Action Company Oscar (CACO) was the unit operating in the Khe Sanh area. A Regional Forces company was comprised of local South Vietnamese soldiers along with their American and ARVN advisors who were under the operational control of the Vietnamese Province Chief.

North Vietnamese offensive designed to overrun Khe Sanh. What later became known as the "Hill Fights" had begun. In retrospect, it appears that the drive toward Khe Sanh was but one prong of the enemy's winter-spring offensive, the ultimate objective of which was the capture of Dong Ha, Quang Tri City, and eventually, Hue-Phu Bai.(*) That portion of the enemy plan which pertained to Khe Sanh involved the isolation of the base by artillery attacks on the Marine fire support bases in the eastern DMZ area (e.g., Camp Carroll, Con Thien, Gio Linh, etc.). These were closely coordinated with attacks by fire on the logistical and helicopter installations at Dong Ha and Phu Bai. Demolition teams cut Route 9 between Khe Sanh and Cam Lo to prevent overland reinforcement and, later, a secondary attack was launched against the camp at Lang Vei, which was manned by Vietnamese CIDG personnel and U. S. Army Special Forces advisors. Under cover of heavy fog and low overcast which shrouded Khe Sanh for several weeks, the North Vietnamese moved a regiment into the Hill 881/861 complex and constructed a maze of heavily reinforced bunkers and gun positions from which they intended to provide direct fire against the KSCB in support of their assault troops. All of these efforts were ancillary to the main thrust--a regimental-sized ground attack--from the <u>325C NVA Division</u> which would sweep in from the west and seize the airfield.(**)(9) (See Map 4).

The job of stopping the NVA was given to Colonel John P. Lanigan and his 3d Marines. Although he probably did not know it when he arrived at Khe Sanh, this assignment would not be unlike one which 22 years before had earned him a Silver Star on Okinawa. Both involved pushing a fanatical enemy force off a hill.

(*) The III MAF and enemy operations during the period of the NVA/VC winter-spring offensive (1966-1967) will be the subject of a separate monograph prepared by the Historical Branch.

(**) The diversionary attacks were all launched apparently on schedule. On 27 and 28 April, the previously mentioned Marine fire support and supply bases were hit by some 1,200 rocket, artillery, and mortar rounds. Route 9 was cut in several places. The Special Forces Camp at Lang Vei was attacked and severely mauled on 4 May. Only the main effort was detected and subsequently thwarted.

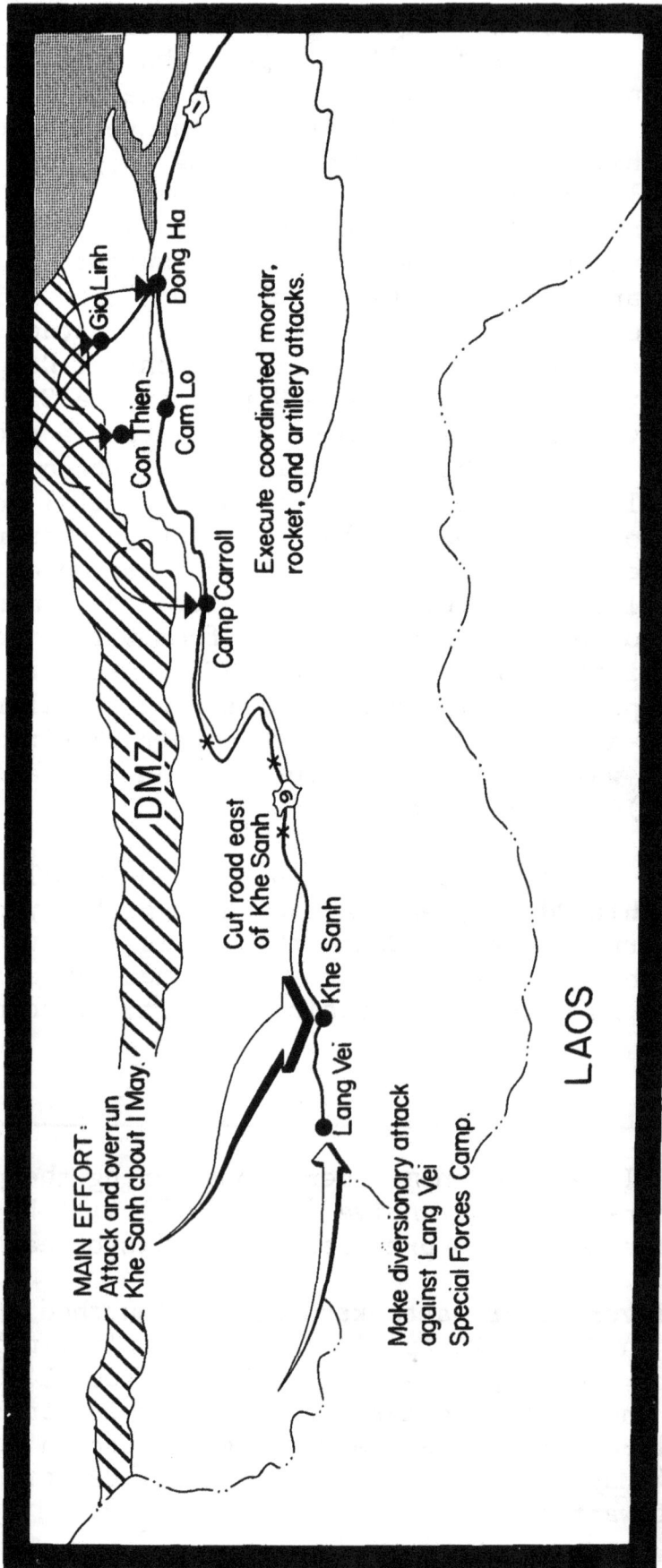

THE ENEMY PLAN

MAP 4

K.W.White

12

On 25 April, the lead elements of the 3d Battalion, 3d Marines, commanded by Lieutenant Colonel Gary Wilder, arrived at Khe Sanh. The following day, 2/3, commanded by Lieutenant Colonel Earl R. De Long, which was taking part in Operation BEACON STAR east of Quang Tri City was airlifted to the combat base. On the 27th, a fresh artillery battery, B/1/12, arrived and reinforced F/2/12; by the end of the day, the two units had been reorganized into an artillery group with one battery in direct support of each battalion.(10)

Late in the afternoon of the 28th, the Marine infantrymen were ready to drive the enemy from the hill masses. These hills formed a near-perfect right triangle with Hill 881 North (N) at the apex and the other two at the base. Hill 861 was the closest to the combat base, some 5,000 meters northwest of the airstrip. Hill 881 South (S) was approximately 3,000 meters west of 861 and 2,000 meters south of 881N.

The concept of operations entailed a two-battalion (2/3 and 3/3) assault for which Hill 861 was designated Objective 1; Hill 881S was Objective 2 and Hill 881N was Objective 3. From its position south of Hill 861, 2/3 would assault and seize Objective 1 on 28 April. The 3d Battalion would follow in trace of 2/3 and, after the first objective was taken, 3/3 would wheel to the west, secure the terrain between Hills 861 and 881S, then assault Objective 2 from a northeasterly direction. Coordinated with the 3/3 attack, 2/3 would consolidate its objective then move out toward Hill 881N to screen the right flank of the 3d Battalion and reinforce if necessary. When Objectives 1 and 2 were secured, 3/3 would move to the northwest and support 2/3 while it assaulted Objective 3. (See Map 5).

After extremely heavy preparatory artillery fires and massive air strikes, the 3d Marines kicked off the attack. On the 28th, 2/3 assaulted and seized Hill 861 in the face of sporadic resistance. Most of the enemy troops had been literally blown from their positions by heavy close air support strikes of the 1st Marine Aircraft Wing. The operation continued with a thrust against Hill 881S by 3/3. This area was the scene of extremely bitter fighting for several days, because, by this time, the NVA regiment which was originally slated for the attack on the airfield had been thrown into the hill battles in a vain effort to stop the Marines. After tons of artillery shells and aerial bombs had been employed against the hill, Lieutenant Colonel Wilder's battalion bulled its way to the summit and, on 2 May, secured the objective. In the meantime,

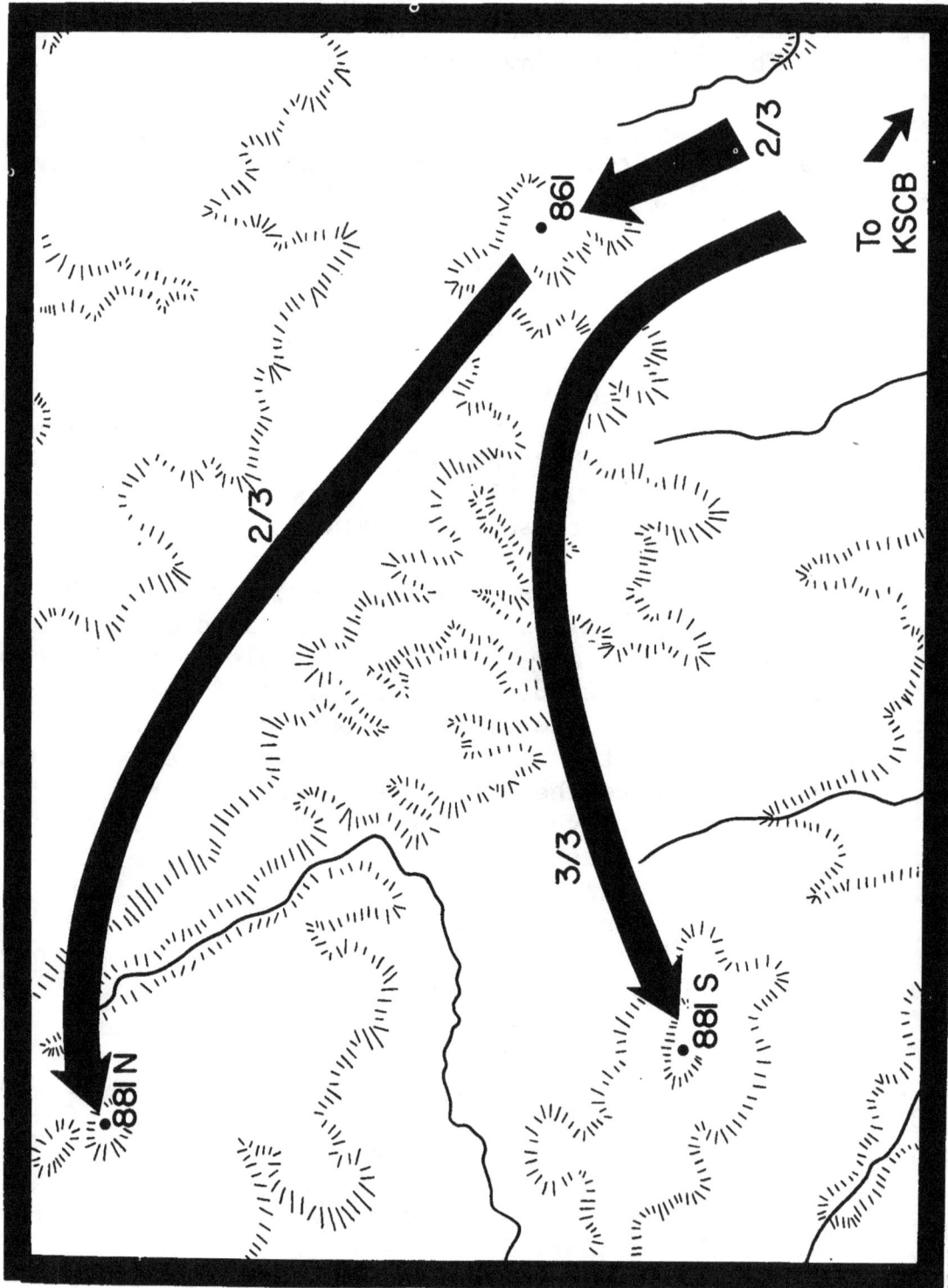

CONCEPT OF OPERATIONS DURING HILL FIGHTS

MAP 5

KWWhite

Marines of Company G, 2d Battalion, 3d Marines inch their way toward the summit of Hill 881N during the Hill fights. (USMC Photo A189161)

Close air support strikes of the 1st Marine Aircraft Wing and massive artillery fires paved the way for infantry assaults. (USMC Photo A421953)

Lieutenant Colonel De Long's battalion pushed along the ridge-line leading from Hill 861 to 881N. After smashing a determined NVA counterattack on 3 May, the 2d Battalion battered its way to the crest of Hill 881N and secured the final objective on the afternoon of the 5th. The three hills belonged to the Marines.(11)

The supporting arms had done a good job, for the top of each hill looked like the surface of the moon. The color of the summit had changed from a vivid green to a dull, ugly brown. All of the lush vegetation had been blasted away, leaving in its place a mass of churned-up dirt and splintered trees. Hundreds of craters dotted the landscape serving as mute witnesses to the terrible pounding that the enemy had taken. What the NVA learned during the operation was something the Marine Corps had espoused for years--that bombs and shells were cheaper than blood.

Thus, the "Hill Fights" ended and the first major attempt by the NVA to take Khe Sanh was thwarted. All intelligence reports indicated that the badly mauled 325C NVA Division had pulled back to lick its wounds, ending the immediate threat in western Quang Tri Province. With the pressure relieved for the time being, General Walt began scaling down his forces at Khe Sanh, because the next phase of the enemy's winter/spring offensive involved a drive through the coastal plain toward Dong Ha.

From 11-13 May, 1/26 moved into the combat base and the adjacent hills to relieve the 3d Marines. By the evening of the 12th, 2/3 had been airlifted to Dong Ha and one artillery battery, B/1/12, was pulled out by convoy. The following day, 3/3 also returned to Dong Ha by truck. In the meantime, Company A, 1/26, was helilifted to Hill 881S while Company C took up positions on Hill 861. Company B, 1/26, and a skeleton headquarters of the 26th Marines arrived and remained at the base, as did a fresh artillery battery, A/1/13. At 1500 on 13 May, Colonel John J. Padley, Commanding Officer of the 26th Marines, Forward, relieved Colonel Lanigan as the Senior Officer Present at Khe Sanh.(12)

In his analysis of the operation, Colonel Lanigan reported that his men had been engaged in a conventional infantry battle against a well-trained, highly-disciplined, and well-entrenched enemy force. In the past, the NVA had used phantom tactics when engaging U. S. forces--not so at Khe Sanh. The maze of bunker complexes served as a grim reminder of their determination to stay and fight. They openly challenged the Americans to push them off the hills, and the 3d Marines rose to the occasion. The fierce resistance was overcome by aggressive infantry assaults in coordination with artillery and close air support, which according to Colonel Lanigan was the most accurate and devastating he had witnessed in three wars.

The Communists had anticipated a blood letting and they received one. From 24 April through 12 May 1967, the NVA lost 940 confirmed killed.(*) Even for the North Vietnamese, this was a massive defeat which could not be easily absorbed. But the leaders in Hanoi were committed to a course of action which traded human lives for strategic expediency. Just like the monsoon rains, the enemy would come again.(13)

(*) Marine losses were 155 killed and 425 wounded.

PART II

THE LULL BETWEEN THE STORMS

With the departure of the 3d Marines, a relative calm pre-
vailed at Khe Sanh for the remainder of the year. Although
occasional encounters and sightings indicated that the Communists
still had an interest in the area, there was a marked decrease
in large unit contacts and the tempo of operations slackened
to a preinvasion pace. Such was not the case in other portions
of Quang Tri Province.

During the summer and fall of 1967, the center of activity
shifted to the eastern DMZ area. After being battered and
thrown for a loss on their end sweep, the Communists concentrated on the middle of the line again. With an estimated 37
battalions poised along the border, the NVA constituted a
genuine threat to the northernmost province. At times as many
as eight Marine battalions were shuttled into the area for
short-term operations and three or four were there full time,
but the enemy's intensified campaign created a demand for more
troops. As a result, General Westmoreland was forced to make
major force realignments throughout South Vietnam to satisfy
the troop requirements in I Corps.(14)

General Westmoreland drew the bulk of these reinforcements
from areas in Vietnam which, at the time, were under less
pressure than the five northern provinces. During April and
May 1967, Task Force OREGON, comprised of nine U. S. Army battalions from II and III Corps, moved into the Chu Lai-Duc Pho
region and was placed under the operational control of General
Walt. By the end of May, five battalions of the 5th and 7th
Marines at Chu Lai had been released for service further north.
Two of these units moved into the Nui Loc Son Basin northwest
of Tam Ky to conduct offensive operations and support the
sagging Vietnamese Revolutionary Development efforts. The other
three settled in the Da Nang tactical area of responsibility
(TAOR) and in turn released two Marine battalions, 1/1 and 2/1,
which moved to Thua Thien and Quang Tri provinces.

In addition to his in-country assets, General Westmoreland
also called on Admiral U. S. Grant Sharp, Commander in Chief,
Pacific, for reinforcements. Besides the two Special Landing
Forces afloat with the U. S. Seventh Fleet, the Pacific Command

maintained a Marine Battalion Landing Team (BLT 3/4) as an amphibious reserve on Okinawa.(*)(15) Actually, this unit was part of the BLT rotation system whereby battalions were periodically shuttled out of Vietnam for retraining and refurbishing in Okinawa before assignment to the SLF. ComUSMACV needed the unit and got it. On 15 May, 3/4 began an airlift from Okinawa to Dong Ha by Air Force and Marine C-130 aircraft and within 31 hours the 1,233-man force was in-country. After the realignment of units in I Corps was complete, there was a net increase of four USMC battalions in the DMZ area making a total of seven. Additionally, the SLFs, cruising off the Vietnamese coast, provided two more battalions which could be landed quickly and added to the III MAF inventory. SLF Alpha (BLT 1/3 and HMM-362) was placed on 24-hour alert to come ashore and SLF Bravo (BLT 2/3 and HMM-164) was given a 96-hour reaction time.(16)

During the second half of 1967, the enemy offensive south of the DMZ was a bloody repetition of the previous year's effort. With more courage than good sense, the NVA streamed across the DMZ throughout the summer only to be met and systematically chewed up in one engagement after another. In July, the enemy, supported by his long-range artillery along the Ben Hai, mounted a major thrust against the 9th Marines near the strongpoint of Con Thien. Reinforced by SLFs Alpha and Bravo, the 9th Marines countered with Operation BUFFALO and, between the 2d and 14th of July, killed 1,290 NVA. Marine losses were 159 dead and 345 wounded.(17)

After this crushing defeat, the NVA shifted its emphasis from direct infantry assaults to attacks by fire. Utilizing

_____

(*) The two Special Landing Forces of the Seventh Fleet are each comprised of a Marine Battalion Landing Team and a Marine helicopter squadron, and provide ComUSMACV/CG, III MAF with a highly-flexible, amphibious striking force for operations along the South Vietnam littoral. During the amphibious operation, operational control of the SLF remains with the Amphibious Task Force Commander designated by Commander, Seventh Fleet. This relationship may persist throughout the operation if coordination with forces ashore does not dictate otherwise. When the Special Landing Force is firmly established ashore, operational control may be passed to CG, III MAF who, in turn, may shift this control to the division in whose area the SLF is operating. Under such circumstances, operational control of the helicopter squadron is passed by CG III MAF to the 1st Marine Aircraft Wing.

Action near the DMZ was characterized by hard fighting in
rugged terrain. A Marine of 3/4 moves forward during
Operation PRAIRIE. (USMC Photo A187904)

Marine Battalion Landing Teams aboard U. S. Seventh Fleet
shipping augmented III MAF forces. USS Iwo Jima stands
off South Vietnamese coast. (USMC Photo A650016)

long-range rockets and artillery pieces tucked away in caves and treelines along the DMZ, the enemy regularly shelled Marine fire support and logistical bases from Cam Lo to Cua Viet. One of the most destructive attacks was against Dong Ha where, on 3 September, 41 enemy artillery rounds hit the base and touched off a series of spectacular explosions which lasted for over four hours. Several helicopters were damaged but, more important, a fuel farm and a huge stockpile of ammunition went up in smoke. Thousands of gallons of fuel and tons of ammunition were destroyed. The enormous column of smoke from the exploding dumps rose above 12,000 feet and was visible as far south as Hue-Phu Bai.(18)

The preponderance of enemy fire, however, was directed against Con Thien. That small strongpoint, never garrisoned by more than a reinforced battalion, was situated atop Hill 158, 10 miles northwest of Dong Ha and, from their small perch, the Marines had a commanding view of any activity in the area. In addition, from one to three battalions were always in the immediate vicinity and deployed so that they could outflank any major enemy force which tried to attack the strongpoint. Con Thien also anchored the western end of "the barrier," a 600-meter-wide trace which extended eastward some eight miles to Gio Linh. This strip was part of an anti-infiltration system and had been bulldozed flat to aid in visual detection.(*)(19)

Because of its strategic importance, Con Thien became the scene of heavy fighting. The base itself was subjected to several ground attacks, plus an almost incessant artillery bombardment which, at its peak, reached 1,233 rounds in one 24-hour period. Most of the NVA and Marine casualties, however, were sustained by maneuver elements in the surrounding area. Operation KINGFISHER, which succeeded BUFFALO, continued around Con Thien and by 31 October, when it was superseded by two new operations, had accounted for 1,117 enemy dead. Marine losses were 340 killed.(**)(20)

(*)   The system was an anti-infiltration barrier just south of the DMZ. Obstacles were used to channelize the enemy. Strong-points, such as Con Thien, served as patrol bases and fire support bases.

(**)   In addition to the action near the DMZ, there was one other area in I Corps that was a hub of activity. The Nui Loc Son Basin, a rice rich coastal plain between Hoi An and Tam Ky, was the operating area of the 2d NVA Division. Between April and

21

While heavy fighting raged elsewhere, action around Khe
Sanh continued to be light and sporadic. Immediately after its
arrival on 13 May, Colonel Padley's undermanned 26th Marines
commenced Operation CROCKETT.(*)(21) The mission was to occupy
key terrain, deny the enemy access into vital areas, conduct
reconnaissance-in-force operations to destroy any elements within the TAOR, and provide security for the base and adjacent outposts. Colonel Padley was to support the Vietnamese irregular
forces with his organic artillery as well as coordinate the
efforts of the American advisors to those units. He also had
the responsibility of maintaining small reconnaissance teams
for long-range surveillance.(22)

To accomplish his mission, the colonel had one infantry
battalion, 1/26, a skeleton headquarters, and an artillery
group under the control of 1/13. The 1st Battalion, 26th Marines,
commanded by Lieutenant Colonel James B. Wilkinson, maintained
one rifle company on Hill 881S and one on 861; a security detachment on Hill 950 to protect a communication relay site; a
rifle company and the Headquarters and Service Company (H&S Co)
for base security; and one company in reserve. The units on
the hill outposts patrolled continuously within a 4,000-meter
radius of their positions. Reconnaissance teams were inserted
further out, primarily to the north and northwest. Whenever
evidence revealed enemy activity in an area, company-sized
search and destroy sweeps were conducted. Although intelligence
reports indicated that the three regiments of the 325C NVA
Division (i.e. 95C, 101D, and 29th) were still in the Khe Sanh
TAOR, there were few contacts during the opening weeks of the
operation.(23)

October 1967, Marine, U. S. Army, and ARVN troops conducted 13
major operations (including 3 SLF landings) in this region and
killed 5,395 enemy soldiers. By the end of the year, the 2d
NVA Division was temporarily rendered useless as a fighting unit.

(*) The official designation of the unit at Khe Sanh was Regimental Landing Team 26 (Forward) which consisted of one battalion
and a lightly staffed headquarters. The other two battalions
were in-country but under the operational control of other units.
The rest of the headquarters, RLT-26 (Rear), remained at Camp
Schwab, Okinawa as a pipeline for replacements. RLT-26 (Forward)
was under the operational control of the 3d MarDiv and the ad-
ministrative control of the 9th MAB. Any further mention of the
26th Marines will refer only to RLT-26 (Forward).

Toward the end of May and throughout June, however, activity picked up. On 21 May, elements of Company A, 1/26, clashed sharply with a reinforced enemy company; 25 NVA and 2 Marines were killed. The same day, the Lang Vei CIDG camp was attacked by an enemy platoon. On 6 June, the radio relay site on Hill 950 was hit by an NVA force of unknown size and the combat base was mortared. The following morning a patrol from Company B, 1/26, engaged another enemy company approximately 2,000 meters northwest of Hill 881S. A platoon from Company A was helilifted to the scene and the two Marine units killed 66 NVA while losing 18 men. Due to the increasing number of contacts, the 3d Battalion, 26th Marines, commanded by Lieutenant Colonel Kurt L. Hoch, was transferred to the operational control of its parent unit and arrived at Khe Sanh on 13 June. Two weeks later, the newly arrived unit got a crack at the NVA when Companies I and L engaged two enemy companies 5,000 meters southwest of the base and, along with air and artillery, killed 35.(24)

Operation CROCKETT continued as a two-battalion effort until 16 July when it terminated. The cumulative casualty figures were 204 enemy KIA (confirmed), 52 Marines KIA, and 255 Marines wounded. The following day, operations continued under a new name--ARDMORE. The name was changed; the mission, the units, and the TAOR remained basically the same. But again the fighting tapered off. Except for occasional contacts by reconnaissance teams and patrols, July and August were quiet.(25)

On 12 August, Colonel David E. Lownds relieved Colonel Padley as the commanding officer of the 26th Marines. At this time the 3d Marine Division was deployed from the area north of Da Nang to the DMZ and from the South China Sea to the Laotian border. In order to maintain the initiative, Lieutenant General Robert E. Cushman, Jr., who had relieved General Walt as CG, III MAF in June, drew down on certain units to provide sufficient infantry strength for other operations. Except for several small engagements Khe Sanh had remained relatively quiet; therefore, on the day after Colonel Lownds assumed command, the regiment was whittled down by two companies when K and L, 3/26, were transferred to the 9th Marines for Operation KINGFISHER. Three weeks later, the rest of 3/26 was also withdrawn and, as far as Marine units were concerned, Colonel Lownds found himself "not so much a regimental commander as the supervisor of a battalion commander." The colonel, however, was still responsible for coordinating the efforts of all the other Allied units (CACO, CIDG, RF, etc) in the Khe Sanh TAOR.(26)

Colonel John J. Padley turns over the colors and
the 26th Marines to Colonel David E. Lownds on 12
August 1967. (Photo courtesy Colonel David E.
Lownds)

As Operation ARDMORE dragged on, the Marines at Khe Sanh concentrated on improving the combat base. The men were kept busy constructing bunkers and trenches both inside the perimeter and on the hill outposts. On the hills, this proved to be no small task as was pointed out by the 1/26 battalion commander, Lieutenant Colonel Wilkinson:

> The monsoon rains had little effect on 881, but when the first torrential rains of the season hit 861 the results were disastrous. The trenchline which encircled the hill washed away completely on one side of the position and caved in on another side. Some bunkers collapsed while others were so weakened they had to be completely rebuilt. Because of the poor soil and the steepness of the terrain, the new bunkers were built almost completely above ground. To provide drainage, twenty-seven 55 gallon steel drums, with the tops and bottoms removed, were installed in the sides of the trenches around 861 so water would not stand in the trenches. (Culvert material was not available.) All bunker materials, as well as other supplies, were delivered to the hills by helicopter. Attempts were made to obtain logs for fighting positions and bunkers in the canopied jungle flanking the hills. This idea was not successful. The trees close to 881 and 861 were so filled with shrapnel from the battles the previous spring that the engineers did not want to ruin their chain saws on the metal....In spite of the shortages, Marines of 1/26 worked extremely hard until every Marine on 881(S) and 861 had overhead cover.(27)

Another bit of foresight which was to prove a God-send in the succeeding months was the decision by higher headquarters to improve the airstrip. The original runway had been a dirt strip on top of which the U. S. Navy Seabees had laid aluminum matting. The 3,900-foot strip, however, did not have a rock base and as a result of the heavy monsoon rains, mud formed under the matting causing it to buckle in several places. Upon direction, Colonel Lownds closed the field on 17 August. His men located a hill 1,500 meters southwest of the perimeter which served as a quarry. Three 15-ton rock crushers, along with other heavy equipment, were hauled in and the Marine and Seabee working parties started the repairs. During September and October, U. S. Air Force C-130s of the 315th Air Division (under the operational control of the 834th Air Division) delivered 2,350 tons of matting, asphalt, and other construction material to the base by paradrops and a special low-altitude extraction system. (See page 76) While the field was shut down, resupply missions were handled by helicopters and C-7 "Caribou" which could land on short segments of the strip. Work continued until 27 October when the field was reopened to C-123 aircraft and later, to C-130s.(28)

On 31 October, Operation ARDMORE came to an uneventful conclusion. The absence of any major engagements was mirrored in the casualty figures which showed that in three and a half months, 113 NVA and 10 Marines were killed. The next day, 1 November, the 26th Marines commenced another operation, new in name only--SCOTLAND I. Again the mission and units remained the same, and while the area of operations was altered slightly, SCOTLAND I was basically just an extension of ARDMORE.(29)

One incident in November which was to have a tremendous effect on the future of the combat base was the arrival of Major General Rathvon McC. Tompkins at Phu Bai as the new Commanding General, 3d Marine Division. General Tompkins took over from Brigadier General Louis Metzger who had been serving as the Acting Division Commander following the death of Major General Bruno Hochmuth in a helicopter crash on 14 November. In addition to being an extremely able commander, General Tompkins possessed a peppery yet gentlemanly quality which, in the gloom that later shrouded Khe Sanh, often lifted the spirits of his subordinates. His numerous inspection trips, even to the most isolated units, provided the division commander with a first-hand knowledge of the tactical situation in northern I Corps which would never have been gained by simply sitting behind a desk. When the heavy fighting broke out at Khe Sanh, the general visited the combat base almost daily. Few people were to influence the coming battle more than General Tompkins or have as many close calls.(30)

During December, there was another surge of enemy activity. Reconnaissance teams reported large groups of NVA moving into the area and, this time, they were not passing through; they were staying. There was an increased number of contacts between Marine patrols and enemy units. The companies on Hills 881S and 861 began receiving more and more sniper fire. Not only the hill outposts, but the combat base itself, received numerous probes along the perimeter. In some cases, the defensive wire was cut and replaced in such a manner that the break was hard to detect. The situation warranted action, and again General Cushman directed 3/26 to rejoin the regiment. On 13 December, the 3d Battalion, under its new commander, Lieutenant Colonel Harry L. Alderman (who assumed command 21 August), was airlifted back to Khe Sanh and the 26th Marines.(31)

On the 21st, the newly-arrived Marines saddled up and took to the field. This was the first time that Colonel Lownds had been able to commit a battalion-sized force since 3/26 had left Khe Sanh in August. Lieutenant Colonel Alderman's unit was helilifted to 881S where it conducted a sweep toward Hill 918, some 5,100 meters to the west, and then returned to the combat base by the way of Hill 689. The 3d Battalion made no contact with the enemy during the five-day operation but the effort proved to be extremely valuable. First of all, the men of 3/26 became familiar with the terrain to the west and south of Hill 881S--a position which was later occupied by elements of the 3d Battalion. The Marines located the best avenues of approach to the hill, as well as probable sites for the enemy's supporting weapons. Secondly, and most important, the unit turned up evidence (fresh foxholes, well-used trails, caches, etc.) which indicated that the NVA was moving into the area in force. These signs further strengthened the battalion and regimental commanders' belief that "things were picking up," and the confrontation which many predicted would come was not far off. Captain Richard D. Camp, the company commander of L/3/26 put it a little more bluntly: "I can smell.../the enemy7."(32)

General Leonard F. Chapman, Jr., Commandant of the Marine Corps, talks with his son, First Lieutenant Walton F. Chapman, during the General's visit to Khe Sanh in January 1968. Lieutenant Chapman served with the 1st Battalion, 26th Marines and spent a good portion of the siege on Hill 950. (USMC Photo A190283)

PART III

THE BUILDUP AND THE OPENING ROUND

With the beginning of the new year, Khe Sanh again became
the focal point of enemy activity in I Corps. All evidence
pointed to a North Vietnamese offensive similar to the one in
1967, only on a much larger scale. From various intelligence
sources, the III MAF, 3d Marine Division, and 26th Marines
Headquarters learned that NVA units, which usually came down
the "Santa Fe Trail" and skirted the combat base outside of
artillery range, were moving into the Khe Sanh area and staying.(*)(33) At first, the reports showed the influx of individual regiments, then a division headquarters; finally a
front headquarters was established indicating that at least
two NVA divisions were in the vicinity. In fact, the 325C NVA
Division had moved back into the region north of Hill 881N while
a newcomer to the area, the 304th NVA Division, had crossed
over from Laos and established positions southwest of the base.
The 304th was an elite home guard division from Hanoi which had
been a participant at Dien Bien Phu.(**)(34) The entire force
included six infantry regiments, two artillery regiments, an
unknown number of tanks, plus miscellaneous support and service
units. Gradually, the enemy shifted his emphasis from reconnaissance and harassment to actual probes and began exerting more
and more pressure on Allied outposts and patrols. One incident
which reinforced the belief that something big was in the wind
occurred on 2 January near a Marine listening post just outside
the main perimeter.(35)

(*) The Santa Fe Trail is a branch of the Ho Chi Minh Trail
which closely parallels the South Vietnam/Laos border.

(**) In addition, one regiment of the 324th Division was located in the central DMZ some 10-15 miles from Khe Sanh and
maintained a resupply role. In the early stages of the siege,
the presence of the 320th Division was confirmed north of the
Rockpile within easy reinforcing distance of Khe Sanh; thus,
General Westmoreland and General Cushman were initially faced
with the possibility that Khe Sanh would be attacked by three
divisions plus a regiment. General Tompkins, however, kept
constant pressure on these additional enemy units and alleviated
their threat.

The post was located approximately 400 meters from the western end of the airstrip and north of where the Company L, 3/26 lines tied in with those of 1/26. At 2030, a sentry dog was alerted by movement outside the perimeter and a few minutes later the Marines manning the post reported that six unidentified persons were approaching the defensive wire. Oddly enough, the nocturnal visitors were not crawling or attempting to hide their presence; they were walking around as if they owned the place. A squad from L/3/26, headed by Second Lieutenant Nile B. Buffington, was dispatched to investigate. Earlier in the day the squad had rehearsed the proper procedure for relieving the listening post and had received a briefing on fire discipline. The training was shortly put to good use.

Lieutenant Buffington saw that the six men were dressed like Marines and, while no friendly patrols were reported in the area, he challenged the strangers in clear English to be sure. There was no reply. A second challenge was issued and, this time, the lieutenant saw one of the men make a motion as if going for a hand grenade. The Marines opened fire and quickly cut down five of the six intruders. One enemy soldier died with his finger inserted in the pin of a grenade. The awesome hitting power of the M-16 rifle was quite evident since all five men were apparently dead by the time they hit the ground. The lone survivor was wounded but managed to escape after retrieving some papers from a mapcase which was on one of the bodies. Using a sentry dog, the Marines followed a trail of blood to the southwest but gave up the hunt in the darkness. The direction the enemy soldier was heading led the Marines to believe that his unit was located beyond the rock quarry.

The importance of the contact was not realized until later when intelligence personnel discovered that all five of the enemy dead were officers including an NVA regimental commander, operations officer, and communications officer. The fact that the North Vietnamese would commit such key men to a highly dangerous, personal reconnaissance indicated that Khe Sanh was back at the top of the Communists' priority list.(36)

This series of events did not go unnoticed at higher headquarters. General Cushman saw that Colonel Lownds had more on his hands than could be handled by two battalions and directed that 2/26 be transferred to the operational control of its parent unit. On 16 January, 2/26, commanded by Lieutenant Colonel Francis J. Heath, Jr., landed at the Khe Sanh Combat Base; its arrival marked the first time that the three battalions of the

30

26th Marines had operated together in combat since Iwo Jima. The rapid deployment of Lieutenant Colonel Heath's unit was another example of the speed with which large number of troops could be committed to battle. The regimental commander knew that he would be getting reinforcements but he did not know exactly when they would arrive; he was informed by telephone just as the lead transports were entering the landing pattern. The question that then arose was: "Where could the newcomers do the most good?"(37)

Outside of the combat base itself, there were several areas which were vital. The most critical points were the hill outposts, because both General Tompkins and Colonel Lownds were well aware of what had happened at Dien Bien Phu when the Viet Minh owned the mountains and the French owned the valley. It was essential that the hills around Khe Sanh remain in the hands of the Marines. Shortly after its arrival in mid-December 1967, 3/26 had relieved 1/26 of most of this responsibility. Company I, 3/26, along with a three-gun detachment of 105mm howitzers from Battery C, 1/13, was situated atop Hill 881S; Company K, 3/26, with two 4.2-inch mortars, was entrenched on Hill 861; and the 2d Platoon, A/1/26 defended the radio-relay site on Hill 950. This arrangement still left the NVA with an excellent avenue of approach through the Rao Quan Valley which runs between Hills 861 and 950. The regimental commander decided to plug that gap with the newly arrived 2d Battalion.(38)

At 1400 the day it arrived, Company F, 2/26, conducted a tactical march to Hill 558--a small knob which sat squarely in the middle of the northwestern approach. The rest of the battalion spent the night in an assembly area approximately 1,300 meters west of the airstrip. The following day, Lieutenant Colonel Heath moved his three remaining companies and the CP group overland to join Company F. Once the Marines were dug in, the perimeter completely encompassed Hill 558 and blocked enemy movement through the Rao Quan Valley.(39)

Even with 2/26 in position, there was still a flaw in the northern screen. The line of sight between K/3/26, on Hill 861, and 2/26 was masked by a ridgeline which extended from the summit of 861 to the northeast. This stretch of high ground prevented the two units from supporting each other by fire and created a corridor through which the North Vietnamese could maneuver to flank either Marine outpost. About a week after his arrival on Hill 558, Captain Earle G. Breeding was ordered to take his company, E/2/26, and occupy the finger at a point approximately 400-500 meters northeast of K/3/26. From this new vantage point, dubbed Hill 861A, Company E blocked the ridgeline and was in a good position to protect the flank of 2/26. Because of its proximity to K/3/26, Company E, 2/26, was later transferred to the operational control of the 3d Battalion. Although these units did not form one continuous defensive line, they did occupy the key terrain which overlooked the valley floor.(40)

With the primary avenue of approach blocked, Colonel Lownds utilized his remaining assets to provide base security and conduct an occasional search and destroy mission. The 1st Battalion was given the lion's share of the perimeter to defend with lines that extended around three sides of the airstrip. Lieutenant Colonel Wilkinson's Marines occupied positions that paralleled the runway to the north (Blue Sector), crossed the eastern end of the strip, and continued back to the west along the southern boundary of the base (Grey Sector). The southwestern portion of the compound was manned by Forward Operating Base-3 (FOB-3), a conglomeration of indigenous personnel and American advisors under the direct control of a U. S. Army Special Forces commander. FOB-3 tied in with 1/26 on the east and L/3/26 on the west. Company L, 3/26, was responsible for the northwestern section (Red Sector) of the base and was thinly spread over approximately 3,000 meters of perimeter. The remaining company from the 3d Battalion, M/3/26, was held in reserve until 19 January when two platoons and a command group were helilifted to 881S. Even though it held a portion of the perimeter, Company D, 1/26 became the reserve and the remaining platoon from M/3/26 also remained at the base as a reaction force.(*)(41)

In addition to his infantry units, the regimental commander had an impressive array of artillery and armor. Lieutenant Colonel John A. Hennelly's 1/13 provided direct support for the 26th Marines with one 4.2-inch mortar battery, three 105mm howitzer batteries, and one provisional 155mm howitzer battery (towed). The 175mm guns of the U. S. Army's 2d Battalion, 94th

---

(*) On the 21st, a platoon from A/1/26 reinforced K/3/26 on Hill 861 and a second platoon from Company A later followed suit. Throughout most of the siege the line up on the hill outpost remained as follows: Hill 881S--Company I, 3/26 plus two platoons and a command group from Company M 3/26; Hill 861--Company K, 3/26 plus two platoons from Company A, 1/26; Hill 861A--Company E, 2/26; Hill 558--2/26 (minus the one company on 861A); Hill 950--one platoon from 1/26.

Artillery at Camp Carroll and the Rockpile were in general support. Five 90mm tanks from the 3d Tank Battalion, which had been moved to Khe Sanh before Route 9 was cut, were attached to the 26th Marines along with two Ontos platoons from the 3d Antitank Battalion.(*) These highly mobile tracked vehicles could be rapidly mustered at any threatened point so Colonel Lownds generally held his armor in the southwestern portion of the compound as a back-up for L/3/26 and FOB-3. All told, the Khe Sanh defenders could count on fire support from 46 artillery pieces of varied calibers, 5 90mm tank guns, and 92 single or Ontos-mounted 106mm recoilless rifles. With an estimated 15,000 to 20,000 North Vietnamese lurking in the surrounding hills, the Marines would need it all.(42)

Ironically, the incidents which heralded the beginning of full-scale hostilities in 1968 occurred in the same general area as the encounter which touched off the heavy fighting in 1967. On 19 January 1968, the 3d Platoon, I/3/26 was patrolling along a ridgeline 700 meters southwest of Hill 881N where, two days before, a Marine reconnaissance team had been ambushed. The team leader and radioman were killed and, while the bodies had been recovered, the radio and a coded frequency card were missing. The 3d Platoon was scouring the ambush site for these items when it was taken under fire by an estimated 25 NVA troops. The Marines returned fire, then broke contact while friendly artillery plastered the enemy positions.

The next morning, Company I, commanded by Captain William H. Dabney, returned to the scene in force. The captain actually had two missions: first, to try and make contact with the enemy, and, second, to insert another reconnaissance team in the vicinity of the ambush site. Two platoons and a command group from Company M, 3/26, commanded by Captain John J. Gilece, Jr. were helilifted to 881S and manned the perimeter while Company I moved out to the north.(**) The terrain between 881S and its northern twin dropped off into a deep ravine and then sloped gradually upward to the crest of 881N. The southern face of 881N had two parallel

---

(*) The Ontos is a lightly armored tracked vehicle armed with six 106mm recoilless rifles. Originally designed as a tank killer, it is primarily used in Vietnam to support the infantry.

(**) Captain Gilece was wounded by sniper fire and on 1 February, First Lieutenant John T. Esslinger, the executive officer, assumed command.

Five M-48 tanks of the 3d Tank Battalion lent the weight of their 90mm guns to the defense of the combat base. (USMC Photo A190384)

Two Ontos platoons of the 3d Antitank Battalion were on hand at Khe Sanh. The Ontos sports six 106mm recoilless rifles with coaxially mounted .50 caliber spotting rifles. (USMC Photo A369169)

ridgelines about 500 meters apart which ran up the hill and provided the company with excellent avenues of approach. These two fingers were dotted with a series of small knobs which Captain Dabney had designated as intermediate objectives.

The Marines moved out at 0500 proceeding along two axes with the 1st and 2d Platoons on the left ridgeline and the 3d Platoon on the right. The ground fog was so thick that the men groped along at a snail's pace probing to their front with extended rifles much the same way a blind man uses a walking cane. For that reason, Captain Dabney had placed Second Lieutenant Harry F. Fromme's 1st Platoon and Second Lieutenant Thomas D. Brindley's 3d Platoon in the lead because both units had patrolled this area frequently and the commanders knew the terrain like the back of their hands. In spite of this, by 0900 the entire force had covered only a few hundred meters but then the fog began to lift enabling the Marines to move out at a brisker pace. The company swept out of the draw at the northern base of 881S, secured its first intermediate objective without incident, and then advanced toward a stretch of high ground which was punctuated by four innocent-looking little hills. These formed an east-west line which ran perpendicular to and bisected the Marines' intended route of march. As it turned out this area was occupied by elements of an NVA battalion and each mound was a link in a heavily-fortified defensive chain.(43)

As the element on the right moved forward after a precautionary 105mm artillery concentration, the enemy opened up with small arms, .50 caliber machine guns, and grenade launchers (RPGs). The resistance was so stiff that Captain Dabney ordered Lieutenant Brindley to hold up his advance and call for more artillery while the force on the left pushed forward far enough to place flanking fire on the NVA position. The 1st and 2d Platoons, however, fared no better; volleys of machine gun fire from the other enemy-owned hills cut through the Marine ranks like giant scythes and, in less than 30 seconds, 20 men were out of action, most with severe leg wounds. Caught in a cross fire, the captain ordered Fromme to hold up and evacuate his wounded. Again, Lieutenant Brindley's men on the right surged forward in the wake of 155mm prep fires. The assault, as described by one observer, was like a "page out of /the life of/ Chesty Puller."(*)

(*) Lieutenant General Lewis B. "Chesty" Puller, a legendary figure in Marine Corps history, is the only Marine to have won the Navy Cross five times.

The ambush of a Marine reconnaissance team near 881N on 17 January 1968 was the prelude to the opening battle three days later. (USMC Photo   A188243)

A view of Hill 881N (1) from its southern twin. Action on 20 January took place on ridgelines (2) and (3). (Photo courtesy Major William H. Dabney)

Brindley was everywhere; he moved from flank to flank slapping his men on the back and urging them on. The lieutenant led his platoon up the slope and was the first man on top of the hill but, for him, the assault ended there--he was cut down by a sniper bullet and died within minutes.(*)

During the advance, the recon team, which had volunteered to join the attack, veered off to the right into a small draw and became separated from the rest of the platoon. When the enemy troops were finally driven off the hill, they fled to the east and inadvertently smashed headlong into the isolated team. After a brief but savage fight, the North Vietnamese over-ran the team and made good their escape; most of the recon Marines were seriously wounded and lay exposed to direct fire from the enemy on the easternmost hill. Several other men in the 3d Platoon were hit during the wild charge and by the time the objective had been taken, the radioman--a corporal--discovered that he was the senior man in the platoon. He quickly reported that fact to Captain Dabney.

The company commander saw that the enemy defense hinged on the center hill which the 3d Platoon had just taken. If he could consolidate that objective, Dabney would have a vantage point from which to support, by fire, assaults on the other three NVA positions. Second Lieutenant Richard M. Foley, the Company I Executive Officer, had moved up to take command of the 3d Platoon and he reported that while the unit had firm pos-session of the hill, there were not enough men left to evacuate the casualties. In addition, he could not locate the recon team and his ammunition was running low. Dabney, therefore, ordered Lieutenant Fromme's 1st Platoon to remain in place and support the left flank of the 3d Platoon by fire. With Second Lieu-tenant Michael H. Thomas' 2d Platoon which had been in reserve on the left, the company commander pulled back to the south, hooked around to the east and joined Foley's unit on its objec-tive. The officers tried to evacuate the wounded and reorganize but this attempt was complicated by the fact that one half of the hastily formed perimeter was being pelted by .50 caliber machine gun and sniper fire from the enemy's easternmost position.

At this point, there were two acts of extraordinary heroism. Lieutenant Thomas, who was crouched in a crater alongside the company commander, was informed of the wounded recon Marines who

_____

(*) Lieutenant Brindley was posthumously awarded the Navy Cross.

lay in the open at the eastern base of the hill. Even though it was courting certain death to do so, Thomas jumped out of the hole without hesitation and started down the hill. He had only gotten a few steps when an enemy sniper shot him through the head killing him instantly.(*) In spite of what happened to the lieutenant, Sergeant Daniel G. Jessup quickly followed his lead. While the NVA hammered away at the exposed slope with continuous machine gun and sniper fire, the sergeant slithered over the crest and crawled down the hill to locate the recon unit. Once at the bottom, he found the team in a small saddle which was covered with elephant grass; two of the Marines were dead and five were seriously wounded. Jessup hoisted one of the wounded men onto his back and made the return trip up the fire-swept slope. Gathering up a handful of Marines, the sergeant returned and supervised the evacuation of the entire team. When all the dead and wounded had been retrieved, Jessup zig-zagged down the hill a third time to gather up weapons and insure that no one had been left behind. For his calm courage and devotion to his comrades, Sergeant Jessup was later awarded the Silver Star.

The heavy fighting raged throughout the afternoon. Lieutenant Colonel Alderman, his operations officer, Major Matthew P. Caulfield, and representatives of the Fire Support Coordination Center (FSCC) flew from Khe Sanh to Hill 881S by helicopter so they could personally oversee the battle. During the action, Company I drew heavy support from the recoilless rifles, mortars, and 105mm howitzers on Hill 881S, as well as the batteries at Khe Sanh. In addition, Marine jets armed with 500-pound bombs streaked in and literally blew the top off of the easternmost enemy hill, while other fighter/bombers completely smothered one NVA counterattack with napalm. A CH-46 helicopter from Marine Aircraft Group 36 was shot down while attempting to evacuate casualties but another Sea Knight swooped in and picked up the pilot and copilot. The crew chief had jumped from the blazing chopper while it was still airborne and broke his leg; he was rescued by Lieutenant Fromme's men. This, however, was the only highlight for the North Vietnamese because Company I had cracked the center of their defense and, under the savage air and artillery bombardment, the rest of the line was beginning to crumble.(46)

Lieutenant Colonel Alderman realized that his men were gaining the advantage and requested reinforcements with which

---

(*) For his actions throughout the battle, Lieutenant Thomas was posthumously awarded the Navy Cross.

to exploit the situation. Colonel Lownds, however, denied the request and directed the 3/26 commander to pull Company I back to Hill 881S immediately. The order was passed on to Captain Dabney and it hit him like a thunderbolt. His men had been fighting hard all day and he hated to tell them to call it off at that point. Nonetheless, he rapidly disengaged, collected his casualties, and withdrew. The struggle had cost the enemy dearly: 103 North Vietnamese were killed while friendly losses were 7 killed, including two platoon commanders, and 35 wounded. As the weary Marines trudged back to Hill 881S, they were understandably disappointed at not being able to continue the attack. It wasn't until later that they learned why they had been halted just when victory was in sight.(*)(47)

Colonel Lownds' decision to break off the battle was not born out of faintheartedness, but was based on a valuable piece of intelligence that he received earlier in the afternoon. That intelligence came in the form of a NVA first lieutenant who was the commanding officer of the 14th Antiaircraft Company, 95C Regiment, 325C NVA Division; at 1400, he appeared off the eastern end of the runway with an AK-47 rifle in one hand and a white flag in the other. Under the covering guns of two Ontos, a fire team from the 2d Platoon, Company B, 1/26, took the young man in tow and, after Lieutenant Colonel Wilkinson had questioned him briefly, the lieutenant was hustled off to the regimental intelligence section for interrogation. The lieutenant had no compunction about talking and gave the Marines a detailed description of the forthcoming Communist offensive. As it turned out, the accuracy of the account was surpassed only by its timeliness, because the first series of attacks was scheduled for that very night--against Hills 861 and 881S. At the time Colonel Lownds received this news, Company I was heavily engaged 1,000 meters north of its defensive perimeter and he definitely did not want Captain Dabney and his men to be caught away from their fortified outpost when the NVA struck. Consequently, Lieutenant Colonel Alderman's request for reinforcements to press his advantage was denied.(48)

When the first enemy rounds began falling on Hill 861 shortly after midnight, Marines all along the front were in bunkers and trenches--waiting. The heavy mortar barrage lasted

---

(*) NVA casualties were obviously much greater than 103 dead because the Marines counted only those bodies found during the withdrawal.

about 30 minutes and was supplemented by RPG, small arms, and automatic weapons fire. This was followed by approximately 300 NVA troops who assaulted Hill 861. The van of the attacking force was made up of sapper teams that rushed forward with bangalore torpedoes and satchel charges to breach the defensive wire. Assault troops then poured through the gaps but were met and, in most sectors, stopped cold by interlocking bands of grazing machine gun fire.

In spite of the defensive fire, enemy soldiers penetrated the K/3/26 lines on the southwestern side of the hill and overran the helo landing zone. The Company K perimeter encompassed a saddle, thus the crest of 861 was actually two hills; the landing zone was on the lower one and the company CP was perched atop a steep rise to the northeast. Before the enemy could exploit the penetration, the Marines counterattacked down the trenchline and pinched off the salient. After vicious hand-to-hand fighting, the men of Company K isolated the pocket and wiped out the North Vietnamese. Had the enemy been able to flood the breach with his reserves, the situation might have become extremely critical. When the fighting subsided, 47 NVA bodies were strewn over the hilltop while four Marines died holding their ground.(*)(49)

During the attack on 861, the 3d Battalion command group remained on Hill 881S because bad weather prevented Lieutenant Colonel Alderman and his operations officer from returning to the combat base.(**)(50) Major Caulfield contacted the Company K command post by radio and found out that the fighting was indeed heavy. The company commander, Captain Norman J. Jasper, Jr., had been hit three times and was out of action; the executive officer, First Lieutenant Jerry N. Saulsbury, was running the show. The company gunnery sergeant was dead, the first sergeant was badly wounded, and the radio operator had been blinded by powder burns. Major Caulfield later recalled that the young Marine remained at his post for almost two hours before being

---

(*)   Many more North Vietnamese died that night than were found. The stench from the bodies decaying in the jungle around the hill became so strong that the men of K/3/26 were forced to wear their gas masks for several days.

(**)   Throughout the night, Lieutenant Colonel Alderman supervised defensive operations from 881S and was assisted by an alternate battalion command group at the base which was headed by the 3/26 Executive Officer, Major Joseph M. Loughran, Jr.

relieved and was "as calm, cool, and collected as a telephone operator in New York City," even though he could not see a thing.(51)

Some men on the hill had a rather unusual way of keeping their spirits up during the fight as First Sergeant Stephen L. Goddard discovered. The first sergeant had been hit in the neck and was pinching an artery shut with his fingers to keep from bleeding to death. As he moved around the perimeter, the Top heard a sound that simply had no place on a battlefield--somebody was singing. After tracing the sound to a mortar pit, Goddard peered into the emplacement and found the gunners bellowing out one stanza after another as they dropped rounds into the tubes. The "ammo humpers" were also singing as they broke open boxes of ammunition and passed the rounds to the gunners. Naturally, the name of the song was "The Marines Hymn."(52)

One decisive factor in this battle was that Hill 881S was not attacked. Company I did not receive a single mortar round and the reprieve left the Marines free to lend unhindered support to their comrades on 861. The bulk of this fire came from the Company I 81mm mortar section. Since Lieutenant Colonel Alderman and Major Caulfield were concerned about the possibility of their position being attacked, they were careful not to deplete their ammunition. Major Caulfield personally authorized the expenditure of every 20-round lot so he knew exactly how many mortar rounds went out that night--680. The mortar tubes became so hot that the Marines had to use their precious drinking water to keep them cool enough to fire; after the water, the men used fruit juice. When the juice ran out, they urinated on the tubes. The spirited support of Company I and its attached elements played a big part in blunting the attack.(53)

There are two plausible explanations for the enemy's failure to coordinate the attack on Hill 861 with one on 881S. Lieutenant Colonel Alderman and Major Caulfield felt that Captain Dabney's fight on the afternoon of 20 January had crippled the NVA battalion which was slated for the attack on Hill 881S and disrupted the enemy's entire schedule. On the other hand, Company I had emerged from the engagement with relatively light casualties and was in fighting trim on the morning of the 21st. Another possibility was the manner in which Colonel Lownds utilized artillery and aircraft. The regimental commander did not use his supporting arms to break up the attack directly; he left that job up to the defenders themselves. Instead, the

colonel called in massive air and artillery concentrations on
points where the enemy would more than likely marshal his reserves. Much of the credit belong to Lieutenant Colonel
Hennelly's batteries at the base. One infantry officer on Hill
881S, who observed the fire, described the Marine artillery as
"absolutely and positively superb." Throughout the battle, the
North Vietnamese assault commander was heard frantically scream-
ing for his reserves--he never received an answer. The fact
that the initial attack on 861 was not followed up by another
effort lent credence to the theory that the backup force was
being cut to pieces to the rear while the assault troops were
dying on the wire.(54)

The Marines did not have long to gloat over their victory
because at 0530 on the 21st the KSCB was subjected to an intense barrage. Hundreds of 82mm mortar rounds, artillery shells,
and 122mm rockets slammed into the compound as Marines dived into
bunkers and trenches.(*)(55) Damage at "ground zero" was extensive: several helicopters were destroyed, trucks and tents
were riddled, one messhall was flattened, and fuel storage areas
were set ablaze. Colonel Lownds' quarters were demolished but,
fortunately, the regimental commander was not in his hut at the
time. One of the first incoming rounds found its mark scoring
a direct hit on the largest ammunition dump, which was situated
near the eastern end of the runway. The dump erupted in a series
of blinding explosions which rocked the base and belched thousands
of burning artillery and mortar rounds into the air. Many of
these maverick projectiles exploded on impact and added to the
devastation. Thousands of rounds were destroyed and much of
this ammunition "cooked off" in the flames for the next 48 hours.
In addition, one enemy round hit a cache of tear gas (CS) re-
leasing clouds of the pungent vapor which saturated the entire
base.(56)

The main ammunition dump was just inside the perimeter
manned by Company B, 1/26, and the 2d Platoon, commanded by

(*) On Hill 881S, Captain Dabney watched several hundred 122mm
rockets lift off from the southern slope of 881N--a scant 300
meters beyond the farthest point of his advance the day before.
The enemy defensive positions between the two hills were obviously designed to protect these launching sites. At the combat
base, the barrage did not catch the Marines completely by surprise; the regimental intelligence section had warned that an
enemy attack was imminent and the entire base was on Red Alert.

Second Lieutenant John W. Dillon, was in the hotseat throughout
the attack. The unit occupied a trenchline which, at places,
passed as close as 30 meters to the dump. In spite of the
proximity of the "blast furnace," Lieutenant Dillon's men stayed
in their positions, answered with their own mortars, and braced
for the ground attack which never came. Throughout the ordeal,
the 2d Platoon lines became an impact area for all sizes of duds
from the dump which literally filled the trenchline with un-
exploded ordnance. In addition, the men were pelted by tiny
slivers of steel from the exploding antipersonnel ammunition
which became embedded in their flak jackets, clothing, and bare
flesh.(57)

The fire raging in the main dump also hampered the rest of
the 1st Battalion. The 81mm mortar platoon fired hundreds of
rounds in retaliation but the ammo carriers had to crawl to and
from the pits because of the exploding ammunition. Captain
Kenneth W. Pipes, commanding officer of Company B, had to dis-
place his command post three times when each position became
untenable. Neither was the battalion CP exempt; at about 1000,
a large quantity of C-4 plastic explosives in the blazing dump
was touched off and the resulting shock waves cracked the timbers
holding up the roof of Lieutenant Colonel Wilkinson's command
bunker. As the roof settled, several members of the staff were
knocked to the floor. For a moment it appeared that the entire
overhead would collapse but after sinking about a foot, the
cracked timbers held. With a sigh of relief, the men inside
quickly shored up the roof and went about their duties.(58)

The sudden onslaught produced a number of heroes, most of
whom went unnoticed. Members of Force Logistics Group Bravo,
and other personnel permanently stationed at the ammunition dump,
charged into the inferno with fire extinguishers and shovels to
fight the blaze. Motor transport drivers darted from the safety
of their bunkers to move trucks and other vehicles into revetments. Artillerymen quickly manned their guns and began returning fire. The executive officer of 1/13, Major Ronald W.
Campbell, ignored the heavy barrage and raced from one shell
hole to another analyzing the craters and collecting fragments
so that he could determine the caliber of the enemy weapons as
well as the direction from which they were being fired. Much
of the counterbattery fire was a direct result of his efforts.(59)

Three other artillerymen from Battery C, 1/13, performed
an equally heroic feat in the midst of the intense shelling.
When the dump exploded, the C/1/13 positions, like those of 1/26,

were showered with hundreds of hot duds which presented a grave danger to the battery. The battery commander, Captain William J. O'Connor, the executive officer, First Lieutenant William L. Everhart, and the supply sergeant, Sergeant Ronnie D. Whiteknight, immediately began picking up the burning rounds and carrying them to a hole approximately 50 meters behind the gun pits. For three hours, these Marines carried out between 75 and 100 duds and disposed of them, knowing that any second one might explode. When the searing clouds of tear gas swept over the battery, many gunners were cut off from their gas masks. Lieutenant Everhart and Sergeant Whiteknight quickly gathered up as many masks as they could carry and distributed them to the men in the gun positions. The "cannon cockers" donned the masks and kept their howitzers in action throughout the attack.(60)

By this time, most of 1/13 had ceased firing counterbattery missions and was supporting the defense force at Khe Sanh Village. An hour after the KSCB came under attack, the Combined Action Company (CACO) and a South Vietnamese Regional Forces (RF) company stationed in the village were hit by elements of the 304th NVA Division. The enemy troops breached the defensive wire, penetrated the compound, and seized the dispensary. Heavy street fighting ensued and, at 0810, the defenders finally drove the enemy force from the village. Later that afternoon, two NVA companies again assaulted the village but, this time, artillery and strike aircraft broke up the attack. Upon request of the defenders, Lieutenant Colonel Hennelly's battalion fired over 1,000 artillery rounds with variable time fuzes which resulted in airbursts over the defensive wire. During the action, a single Marine A-6A "Intruder" knifed through the ground fire and killed about 100 of the attackers. Those enemy soldiers who persisted were taken care of by close-in defensive fires and, when the fighting subsided, an American advisor counted 123 North Vietnamese bodies on or around the barbed wire.(61)

Following the second attack, Colonel Lownds decided to withdraw these isolated units to the confines of the KSCB. The village, which was the seat of the Huong Hoa District Headquarters, was not an ideal defensive position. The Allies were hampered by restricted fields of fire and there was a temple just outside the village which overlooked the perimeter. Most important, a regiment of the 304th NVA Division was operating in the immediate vicinity. The colonel decided that he would rather evacuate the village while he could, instead of waiting until its occupants were surrounded and fighting for their lives. Helicopters flew in and picked up the Marines and U. S. Army advisors; the Vietnamese troops and officials of the local government moved overland.

Upon arrival, the CACO and RF companies, which totaled about 250 men, took up positions in the southwestern sector of the base and were absorbed by FOB-3.(*)(62)

There was one other encounter on the 21st. At 1950, the 2d Platoon, L/3/26, reported 25-30 enemy soldiers crawling toward the wire bordering Red Sector. The Marines opened fire and, within an hour, killed 14 North Vietnamese. Remnants of the attacking force were seen dragging dead and wounded comrades from the battlefield. Cumulative friendly casualties for the day, including those incurred on Hill 861, were 9 killed, 37 wounded and evacuated (Medevaced), plus 38 wounded but returned to duty.(63)

When the events of the 21st were flashed to the world via the news media, many self-appointed experts in the United States began to speak out concerning the feasibility of maintaining the garrison at Khe Sanh. Those who opposed the planned defense felt that the Marines had been able to remain there only at the pleasure of the NVA. They pointed out that, in the preceding months, the installation had been of little concern to the North Vietnamese because it was ineffective as a deterrent to infil- tration. The undermanned 26th Marines could not occupy the perimeter, man the hill outposts, and simultaneously conduct the constant, large-unit sweeps necessary to control the area. Therefore, the enemy could simply skirt the base and ignore it. A build-up, however, would make the prize worthwhile for the NVA, which badly needed a crushing victory over the Americans for propaganda purposes. By concentrating forces at Khe Sanh, the theory went, the Allies would be playing into the enemy's hands because the base was isolated and, with Route 9 inter- dicted, had to be completely supplied by air. Fearing that Khe Sanh would become an American Dien Bien Phu, the critics favored a pull-out.

In Vietnam, where the decision was being made, there was little disagreement. The two key figures, General Westmoreland and General Cushman, "after discussing all aspects of the situ- ation, were in complete agreement from the start."(64) There were several reasons they decided to hold Khe Sanh at that time. The base and adjacent outposts commanded the Khe Sanh Plateau and the main avenue of approach into eastern Quang Tri

_____

(*)   The Huong Hoa District Headquarters operated from within the KSCB throughout the siege.

Lieutenant General Robert E. Cushman,
Jr., CG, III MAF (USMC Photo A190016)

General William C. Westmoreland,
ComUSMACV (Photo courtesy Office of
the Chief of Staff, U. S. Army)

Province. While the installation was not 100 percent effective as a deterrent to infiltration, it was a solid block to enemy invasion and motorized supply from the west. Had the Allies possessed greater strength in the northern provinces, they might have achieved the same ends with large and frequent airmobile assaults--a concept which General Cushman had advocated for some time. In January 1968, he had neither the helicopter resources, the troops, nor the logistical bases for such operations. The weather was another critical factor because the poor visibility and low overcasts attendant to the monsoon season made helicopter operations hazardous to say the least. Even if the III MAF commander had the materiel and manpower for such large airmobile assaults, the weather precluded any such effort before March or April. Until that time, the job of sealing off Route 9 would have to be left up to the 26th Marines.(65)

An additional consideration for holding the base was the rare and valuable opportunity to engage and destroy an, heretofore, elusive foe. Up to this time, there was hardly a commander in Vietnam who, at one time or another, had not been frustrated in his attempts to box in the slippery NVA and VC units. At Khe Sanh, the enemy showed no desire to hit and run but rather to stand and fight; it was a good idea to oblige him. In effect, the 26th Marines would fix the enemy in position around the base while Allied air and artillery battered him into senselessness. Furthermore, the defense was envisioned as a classic example of economy of force. Although there was conjecture that the NVA was trying to draw American units to the DMZ area, the fact remained that two crack NVA divisions, which otherwise might have participated in the later attacks on Hue and Quang Tri City, were tied down far from the vital internal organs of South Vietnam by one reinforced Marine regiment.(66)

Thus, with only two choices available--withdraw or reinforce --ComUSMACV chose the latter. In his "Report On The War In Vietnam," General Westmoreland stated:

> The question was whether we could afford the troops to reinforce, keep them supplied by air, and defeat an enemy far superior in numbers as we waited for the weather to clear, build forward bases, and made preparations for an overland relief expedition. I believed we could do all of those things. With the concurrence of the III Marine Amphibious Force Commander, Lieutenant General Robert E. Cushman, Jr., I made the decision to reinforce and hold the area while destroying the enemy with our massive firepower

47

and to prepare for offensive operations when the weather became favorable.

General Westmoreland reported his decision to Washington and more troops began to pour into the combat base.(67)

On 22 January, the 1st Battalion, 9th Marines, commanded by Lieutenant Colonel John F. Mitchell, was transferred to the operational control of the 26th Marines and arrived at 1900 the same day. Ever since the three high ranking NVA officers were killed outside Red Sector, General Tompkins and Colonel Lownds were concerned over the unhealthy interest that the North Vietnamese were showing in the western perimeter. When 1/9 arrived, the colonel directed the battalion commander to establish defensive positions at the rock quarry, 1,500 meters southwest of the strip. Lieutenant Colonel Mitchell moved his unit overland and set up a kidney-shaped perimeter around the quarry with his CP perched atop a hill. In addition, he dispatched a platoon from Company A approximately 500 meters further west to set up a combat outpost on a small knob. The 1/9 lines curved near, but did not tie in with, those of L/3/26; the small gap, however, could easily be covered by fire. The western approach was firmly blocked.(68) (See Map 6).

General Tompkins and Colonel Lownds also discussed plans for the opposite side of the compound. This approach would have been the most difficult for the North Vietnamese to negotiate because the terrain east of the runway dropped off sharply to the river below. This steep grade, however, was heavily wooded and provided the enemy with excellent concealment. The NVA troops, masters at the art of camouflage, could have maneuvered dangerously close to the Marine lines before being detected.

The main reason for concern, however, was the testimony of the cooperative NVA lieutenant who had surrendered on the 20th. According to the lieutenant, the eastern avenue of approach was the key with which the Communists hoped to unlock the Khe Sanh defenses. First, the NVA intended to attack and seize Hills 861 and 881S, both of which would serve as fire support bases. From these commanding positions, the enemy would push into the valley and apply pressure along the northern and western portion of the Marines' perimeter. These efforts, however, were simply a diversion to conceal the main thrust--a regimental ground attack from the opposite quarter. An assault regiment from the 304th Division would skirt the base to the south, hook around to the east, and attack paralleling the runway through the 1/26 lines.

Two key figures in the defense of Khe Sanh: Major General Rathvon McC. Tompkins (L), CG, 3d MarDiv, and Colonel David E. Lownds (R), CO, 26th Marines. (Photo courtesy Colonel David E. Lownds)

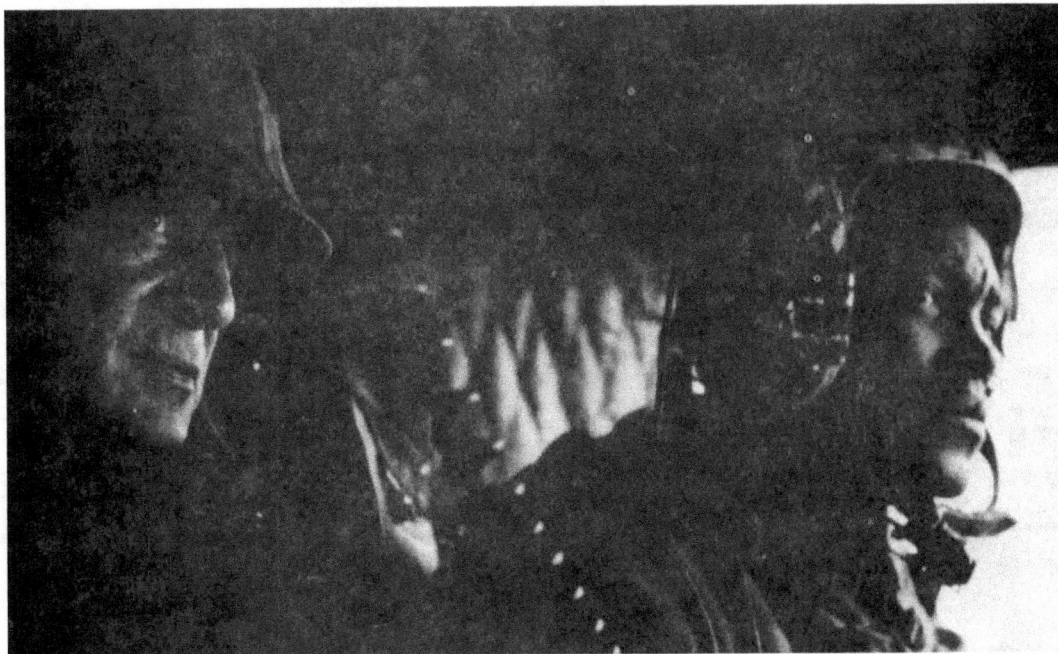

General Tompkins (L) made helicopter trips into Khe Sanh almost daily in spite of heavy enemy fire. (Photo courtesy David D. Duncan)

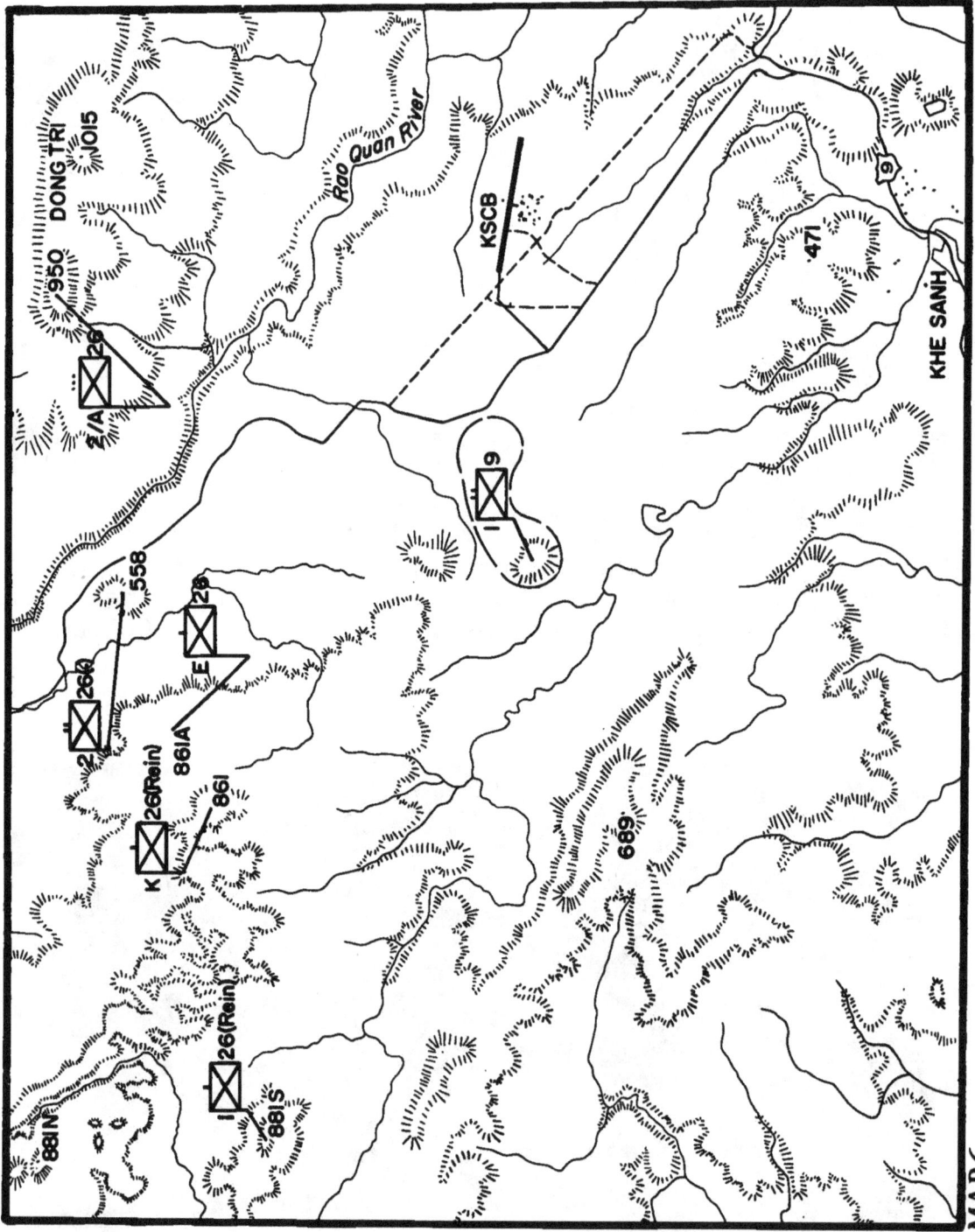

MAP 6

LOCATION OF OUTPOSTS

E. L. WILSON

Once the compound was penetrated, the North Vietnamese anticipated that the entire Marine defense system would collapse.(69)

On 27 January, the 37th ARVN Ranger Battalion, the fifth and
final battalion allotted for Khe Sanh, arrived.(*)(70) Understandably, Colonel Lownds moved the ARVN unit into the eastern
portion of the perimeter to reinforce the 1st Battalion. Actually,
the Marines were backing-up the South Vietnamese because the
Ranger Battalion occupied trenches some 200 meters outside the
1/26 lines. Lieutenant Colonel Wilkinson's men had already prepared these defensive positions for the new arrivals. The new
trenchline extended from the northeast corner of Blue Sector,
looped across the runway, paralleled the inner trenchline of
1/26, and tied back in with the Marine lines on the southeastern
corner of Grey Sector. (See Map 7) The only gap was where the
runway extended through the ARVN lines; this section was covered
by two Ontos. At night, the gap was sealed off with strands of
German Tape--a new type of razor-sharp barbed wire which was extremely difficult to breach. The North Vietnamese would now have
to penetrate two lines of defense if they approached from the
east.(71)

As January drew to a close, the situation at Khe Sanh could
be summed up in three words--enemy attack imminent. As a result
of rumblings of a large-scale Communist offensive throughout
South Vietnam, the scheduled Vietnamese Lunar New Year (TET)
ceasefire was cancelled in I Corps and the 26th Marines braced
for the inevitable. While they waited, they filled sandbags, dug
deeper trenches, reinforced bunkers, conducted local security
patrols, and, in general, established a pattern which would remain unbroken for the next two months. The NVA also established
a routine as enemy gunners daily shelled the base and hill outposts while assault units probed for a soft spot. Thus the two
adversaries faced each other like boxers in a championship bout;
one danced around nimbly throwing jabs while the second stood
fast waiting to score the counterpunch that would end the fight.(72)

(*)   ARVN battalions were considerably smaller than Marine battalions and the 37th Ranger was no exception. Even by Vietnamese
standards, the unit was undermanned; it had 318 men when it arrived.

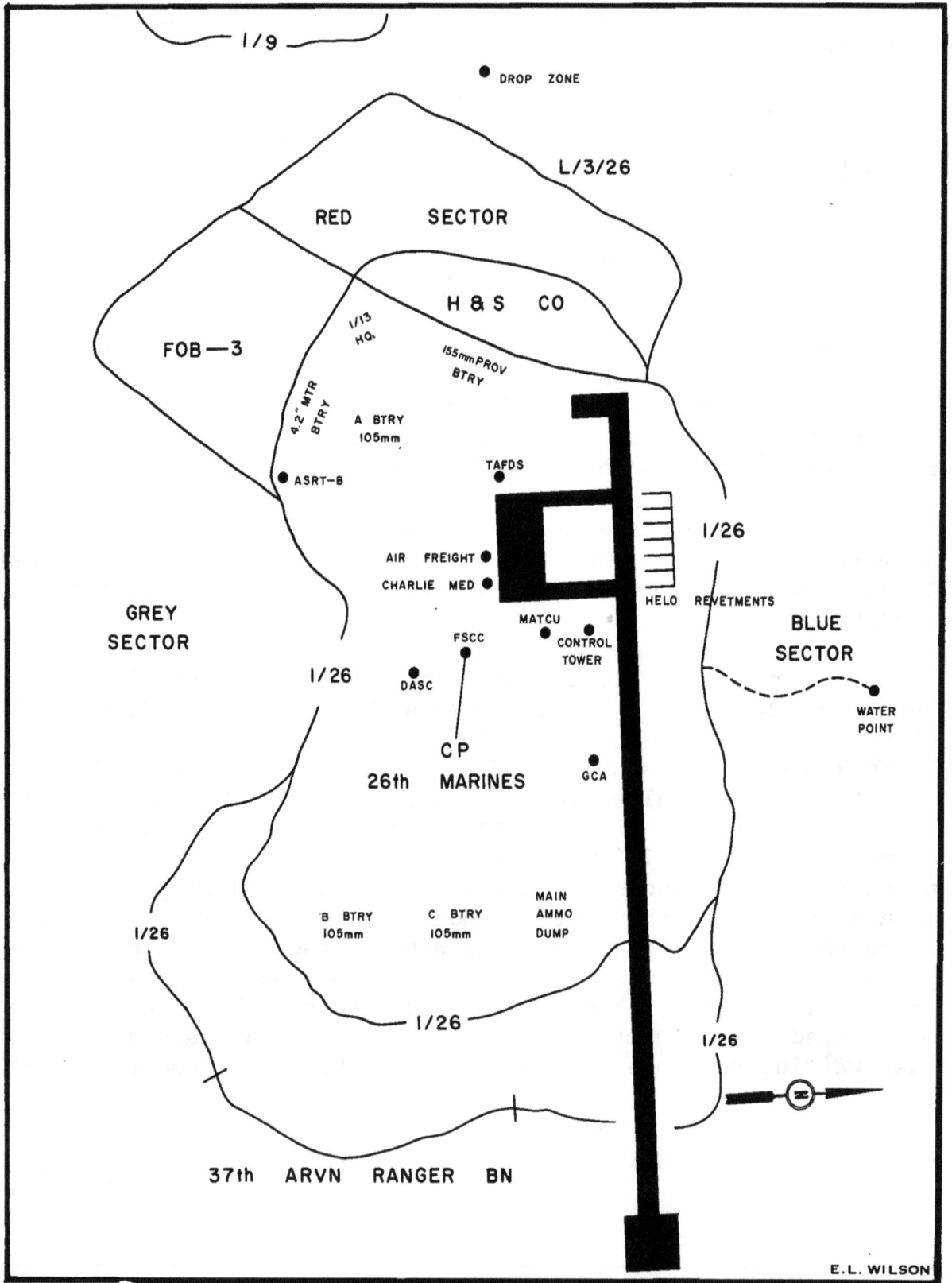

1/9

• DROP ZONE

L/3/26

RED   SECTOR

H & S   CO

1/13
HQ

155mm PROV
BTRY

FOB—3

4.2" MTR
BTRY

A BTRY
105mm

TAFDS •

• ASRT-8

AIR FREIGHT •

CHARLIE MED •

1/26

MATCU

FSCC •
• GCA   CONTROL
              TOWER

HELO   REVETMENTS

GREY
SECTOR

• DASC

BLUE
SECTOR

1/26

WATER
POINT

CP

26th   MARINES

• GCA

B BTRY
105mm

C BTRY
105mm

MAIN
AMMO
DUMP

1/26

1/26

1/26

N

37th   ARVN   RANGER   BN

E.L. WILSON

MAP7

KHE SANH COMBAT BASE

PART IV

THE "SO-CALLED" SIEGE BEGINS

When the Communists launched their TET Offensive on 30
January, they struck in force almost everywhere in South Vietnam
except Khe Sanh. Their prime targets were not military installations but the major population centers--36 provincial capitals,
64 district capitals, and 5 autonomous cities. The leaders in
Hanoi were apparently becoming dissatisfied with their attempts
to win in the South by a protracted war of attrition and decided
on one massive stroke to tip the scales in their favor. Consequently, the enemy unleashed some 62,000 troops, many of whom
infiltrated the cities disguised as civilians, in hopes that
they could foster a public uprising against the central government and encourage mass defections among the Republic of Vietnam
Armed Forces. Virtually all available VC main and local force
units were thrown into the initial attacks. With the exception
of Hue and Da Nang, NVA units were generally committed a few
days later to reinforce the assault troops.(73)

The sudden onslaught initially achieved surprise but, in the
final analysis, the overall military effort failed miserably.
Allied forces reacted quickly and drove the invaders from the
cities and towns, killing approximately 32,000 (as of 11 February)
hard-core guerrillas and North Vietnamese soldiers in the process.
Many Viet Cong units, with no other orders than to take their
initial objectives and hold until reinforcements arrived, were
wiped out completely. Ironically, these elite cadres were the
backbone of the guerrilla infrastructure in the South which the
Communists, up to that point, had tried so hard to preserve. In
Saigon and Hue, die-hard remnants held out for several weeks but,
for the most part, the attacks were crushed within a few days.
The general uprising and mass desertions never materialized; on
the contrary, the offensive tended to galvanize the South
Vietnamese.(74)

Even though he paid an exorbitant price, the enemy did
achieve certain gains. If the Communists' goal was to create
sensational headlines which would stun the American people--they
succeeded. To the strategists in Hanoi, an important byproduct
of any military operation was the associated political ramifications
in the United States; namely, how much pressure would certain
factions put on their leaders to disengage from the struggle in

South Vietnam. To the delight of the Communists, no doubt, the TET Offensive had a tremendous psychological impact in the U. S. and, as usual, the response of the dissidents was vociferous. Much of the reaction was completely out of proportion to the actual military situation but it had a definite demoralizing effect on the American public--the long-range implications of which are still undetermined.(75)

Another casualty of these nation-wide attacks was the pacification program in rural communities. When the Allies pulled back to clear the cities, they temporarily abandoned portions of the countryside to the enemy. Upon return, they found that progress in the so-called "battle for the hearts and minds of the people" had received a temporary set back.(76)

To achieve these ends, however, the enemy troops brought senseless destruction to Vietnamese cities and heaped more suffering upon an already war-weary populace. Thousands of innocent civilians were killed and hundreds of thousands made homeless--mostly in Saigon/Cholon and Hue. Four days after the initial attacks, the central government formed the Central Recovery Committee which, with U. S. assistance, launched Project RECOVERY to help alleviate the misery of the people. Had this program not been implemented, the Communists might have come much closer to achieving their goal of overthrowing the government. In addition to the destruction in the cities, the enemy violated a sacred religious holiday and, what's worse, actually desecrated a national shrine by turning the majestic Hue Citadel into a bloody battlefield. For these acts, the Viet Cong and North Vietnamese earned the deep-seated hatred of many South Vietnamese who in the past had been, at best, neutral.(77)

Whether or not Khe Sanh was, in fact, the ultimate enemy objective or merely a diversion for the TET Offensive has not yet been established with certainty. The U. S. command in Saigon believed that the Communists' goal was to create a general uprising, precipitate mass defections in the RVN armed forces, and then seize power. The concentration of NVA regular forces in the northern two provinces was primarily to support this overall objective but it was also possible that the enemy had a secondary aspiration of shearing off and seizing the Quang Tri-Thua Thien area should his primary effort fail. Thus Khe Sanh was envisioned as an intregal part of the master plan, or as General Westmoreland called it "an option play."

Subsequent events tended to vindicate that evaluation. Since the initial nation-wide attacks had been conducted primarily by Viet Cong guerrillas and main force units, the NVA regular forces remained relatively unscathed and, with two of the four North Vietnamese divisions known to be in I Corps poised around the 26th Marines, there was little doubt as to where the next blow would fall. Furthermore, the enemy's extensive preparations around the base reinforced the belief that this effort was a major offensive and not just a feint. Before investing the garrison, the North Vietnamese dug positions for their long-range artillery pieces. Later, they emplaced countless smaller supporting weapons, established numerous supply depots, and began the ant-like construction of their intricate siege-works. This intensive build-up continued long after most of the fighting associated with the TET Offensive was over.(78)

The enemy had much to gain by taking Khe Sanh. If they could seize any portion of Quang Tri Province, the Communists would have a much stronger bargaining position at any future conference table. In addition, the spectre of Dien Bien Phu which was constantly raised in the American press undoubtedly led the enemy to believe that the coming battle could not only prove successful but decisive. If the garrison fell, the defeat might well turn out to be the coup de grace to American participation in the war. At first, the Marines anticipated a major pitched battle, similar to the one in 1967, but the enemy continued to bide his time and the battle at Khe Sanh settled into one of supporting arms.(79)

At Khe Sanh, the periodic showers of enemy artillery shells were, quite naturally, a major source of concern to General Tompkins and Colonel Lownds and they placed a high priority on the construction of stout fortifications. Understandably, not every newcomer to Khe Sanh immediately moved into a thick bunker or a six-foot trench with overhead cover. The colonel had spent most of his tour with a one-battalion regiment and had prepared positions for that battalion; then, almost overnight, his command swelled to five battalions. The new units simply had to build their own bunkers as quickly as they could.(80)

The regimental commander placed a minimum requirement on his subordinates of providing overhead cover for the troops that would stop, at least, an 82mm mortar round. The FSCC determined that one strip of runway matting and two or three layers of sandbags would fill the requirement. The average bunker usually started as an 8x8 foot dugout with one 6x6 inch timber inserted in each corner and the center for support. The overhead consisted of planks, a strip of runway matting, sandbags, loose dirt,

55

Marines at the combat base run for cover when warning of enemy rocket or artillery attack is sounded. (USMC Photo A190245)

Machine gunners lie on top of trench cover while they search for enemy movement. (USMC Photo A190929)

and more sandbags. Some enterprising Marines piled on more loose dirt, then took discarded 105mm casings and drove them into the top of the bunker like nails. These casings often caused pre-detonation of the heavier-caliber rounds. The combat engineers attached to the 26th Marines could build one of these bunkers in three or four days; the average infantrymen took longer. Overhead cover for the trenchlines consisted of a strip of matting placed across the top of the trench at intervals and reinforced with sandbags. The defenders could stand up in the trench during periods of inactivity and duck under the matting when enemy rounds started to fall.(81)

The Marines were also faced with another question concerning their defenses: "How large an artillery round could you defend against and still remain within the realm of practicality?" Since the 26th Marines was supplied solely by air, building material was a prime consideration. Matting and sandbags were easy enough to come by but lumber was at a premium. Fortifications which could withstand a hit from an 82mm mortar were a must because the North Vietnamese had an ample supply of these weapons but the base was also being pounded, to a lesser degree, by heavier-caliber guns. With the material available to the 26th Marines, it was virtually impossible to construct a shelter that was thick enough or deep enough to stop the heavy stuff.(82)

This fact was borne out when Colonel Lownds decided to build a new regimental CP bunker. The engineers supplied the specifications for an overhead that would withstand a 122mm rocket; to be on the safe side, the colonel doubled the thickness of the roof. The day before the CP was to be occupied, a 152mm round landed squarely on top of the bunker and penetrated both layers.(83)

The massing of enemy artillery made the hill outposts that much more important. Had they been able to knock the Marines from those summits, the North Vietnamese would have been able to fire right down the throats of the base defenders and make their position untenable. As it was, the companies on Hills 881S, 861, 861A, and 558 not only denied the enemy an unobstructed firing platform from which to pound the installation, they also served as the eyes for the rest of the regiment in the valley which was relatively blind to enemy movement. For observation purposes, Hill 881S was the most strategically located and a discussion of the enemy's heavy weaponry will point out why.

While the 60mm and 82mm mortars were scattered around in proximity of the combat base (roughly within a 2,000-3,000 meter radius), the NVA rocket sites and artillery pieces were located well to the west, southwest, and northwest, outside of friendly counterbattery range. One particularly awesome and effective weapon was the Soviet-built 122mm rocket, the ballistic characteristics of which had a lot to do with the way the North Vietnamese employed it. When fired, the projectile was fairly accurate in deflection but, because it was powered by a propellent, the biggest margin of error was in range. Consequently, the North Vietnamese preferred to position their launching sites so the gunners could track along the long axis of a given target; thus, longs and shorts would land "in the ballpark." The KSCB hugged the airstrip and was roughly in the shape of a rectangle with the long axis running east and west. This made the optimum firing positions for the 122mm rocket either to the east or west of the base on line with the runway. There was really only one logical choice because the eastern site would have placed the rockets within range of the Americans' 175s and extended the enemy's supply lines from Laos. To the west, Hills 881S or 861 would have been ideal locations because in clear weather those vantage points provided an excellent view of Khe Sanh and were almost directly on line with the airstrip. Unfortunately for the NVA, the Marines had squatters' rights on those pieces of real estate and were rather hostile to claim jumpers. As an alternative, the North Vietnamese decided on 881N but this choice had one drawback since the line of sight between that northern peak and the combat base was masked by the top of Hill 861. Nevertheless, the enemy emplaced hundreds of launching sites along its slopes and throughout the siege approximately 5,000 122mm rockets rained on Khe Sanh from 881N.(84)

Because of their greater range, the enemy's 130mm and 152mm artillery batteries were located even further to the west. These guns were cleverly concealed in two main firing positions. One was on Co Roc Mountain which was southwest of where Route 9 crossed the Laotian border; the other area was 305, so called because it was on a bearing of 305 degrees (west-northwest) from Hill 881S at a range of about 10,000 meters. While the heavy caliber artillery rounds which periodically ripped into the base were usually referred to as originating from Co Roc, 305 was the source of about 60-70 percent of this fire, probably because it was adjacent to a main supply artery. Both sites were vulnerable only to air attack and were extremely difficult to pinpoint because of the enemy's masterful job of camouflage, his cautious employment, and the extreme distance from friendly observation posts. The NVA gunners fired only a few rounds every hour so that continuous muzzle flashes did not betray their positions and, after each round, quickly scurried out to cover the guns with protective nets and screens. Some pieces, mounted on tracks, were wheeled out of caves in Co Roc Mountain, fired, and returned immediately. Though never used in as great a quantity as the rockets and mortars, these shells wreaked havoc at Khe Sanh because there was very little that they could not penetrate; even duds went about four feet into the ground.(85)

The 3/26 elements on Hill 881S were a constant thorn in the enemy's side because the men on that most isolated of the Marine outposts could observe all three of the main NVA firing positions --881N, 305, and Co Roc. When rockets lifted off of 881N or the guns at Co Roc lashed out, the men of Company I could see the flashes and provided advance warning to the base. Whenever possible they directed retaliatory air strikes on the offenders.(*) Whenever the enemy artillery at 305 opened up, the muzzle flashes were hard to see because of the distance and the everpresent dust from air strikes, but the rounds made a loud rustling noise as they arched directly over 881S on the way to Khe Sanh. When the Marines heard the rounds streak overhead, they passed a warning to the base over the 3d Battalion tactical radio net, provided the net was not clogged with other traffic. The message was short and to the point: "Arty, Arty, Co Roc" or "Arty, Arty, 305."(86)

At the base the Marines had devised a crude but effective early warning system for such attacks. Motor transport personnel had mounted a horn from a two-and-a-half ton truck in the top of a tree and the lead wires were attached to two beer can lids. When a message was received from 881S, a Marine, who monitored the radio, pressed the two lids together and the blaring horn gave advanced warning of the incoming artillery rounds. The radio operator relayed the message over the regimental net and then dived into a hole. Men in the open usually had from five to eighteen seconds to find cover or just hit the deck before "all hell broke loose." When poor visibility obscured the view between 881S and the base, the radio operator usually picked himself up, dusted off, and jokingly passed a three-word message to Company I which indicated that the rounds had arrived on schedule--"Roger India...Splash."(87)

(*) One Marine, Corporal Robert J. Arrota, using a PRC-41 UHF radio which put him in direct contact with the attack pilots, personally controlled over 200 air strikes without the aid of a Tactical Air Controller (Airborne); his peers gave him the title of "The Mightiest Corporal In The World."

"Arty, Arty, Co Roc" was the title
of a popular folksong in 3/26.
(Photo courtesy David D. Duncan)

A Marine forward observer keeps a
watchful eye on enemy trenches.
(USMC Photo A190933)

Water on Hill 881S was scarce and beards flourished. 2dLt Richard M. Foley, XO of India, 3/26. (Photo courtesy Major William H. Dabney)

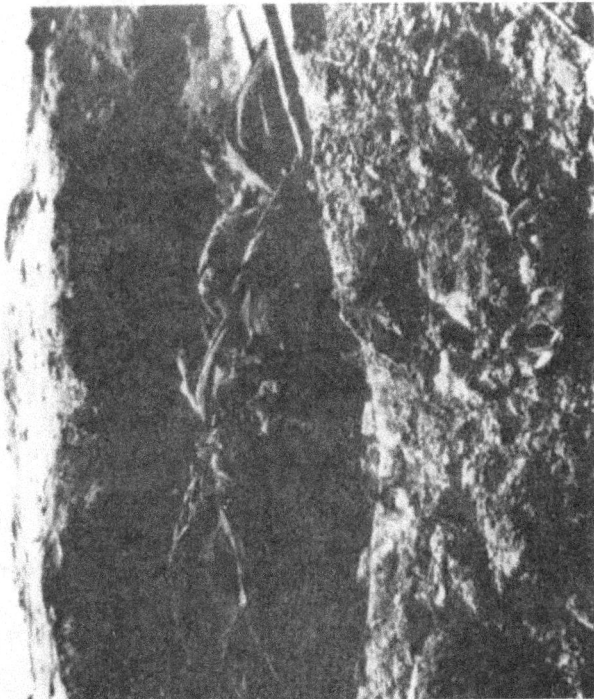

Colors over Hill 881S. (Photo courtesy Major William H. Dabney)

The fact that Company I on 881S was the fly in the enemy's ointment was no secret, especially to the enemy. As a result, North Vietnamese gunners made the Marines' existence there a veritable nightmare. Although no official tally of incoming rounds was recorded, Captain Dabney's position took a much more severe pounding than any of the other hill outposts. Volume, however, was only part of the story because the incoming was almost always the heavier stuff. The hill received little 60mm or 82mm mortar fire but a deluge of 120mm mortar and 100mm artillery rounds. There was also a smattering of 152mm shells from Co Roc. The shelling was the heaviest when helicopters made resupply runs.

The firing position which plagued the Marines the most was located to the southwest of the hill in a U-shaped draw known as "the Horseshoe." There were at least two NVA 120mm mortars in this area which, in spite of an avalanche of American bombs and artillery shells, were either never knocked out or were frequently replaced. These tubes were registered on the hill and harassed Company I constantly. Anyone caught above ground when one of the 120s crashed into the perimeter was almost certain to become a casualty because the explosion produced an extremely large fragmentation pattern. Captain Dabney figured that it took one layer of runway matting, eight of sandbags, and one of either rocks or 105mm casings to prevent penetration of a 120mm with a quick fuze--nothing the Marines had on 881S could stop a round with a delayed fuze. Because of the shape of the hill, the summit was the only defendable terrain and thus provided the enemy with a compact target; this often resulted in multiple casualties when the big rounds landed within the perimeter. The only thing that the Marines had going for them was that they could frequently spot a tell-tale flash of an artillery piece or hear the "thunk" when a mortar round left the tube but the heavy shells took their toll. On Hill 881S alone, 40 Marines were killed throughout the siege and over 150 were wounded at least once.(88)

Considering the sheer weight of the bombardment, enemy shells caused a relatively small number of fatalities at the base. Besides the solid fortifications, there were two factors which kept casualties to a minimum. The first was the flak jacket--a specially designed nylon vest reinforced with overlapping fiberglass plates. The jacket would not stop a high-velocity bullet but it did protect a man's torso and most vital organs against shell fragments. The bulky vest was not particularly popular in hot weather when the Marines were on patrol but

62

in a static, defensive position the jacket was ideal. The second factor was the high quality of leadership at platoon and company level. Junior officers and staff noncommissioned officers (NCOs) constantly moved up and down the lines to supervise the younger, inexperienced Marines, many of whom had only recently arrived in Vietnam. The veteran staff NCOs, long known as the "backbone of the Corps," knew from experience that troops had to be kept busy. A man who was left to ponder his problems often developed a fatalistic attitude that could increase his reaction time and decrease his life time. The crusty NCOs did not put much stock in the old cliche: "If a round has your name on it, there's nothing you can do." Consequently, the Marines worked; they dug trenches, filled sandbags, ran for cover, and returned to fill more sandbags. Morale remained high and casualties, under the circumstances, were surprisingly low.(89)

Although the NVA encircled the KSCB and applied constant pressure, the defenders were never restricted entirely to the confines of the perimeter. The term "siege," in the strictest sense of the word, was somewhat of a misnomer because the Allies conducted a number of daily patrols, often as far as 500 meters from their own lines.(*)(90) These excursions were primarily for security and reconnaissance purposes since General Tompkins did not want his men engaged in a slugging match with the enemy outside the defensive wire. If the North Vietnamese were encountered, the Marines broke contact and withdrew, while supporting arms were employed.(91)

One vital area was the drop zone. When the weather turned bad in February, the KSCB was supplied primarily by parachute drops. Colonel Lownds set up his original zone inside the FOB-3 compound but later moved it several hundred meters west of Red Sector because he was afraid that the falling pallets might injure someone. Lieutenant Colonel Mitchell's 1/9 was given responsibility for security of the drop zone and his patrols conducted daily sweeps along the periphery of the drop area to flush out enemy troops who might try to disrupt the collection of supplies. In addition, combat engineers swept through the zone each morning and cleared out any mines the enemy set in during the night. Thus the defenders at Khe Sanh were never

---

(*) Lieutenant Colonel Mitchell, whose battalion held the rock quarry perimeter, later commented that his troops patrolled out to 1,200 meters. The units at the base never went that far until the siege was lifted.

completely hemmed-in, but the regimental commander admitted that any expedition beyond sight of the base was an invitation to trouble.(92)

The Allies did more than prepare defenses and conduct patrols because the NVA launched three of its heaviest ground attacks during the first week in February. In the predawn hours of 5 February, the North Vietnamese lashed out at the Marine base and adjacent outposts with nearly 200 artillery rounds while a battalion from the 325C NVA Division assaulted Hill 861A. Colonel Lownds immediately placed all units on Red Alert and, within minutes, 1/13 was returning fire in support of E/2/26.

The fight on Hill 861A was extremely bitter. At 0305 the North Vietnamese opened up on Captain Breeding's positions with a tremendous 82mm mortar barrage. This was followed by continuous volleys of RPG rounds which knocked out several Marine crew-served weapons and shielded the advance of the NVA sappers and assault troops. The North Vietnamese blew lanes through the barbed wire along the northern perimeter and slammed into the Company E lines. Second Lieutenant Donald E. Shanley's 1st Platoon bore the brunt of the attack and reeled back to supplementary positions. Quickly the word filtered back to the company CP that the enemy was inside the wire and Captain Breeding ordered that all units employ tear gas in defense but the North Vietnamese were obviously "hopped up" on some type of narcotic and the searing fumes had very little effect. Following the initial assault there was a brief lull in the fighting. The NVA soldiers apparently felt that, having secured the northernmost trenchline, they owned the entire objective and stopped to sift through the Marine positions for souvenirs. Magazines and paperbacks were the most popular. Meanwhile, the temporary reversal only served to enrage the Marines. Following a shower of grenades, Lieutenant Shanley and his men charged back into their original positions and swarmed all over the surprised enemy troops.(93)

The counterattack quickly deteriorated into a melee that resembled a bloody, waterfront barroom brawl--a style of fighting not completely alien to most Marines. Because the darkness and ground fog drastically reduced visibility, hand-to-hand combat was a necessity. Using their knives, bayonets, rifle butts, and fists, the men of the 1st Platoon ripped into the hapless North Vietnamese with a vengeance. Captain Breeding, a veteran of the Korean conflict who had worked his way up through the ranks, admitted that, at first, he was concerned over how his younger, inexperienced Marines would react in their first fight. As it turned out, they were magnificent. The captain saw one of his men come face to face with a North Vietnamese in the inky darkness; the young American all but decapitated his adversary with a crushing, round-house right to the face, then leaped on the flattened soldier and finished the job with a knife. Another man was jumped from behind by a North Vietnamese who grabbed him around the neck and was just about to slit his throat, when one of the Marine's buddies jabbed the muzzle of his M-16 between the two combatants. With his selector on full automatic, he fired off a full magazine; the burst tore hugh chunks from the back of the embattled Marine's flak jacket but it also cut the North Vietnamese in half. Since the fighting was at such close quarters, both sides used hand grenades at extremely short-range. The Marines had the advantage because of their armored vests and they would throw a grenade, then turn away from the blast, hunch up, and absorb the fragments in their flak jackets and the backs of their legs. On several occasions, Captain Breeding's men used this technique and "blew away" enemy soldiers at less than 10 meters.(94)

No one engaged in the donnybrook was exactly sure just how long it lasted--all were too busy fighting to check their watches. More than likely, the enemy was inside the wire less than a half hour. During the fighting, Captain Breeding fed fire team-sized elements from the 2d and 3d Platoons into the fray from both flanks of the penetration. The newcomers appeared to be afraid that they might miss all the action and tore into the enemy as if they were making up for lost time. Even though the E/2/26 company commander was no newcomer to blood and gore, he was awed by the ferocity of the attack. Captain Breeding later said: "It was like watching a World War II movie. Charlie didn't know how to cope with it...we walked all over them."(95) Those dazed NVA soldiers who survived the vicious onslaught retreated into another meatgrinder; as they ran from the hill, they were blasted by recoilless rifle fire from 2/26 which was located on Hill 558.

At approximately 0610, the North Vietnamese officers rallied the battered remnants and tried again, but the second effort was also stopped cold. By this time, Captain Breeding, who was busier than the proverbial one-armed paper hanger, was assisting in the coordination of fire support from five separate sources (i.e. Hills 861A, 881S, 558, the KSCB, and the 175mm gun bases). The Marines of Captain Dabney's I/3/26, located on Hill 881S provided extremely effective and enthusiastic support throughout the attack. In three hours, Captain Dabney's men pumped out close to 1,100 rounds from only three 81mm mortars, and the tubes became so hot that they actually glowed in the dark.(*) Again, the bulk of the heavy artillery fire, along with radar controlled bombing missions, was placed on the northern avenues leading to the hill positions. The enemy units, held in reserve, were thus shredded by the bombardment as they moved up to continue the attack.(96)

After the second assault fizzled out, the North Vietnamese withdrew, but enemy gunners shelled the base and outposts throughout the day. At 1430, replacements from 2/26 were helilifted to Hill 861A. Captain Breeding had lost seven men, most of whom were killed in the opening barrage, and another 35 were medevaced so the new arrivals brought E/2/26 back up to normal strength. On the other hand, the NVA suffered 109 known dead; many still remained in the 1st Platoon area where they had been shot, slashed, or bludgeoned to death. As near as Captain Breeding could tell, he did not lose a single man during the fierce hand-to-hand struggle; all American deaths were apparently the result of the enemy's mortar barrage and supporting fire. The Marines never knew how many other members of the 325C NVA Division had fallen as a result of the heavy artillery and air strikes but the number was undoubtedly high. All in all, it had been a bad day for the Communists.(97)

The North Vietnamese took their revenge in the early morning hours of 7 February; their victims were the defenders of the Special Forces camp at Lang Vei. At 0042, an American advisor reported that the installation was under heavy attack by enemy tanks. This was the first time that the NVA had employed its armor in the south and, within 13 minutes, 9 PT-76 Soviet-built tanks churned through the defensive wire, rumbled over the anti-personnel minefields, and bulled their way into the heart of the compound.(**)(98) A battalion from the 66th Regiment, 304th NVA Division, equipped with satchel charges, tear gas, and flame-throwers, followed with an aggressive infantry assault that was coordinated with heavy attacks by fire on the 26th Marines. Colonel Lownds placed the base on Red Alert and the FSCC called in immediate artillery and air in support of the beleaguered

---

(*)   The men of Company I used the same methods to cool the mortar tubes that they used during the attack against 861 on 21 January.

(**) The defenders later reported knocking out at least one and probably two tanks with rocket launchers.

Lang Vei garrison. Although the Marines responded quickly, the defensive fires had little effect because, by that time, the enemy had overrun the camp.(*)(99) The defenders who survived buttoned themselves up in bunkers and, at 0243, called for artillery fire to dust off their own positions.(100)

Lieutenant Colonel Hennelly's artillerymen responded with scores of deadly air bursts which peppered the target area with thousands of fragments. The 1/13 batteries fired over 300 rounds that morning and the vast fire superiority was echoed in the radio transmission of one Lang Vei defender who said: "We don't know what you're using but for God's sake keep it up." That was one of the last transmissions to Khe Sanh because, at 0310, the Marines lost communications with the camp.(101).

Part of Colonel Lownds' mission as coordinator of all friendly forces in the Khe Sanh area was to provide artillery support for Lang Vei and, if possible, to reinforce the camp in case of attack. Under the circumstances, a relief in strength was out of the question. In early January, when M/3/26 was in reserve, Lieutenant Colonel Alderman and Major Caulfield had conducted a personal reconnaissance of Route 9 between the KSCB and Lang Vei to determine the feasibility of moving a large unit overland. Their opinion was that any such attempt would be suicidal because the terrain bordering Route 9 was so well suited for an ambush it was an "NVA dream." Any column moving down the road, especially at night, would undoubtedly have been ambushed.(**)(102) If the Marines went directly over the mountains, they would have to hack through the dense growth and waste precious hours.(***)(103) A

(*) The 26th Marines FSCC had prepared extensive defensive fire plans for the Lang Vei Camp. In the early stages of the attack, the camp commander did not request artillery and later asked for only a few concentrations. He never asked for the entire schedule to be put into effect.

(**) Documents taken off a dead NVA officer later in the battle indicated that the enemy hoped that the attack on Lang Vei would draw the Marines out of Khe Sanh so he could destroy the relief column.

(***) In November 1967, Lieutenant Colonel Wilkinson, on direction of the regimental commander, had sent a rifle company to determine possible direct routes through the jungle. The company commander, Captain John N. Raymond, reported that his unit, avoiding well-used trails to preclude ambush, had made the trip in about 19 hours.

large-scale heliborne effort was ruled out because the North
Vietnamese apparently anticipated such a move and withdrew
their tanks to the only landing zones near the camp which were
suitable for such an operation. Even with tactical aircraft
providing suppressive fire, a helo assault into the teeth of
enemy armor was ill-advised. The most important factor, however,
was that NVA units in the area greatly outnumbered any force
Colonel Lownds could commit.(104)

Since a relief in force was undesirable, plans for a hit
and run rescue attempt were quickly drawn up at General Cushman's
headquarters. Once General Westmoreland had given the green
light, Major General Norman J. Anderson, commanding the 1st
MAW and Colonel Jonathan F. Ladd of the U. S. Army Special Forces,
worked out the details. Two major points agreed upon were that
the helicopters employed in the operation would be those which
were not essential to the 26th Marines at the moment and that
Marine fixed-wing support would be provided.(105)

As soon as it was light, the survivors of the Lang Vei
garrison managed to break out of their bunkers and work their
way to the site of an older camp some 400-500 meters to the
east. Later that same day, a raiding party composed of 40 CIDG
personnel and 10 U. S. Army Special Forces advisors from FOB-3
boarded Quang Tri-based MAG-36 helicopters and took off for
Lang Vei. A flight of Huey gunships, led by Lieutenant Colonel
William J. White, Commanding Officer of Marine Observation
Squadron 6, as well as jet aircraft escorted the transport
choppers. While the jets and Hueys covered their approach,
the helicopters swooped into a small strip at the old camp and
took on survivors, including 15 Americans. In spite of the heavy
suppressive fire provided by the escorts, three transport helos
suffered battle damage during the evacuation. One overloaded
chopper, flown by Captain Robert J. Richards of Marine Medium
Helicopter Squadron 262, had to make the return trip to Khe
Sanh at treetop level because the excess weight prevented the
pilot from gaining altitude.(106)

(*)   On the return trip to the KSCB, Captain Richards flew
over the outskirts of Khe Sanh Village. A NVA soldier suddenly
stepped out of one hut and sprayed the low-flying chopper with
a burst from his AK-47 assault rifle. The rounds ripped out
part of Richards' instrument panel and one bullet zinged about
two inches in front of his nose before passing through the top
of the cockpit. A Marine gunner on the CH-46 quickly cut down

There was a large number of indigenous personnel--both military and civilian--who could not get out on the helicopters and had to move overland to Khe Sanh. A portion of these were members of the Laotian Volunteer Battalion 33 which on 23 January had been overrun at Ban Houei San, Laos (near the Laotian/ South Vietnam border) by three NVA battalions. The remnants fled across the border and took refuge at Lang Vei and when the Special Forces camp fell, the Laotians continued their trek to the east with a host of other refugees. At 0800 on the 8th, about 3,000 approached the southern perimeter at Khe Sanh and requested admittance. Colonel Lownds, fearing that NVA infiltrators were in their midst, denied them entrance until each was searched and processed. This took place near the FOB-3 compound after which some of the refugees were evacuated. The Laotians were eventually returned to their own country.(107)

Also on the morning of 8 February, elements of the 101D Regiment, 325C Division launched the first daylight attack against the 26th Marines. At 0420, a reinforced battalion hit the 1st Platoon, A/1/9, which occupied Hill 64 some 500 meters west of the 1/9 perimeter. Following their usual pattern, the North Vietnamese tried to disrupt the Marines' artillery support with simultaneous bombardment of the base. To prevent friendly reinforcements from reaching the small hill the enemy also shelled the platoon's parent unit and, during the fight, some 350 mortar and artillery rounds fell on the 1/9 positions. The NVA assault troops launched a two-pronged attack against the northwestern and southwestern corners of the A/1/9 outpost and either blew the barbed wire with bangalore torpedoes or threw canvas on top of the obstacles and rolled over them. The enemy soldiers poured into the trenchline and attacked the bunkers with RPGs and satchel charges. They also emplaced machine guns at the edge of the penetrations and pinned down those Marines in the eastern half of the perimeter who were trying to cross over the hill and reinforce their comrades.(108)

The men in the northeastern sector, led by the platoon commander, Second Lieutenant Terence R. Roach, Jr., counterattacked

---

the North Vietnamese but the damage had already been done. Even though he was shaken by the experience, the pilot nursed his crippled bird back to the base and landed safely. Once on the ground, he quickly switched helicopters and returned to Lang Vei for another evacuation mission. For his actions during the day, Captain Richards was later awarded the Distinguished Flying Cross.

down the trenchline and became engaged in savage hand-to-hand fighting. While rallying his troops and directing fire from atop an exposed bunker, Lieutenant Roach was mortally wounded. From sheer weight of numbers, the North Vietnamese gradually pushed the Marines back until the enemy owned the western half of the outpost. At that point, neither side was able to press the advantage. Pre-registered mortar barrages from 1/9 and artillery fire from the KSCB had isolated the NVA assault units from any reinforcements but at the same time the depleted 1st Platoon was not strong enough to dislodge the enemy.(109)

One Marine had an extremely close call during the fight but lived to tell about it. On the northern side of the perimeter, Private First Class Michael A. Barry of the 1st Squad was engaged in a furious hand grenade duel with the NVA soldiers when a ChiCom grenade hit him on top of the helmet and landed at the young Marine's feet. PFC Barry quickly picked it up and drew back to throw but the grenade went off in his hand. Had it been an American M-26 grenade, the private would undoubtedly have been blown to bits but ChiCom grenades frequently produced an uneven frag pattern. In this case, the bulk of the blast went down and away from the Marine's body; Barry had the back of his right arm, his back, and his right leg peppered with metal fragments but he did not lose any fingers and continued to function for the rest of the battle.(110)

In another section of the trenchline, Lance Corporal Robert L. Wiley had an equally hair-raising experience. Wiley, a shell-shock victim, lay flat on his back in one of the bunkers which had been overrun by the enemy. His eardrums had burst, he was temporarily paralyzed and his glazed eyes were fixed in a corpse-like stare but the Marine was alive and fully aware of what was going on around him. Thinking that Wiley was dead, the North Vietnamese were only interested in rummaging through his personal effects for souvenirs. One NVA soldier found the Marine's wallet and took out several pictures including a snapshot of his family gathered around a Christmas tree. After pocketing their booty, the North Vietnamese moved on; Lance Corporal Wiley was later rescued by the relief column.(111)

At 0730, Lieutenant Colonel Mitchell committed a second platoon, headed by the Company A commander, Captain Henry J. M. Radcliffe, to the action. By 0900, the relief force had made its way to the eastern slope of the small hill and established contact with the trapped platoon. During the advance, Companies B and D, along with one section of tanks, delivered murderous direct fire to the flanks and front of Captain Radcliffe's column, breaking up any attempt by the enemy to interdict the linkup. After several flights of strike aircraft had pasted the reverse slope of the hill, the company commander led his combined forces in a frontal assault over the crest and, within 15 minutes, drove the North Vietnamese from the outpost. Automatic weapons chopped down many North Vietnamese as they fled from the hill. The battered remnants of the enemy force retreated to the west and, once in the open, were also taken under fire by the rest of the Marine battalion. In addition, the artillery batteries at KSCB contributed to the slaughter and, when the smoke cleared, 150 North Vietnamese were dead. Although the platoon lines were restored, Colonel Lownds decided to abandon the position and, at 1200, the two units withdrew with their casualties. Marine losses that morning on the outpost were 21 killed and 26 wounded; at the base, 5 were killed and 6 wounded.(112)

During the next two weeks, the NVA mounted no major ground attack but continued to apply pressure on the KSCB. There were daily clashes along the Marine lines but these were limited to small fire fights, sniping incidents, and probes against the wire. A decrease in activity along the various infiltration routes indicated that the enemy had completed his initial build-up and was busily consolidating positions from which to launch an all-out effort. The Allies continued to improve their defenses and by mid-February most units occupied positions with three or four layers of barbed wire, dense minefields, special detection devices, deep trenches, and mortar-proof bunkers. The battle reverted to a contest of supporting arms and the North Vietnamese stepped up their shelling of the base, especially with direct fire weapons. Attempts to silence the enemy guns were often frustrated because the Marines were fighting two battles during February--one with the NVA, the other with the weather.(113)

PART V

THE AIRLIFT

The weather at Khe Sanh throughout February could be characterized in one word--miserable. General Tompkins remarked that, for combat purposes, the weather was the worst that he'd ever seen. The northeast monsoons had long since spilled over into the Khe Sanh Valley and every morning the base was shrouded with ground fog and low scud layers which dissipated around 1000 or 1100. When the sun finally managed to burn through, the cloud ceiling retreated slightly but still hovered low enough to prevent the unrestricted use of airborne artillery spotters and strike aircraft. It was during these periods, when the overcast was between 100 and 500 feet, that enemy artillery, rocket, and mortar fire was the heaviest. The NVA forward observers, perched along the lower slopes of the surrounding hills, called in and adjusted barrages with little fear of retaliation against their own gun positions. Later in the afternoon, when the fog rolled in again and obscured the enemy's view, the incoming tapered off.(*)(114)

The Marines adjusted their schedule accordingly. They usually worked under the cover of the haze in the morning, went underground during the midday shelling, and returned to their duties later in the afternoon. While the extremely low cloud cover occasionally befriended the men at the base, it constantly plagued the pilots whose mission was to resupply the 26th Marines.

The job of transporting enough "bullets, beans, and bandages" to sustain the 6,680 Khe Sanh defenders fell to the C-130s of Marine Aerial Refueler Transport Squadron 152 and the U. S. Air Force 834th Air Division; the C-123s of the 315th Air Commando Wing; the UH-34, Ch-46, and UH-1E helicopters of Marine Aircraft Group 36 (MAG-36); and the CH-53 choppers of MAG-16.(**)(115)

(*) The weather during February was bad for operations but not particularly uncomfortable. The mean temperature was 71 degrees, the average humidity was 92 percent, and an average weekly rainfall was .04 inches. The wind was out of the east with an average velocity of 6 miles per hour.

(**) Organizationally, the USAF C-130s belonged to the 315th

Ground fog in the morning and late afternoon shrouded the base obscuring the view of both the enemy and the Marines. (Photo courtesy David D. Duncan)

The reduced visibility from fog and haze hampered air operations. Crews of Marine UH-1E gunships wait for ceiling to lift. (Photo courtesy David D. Duncan)

Even under ideal circumstances, the airlift would have been a massive undertaking. The difficulties, however, were compounded by the poor visibility which was below minimum for airfield operations 40 percent of the time and the heavy volume of anti-aircraft and artillery fire directed at the incoming transports. The NVA had moved several antiaircraft units into the hills east of the airstrip forcing the C-130 Hercules, the C-123 Providers, and the helicopters to run the gauntlet during their final approach. Under cover of the heavy fog, some audacious NVA gun crews positioned their antiaircraft weapons just off the eastern threshold of the runway and fired in the blind whenever they heard the drone of incoming planes. Several aircraft were hit while on GCA final and completely in the soup.(*)(116) Immediately after touchdown, the aircraft were subjected to intense mortar and rocket fire; in fact, the incoming was so closely synchronized with their arrival, the fixed-wing transports were nicknamed "mortar magnets" by the Marines.(117)

The key to survival for the pilots was a steep approach through the eastern corridor, a short roll-out, and a speedy turnaround after landing. A small ramp paralleled the western end of the strip which the transport crews used as an unloading point. After roll-out, the pilot turned off the runway onto the easternmost taxiway, then wheeled onto the ramp while the loadmasters shoved the pallets of supplies out the back.(**) All outgoing passengers were loaded on the double because the

---

Air Division but that unit did not operate in Vietnam. Five to seven aircraft from each of the 315th's squadrons were on temporary duty in Vietnam and were under the operational control of the 834th Air Division. The 315th Air Commando Wing and its C-123s were organizationally part of the 834th.

(*)   One NVA gun crew came in too close for its own good. The 1/26 commander, Lieutenant Colonel Wilkinson, dispatched a platoon from Company D to attack this position which was off the northeastern end of the airstrip. While the 81mm mortars of 1/26 provided support, the platoon commander, Second Lieutenant Daniel L. McGravey, and his men aggressively assaulted the position. During a brisk fire fight, they killed several North Vietnamese, captured the antiaircraft weapon, and took the gunner prisoner.

(**)   If a pilot made his approach from the west, which was not often the case, he had to taxi all the way back down the runway to the loading ramp.

View of airstrip at Khe Sanh facing east.
(Photo courtesy David D. Duncan)

U. S. Air Force C-130 about to touch down after approaching from the east. (Photo courtesy David D. Duncan)

planes rarely stopped rolling. The pilot completed the loop by turning back onto the runway via the western taxiway and took off in the opposite direction from which he landed. It was not uncommon for the entire circuit to be completed within three minutes; even then, the planes were tracked by exploding mortar rounds.(118)

On 10 February, a tragedy occurred which resulted in a drastic alteration of the unloading process. A Marine C-130, heavily laden with bladders of fuel for the 26th Marines, was making its approach to the field under intense fire. Just before the giant bird touched down, the cockpit and fuel bags were riddled by enemy bullets. With flames licking at one side, the stricken craft careened off the runway 3,100 feet from the approach end, spun around, and was rocked by several muffled explosions. The C-130 then began to burn furiously. Crash crews rushed to the plane and started spraying it with foam. The pilot, Chief Warrant Officer Henry Wildfang, and his copilot suffered minor burns as they scrambled out the overhead hatch in the cockpit. Fire fighters in specially designed heat suits dashed into the flaming debris and pulled several injured crewmen and passengers to safety--rescue attempts came too late for six others. One of those killed in the crash, Lieutenant Colonel Carl E. Peterson, the 1st MAW Engineer Officer, was a reserve officer who only a few months before had volunteered for active duty. As a result of this accident and damage sustained by other transports while on the ground, C-130 landings at Khe Sanh were suspended.(119)

With the field closed to C-130s, a U. S. Air Force innovation--the Low Altitude Parachute Extraction System or LAPES--was put into effect. This self-contained system, which had been used extensively during the renovation of the airstrip in the fall of 1967, enabled the aircraft to unload their cargo without landing. When making a LAPES run, the Hercules pilot made his approach from the east during which he opened the tail ramp and deployed a reefed cargo parachute. Prior to touchdown, he added just enough power to hold the aircraft about five feet above the ground. As the plane skimmed over the runway and approached the intended extraction point, the pilot electrically opened the streaming chute which was attached to the roller-mounted cargo pallets. The sudden jolt of the blossoming chute snatched the cargo from the rear hatch and the pallets came to a skidding halt on the runway. The pilot then jammed the throttles to the firewall, eased back on the yoke, and executed a high-angle, westerly pull-out to avoid ground fire while the Marines moved

Death of a Hercules. A C-130 of Marine Aerial Refueler Transport Squadron 152 burns after crashing at the base. (Photo courtesy David D. Duncan)

Crash crew at Khe Sanh pours foam on a burning CH-46 helicopter following an enemy artillery attack. (USMC Photo A190350)

onto the runway with forklifts and quickly gathered in the
supplies. The system was quite ingenious and allowed the aircraft to pass through the V-ring in a matter of seconds.(*)
Even though the airmen could not control the skidding pallets
after release, some pilots perfected their individual technique
and were able to place the cargo on a 25-meter square with con-
sistency. On one occasion, however, an extraction chute mal-
functioned and the cargo rocketed off the western end of the
runway; the eight-ton pallet of lumber smashed into a messhall
located near the end of the strip and crushed three Marines
to death.(120)

Another technique--the Ground Proximity Extraction System
or GPES--was also used but to a lesser degree than the LAPES.
(15 GPES deliveries during the siege as compared to 52 LAPES.)
Both utilized the low approach but with GPES the cargo was extracted by a hook extended from a boom at the rear of the aircraft. As the C-130 swooped low over the runway, the pilot tried
to snag an arresting cable similar to the one used on aircraft
carriers; only his hook was attached to the cargo bundles and
not the plane. Upon engagement, the pallets were jerked from
the rear hatch and came to a dead stop on the runway. With the
GPES, the chance of a pallet skidding out of control or over-
turning was greatly reduced. The only problem that occurred was
not with the system itself but with faulty installation. The
Marines who initially emplaced the GPES were frequently chased
away from their work by incoming mortar rounds and, as a result
of the periodic interruptions, the cable was not anchored properly.
The first C-130 that snagged the wire ripped the arresting gear
out by the roots. After the initial bugs were remedied, the
system worked so successfully that, on one pass, a load containing 30 dozen eggs was extracted without a single eggshell
being cracked.(121)

Most of the time, however, the low overcast precluded the
use of either extraction system and the preponderance of supplies
was delivered by paradrops. This technique called for close
air/ground coordination and the C-130 pilots relied on the Marine
Air Traffic Control Unit (MATCU) at Khe Sanh to guide them in
to the drop zones. The Marine ground controller lined the aircraft up on the long axis of the runway for a normal instrument
approach and when the Hercules passed a certain point over the

_____

(*) V-ring is a term used on the rifle range to describe the
bull's-eye of a target.

eastern threshold of the field, the controller called "Ready, Ready, Mark." At "Mark," the pilot pushed a stop watch, activated his Doppler navigational system, turned to a predetermined heading and maintained an altitude of between 500 and 600 feet. The Doppler device indicated any deviation from the desired track to the drop zone, which was west of Red Sector, and the release point was calculated by using the stop watch--20 to 26 seconds from "Mark," depending on the winds. At the computed release point, the pilot pulled the C-130 into an 8-degree nose-up attitude and 16 parachute bundles, containing 15 tons of supplies, slid from the rear of the aircraft and floated through the overcast into the 300-meter-square drop zone. Under Visual Flight Rules (VFR), the average computed error for the drops was only 95 meters. Even when these missions were executed completely under Instrument Flight Rules (IFR), the average distance that the bundles landed from the intended impact point was 133 meters--well inside the drop zone. On a few occasions, however, the parachute bundles missed the zone and drifted far enough away from the base to preclude a safe recovery. In these rare instances, friendly artillery and air strikes were brought to bear on the wayward containers to keep them from falling into the hands of the enemy. During the siege, Air Force C-130 crews conducted a total of 496 paradrops at Khe Sanh.(*)(122)

Although the paradrops were sufficient for bulk commodities such as rations and ammunition, there were certain items which had to be delivered or picked up personally. Medical supplies, special ammunition, and other delicate cargo would not withstand the jolt of a parachute landing. In addition, there were

---

(*) Disparities in official records make it difficult to determine the exact tonnage delivered to Khe Sanh by air. The USAF Historical Division Liaison Office states that, of the 14,356 tons delivered during the siege, Air Force planes were responsible for 12,430 tons (8,120 tons by paradrop, LAPES and GPES; 4,310 by aircraft landing at the field). On the other hand, 1st Marine Aircraft Wing records show that Marine helicopters alone carried 4,661 tons of cargo. About three-fourths of the helicopter tonnage, however, was lifted directly from Dong Ha to the hill outposts and thus did not pass through the main base at Khe Sanh. Neither total includes the contributions made by Marine Aerial Refueler Transport Squadron 152; the records of that unit only indicate the tonnage transported throughout the whole of I Corps and do not break it down to the amount delivered to individual bases such as Khe Sanh.

replacements to be shuttled into the base and casualties to be evacuated. With the cancellation of all C-130 landings, this job was left up to the sturdy C-123 Providers of the 315th Air Commando Wing as well as MAG-36 and MAG-16 helicopters. The choppers could maneuver around areas of heavy ground fire, land, unload, take on medevacs, and depart very quickly but their pay-loads were limited. On the other hand, the C-123s had a larger cargo capacity but were restricted to a more rigid approach and provided better targets both in the pattern and on the ground. (*)(123) The Providers, however, required much less runway from which to operate than the C-130s and could land and take off using only 1,400 of the 3,900 foot strip. This saving feature enabled the pilots to make a steep approach, short roll-out, and rapid turnaround. The crews still had to undergo those frantic moments on the ground when the geysers of dirty-black smoke bracketed their aircraft. Nevertheless, the dauntless C-123 crews continued their perilous missions throughout the siege with great success.(124)

No discussion of the airlift would be complete without mention of the MAG-36 and MAG-16 helicopter pilots who flew in and out of Khe Sanh daily delivering supplies, delicate cargo, reinforcements, and evacuating casualties. The chopper crews were faced with the same problems that plagued the fixed-wing transports--low ceilings and enemy ground fire--but to a greater degree because of their slow speed and vulnerability. MAG-36 operated primarily from Quang Tri and Dong Ha, and was reinforced from the group's main base at Phu Bai. These valiant pilots and crewmen in their Huey gunships, CH-46 transports, and UH-34s flew long hours, day and night, in all kinds of weather to sustain the Marines in and around Khe Sanh. The CH-53s of Da Nang-based MAG-16, with their heavier payload, also made a sizeable contribution to this effort.(125)

The resupply of the hill outposts was a particularly hazardous aspect of the overall mission. Approximately 20 per-cent of Colonel Lownds' personnel occupied these redoubts and, for all practical purposes, were cut off from the rest of the garrison. The road north of the base was not secure and the perimeters atop the hills were too small and irregular for para-chute drops; the only way that the isolated posts could be

---

(*) This resulted in another fiery crash on 6 March when a C-123 was shot down while on approach to the field and all aboard (43 USMC, 1 USN, and 4 USAF) were killed.

80

A UH-34 of MAG-36 departs Khe Sanh on its way to the hill outposts. (Photo courtsey David D. Duncan)

C-130 Hercules conducts paradrops west of Red Sector. (USMC Photo A190803)

sustained was by helicopter. When the dense monsoon clouds rolled into the valley, the mountain tops were the first to become submerged and, as the overcast lifted, the last to reappear. During February, several of the outposts were completely obscured for more than a week and resupply was impossible. During these periods, the North Vietnamese took advantage of the reduced visibility and emplaced heavy automatic weapons along the neighboring peaks and waited for the ceiling to lift which invariably heralded the arrival of helicopters. As a result, the UH-1Es, UH-34s, and CH-46s were subjected to a hail of enemy bullets during each mission.(126)

When the helicopters proceeded to the hills singly or in small groups, each mission was a hair-raising experience for both the chopper crews and the men on the ground. A good example of what often transpired during those frantic moments occurred early in the siege on Hill 881S when Captain Dabney called for a chopper to evacuate a badly wounded Marine. One corporal was assigned as a stretcher bearer because he had a badly impacted wisdom tooth and, once aboard, he could ride out on the helicopter and have the tooth extracted at the main base.(*) Because of the 120mm mortars located in the Horseshoe and the antiaircraft guns which ringed the hill, the men on 881S had to employ a variety of diversions to keep the enemy gunners from getting the range of the incoming choppers. In this instance, they threw a smoke grenade a good distance away from the actual landing zone in hopes that the gunners would register on the smoke and the helicopter would be in and out before the North Vietnamese could readjust. This meant that the helo had about 19 seconds to get off the ground.(127)

The ruse did not come off as planned. The stretcher bearers had barely loaded the wounded man aboard the helicopter, a CH-46, when 120mm mortar rounds bracketed the aircraft and spurred the pilot to action. The helo lurched into the air and the sudden jolt rolled the corporal with the bad tooth over the

---

(*)   Having the ambulatory cases serve as stretcher bearers was standard operating procedure on 881S. These men stayed on the chopper and did not have to make the return trip to their trenches under fire. When uninjured Marines served in this capacity there was the added danger that the helicopter would take off before they could debark and they would end up at Khe Sanh. In one instance after the siege was lifted, Captain Dabney spent a day at the combat base because he did not get off a medevac chopper fast enough.

edge of the tail ramp; he held on desperately for a few seconds but finally let go and fell about 20 feet to the ground. Cursing to himself, the young man limped back to his trench and waited for another chance.

Later that day, a UH-34 swooped in to pick up another casualty and the prospective dental patient quickly scrambled aboard. This trip also covered about 20 feet--10 feet up and 10 feet down--because the tail rotor of the UH-34 was literally sawed off by a burst from an enemy machine gun just after the bird became airborne. After the swirling craft came to rest, the passengers and the three-man crew quickly clamored out the hatch and dived into a nearby trench. A heavy mortar barrage ensued during which several more men were hit.

By the time another CH-46 arrived on the scene, the passenger list had grown to 14, including 10 casualties, the crew of the downed helo, and the original dental case. Because of the heavy concentration of enemy fire in the original zone, the Marines had blasted out another landing site on the opposite side of the hill. The chopper touched down and 13 of the 14 Marines boarded before the crew chief stated emphatically that the aircraft was full. As luck would have it, the young Marine with the swollen jaw was the 14th man. Thoroughly indignant, the three-time loser returned to his position and mumbled that he would rather suffer from a toothache than try and get off the hill by helicopter.(*)(128)

It was the consensus of both the ground commanders and pilots alike that the problem of getting helicopters to and from the hills was becoming critical. The technique then employed was resulting in casualties among both the air crews

---

(*)   During the course of the battle, 881S became a small grave-yard for helicopters; at least five were downed on or around the hill. Consequently, Company I gained a reputation among chopper crews which lasted long after the siege was over. When the 3d Battalion later departed Khe Sanh, Company I eventually moved to Hill 55 near Da Nang. One afternoon, while evacuating a wounded Marine, a CH-46 developed engine trouble and the pilot decided to shut down for repairs. Another flight was sent to pick up the wounded man and as the lead pilot approached he came up over the radio and asked his wingman where the landing zone was. The wingman replied: "Just look for the downed chopper, India /Company I/ always marks their zones that way."

and the infantry units, as well as a rapid rise in the attrition of MAG-36 helicopters. The Huey gunships, though putting forth a valiant effort, did not possess the heavy volume of fire required to keep the approach lanes open. As a result, the 1st MAW adopted another system which provided more muscle.(129)

The solution was basically a page out of the Fleet Marine Force Manual for Helicopter Support Operations. All helicopter flights to the hill outposts were to be escorted by strike aircraft which would provide suppressive fire. The A-4 Skyhawks of Chu Lai-based MAG-12 were selected as the fixed-wing escorts and the little jet was perfect for the job. Affectionately referred to as "Scooters" by their pilots, the A-4 was a highly maneuverable attack aircraft; its accuracy, dependability, and varied ordnance load had made it the workhorse of Marine close air support for many years.

Generals Cushman and Anderson conceived the idea and the details were worked out by Colonel Joel B. Bonner, Lieutenant Colonel William J. White, and Lieutenant Colonel Richard E. Carey at 1st MAW Headquarters. The operation went into effect on 24 February. Because of the large number of aircraft utilized in each mission--12 A-4s, 1 TA-4, 12 CH-46s, and 4 UH-1E gunships--the overall effort was nicknamed the Super Gaggle by its planners. The difficulty in execution was primarily one of coordination and control because of the various agencies (i.e. MAG-36, MAG-12, 3d MarDiv G-4, Dong Ha Logistics Support Area, and the units on the hill outposts) which were involved. Additional factors that had to be considered were departure weather, destination weather, and coordination of friendly artillery and air strikes around Khe Sanh. Lieutenant Colonel Carey, the 1st MAW Operations Officer and one of the planners, later described the mechanics of the Super Gaggle:

Success of the effort was predicated on timing, coordination, and often times luck. Luck, as used, refers to the ability to guess whether the weather would hold long enough to complete an effort once it got underway. The effort began with the TA-4 on station determining if sufficient ceiling existed for the "Scooters" of MAG-12 to provide sufficient suppressive fires to assure success... Once the TA-4 called all conditions go, an "H" hour was set and the Super Gaggle began. Twelve A-4s would launch from Chu Lai while simultaneously 100 miles to the north 12-16 helos would launch from the Quang Tri helo base and proceed to the Dong Ha LSA (Logistics Support Area) for supply pickup. The object was for all aircraft to arrive

After introduction of the Super Gaggle, CH-46 helicopters
with their 4,000-pound external loads proceeded to the
hill outposts in convoy. (USMC Photo A422061)

A-4 Skyhawks of Marine Aircraft Group-12 provided suppressive fire during resupply missions. (USMC Photo
A421671)

in the objective area on a precise schedule. So the operation generally consisted as follows: (1) Softening up known enemy positions by four A-4s, generally armed with napalm and bombs; (2) Two A-4s armed with CS (tear gas) tanks saturate enemy antiaircraft and automatic weapons positions; (3) 30-40 seconds prior to final run in by the helos two A-4s lay a smoke screen along selected avenues of approach....(4) While helos make final run into the target, four A-4s with bombs,rockets, and 20mm guns provide close-in fire suppression.... Once the helos commenced their descent the factors of weather, their 4,000-pound externally carried load, and the terrain would not permit a second chance. If an enemy gun was not suppressed there was no alternative for the helos but to continue. They (the transport pilots) were strengthened with the knowledge that following close on their heels were their gunships ready to pick them up if they survived being shot down. Fortunately, these tactics were so successful that during the entire period of the Super Gaggle only two CH-46s were downed enroute to the hill positions. The crews were rescued immediately by escorting Huey gunships.(*)(130)

These missions, however, looked much more orderly on paper than they did in the air and the operation lived up to its name. Only those who have experienced the hazards of monsoon flying can fully appreciate the veritable madhouse that often exists when large numbers of aircraft are confined to the restricted space beneath a low-hanging overcast. Coupled with this was the fact that the fluffy looking clouds around Khe Sanh housed mountains which ran up to 3,000 feet. No doubt, the aircrews involved in the Gaggle were mindful of the standard warning issued to fledgling aviators: "Keep your eyes out of the cockpit; a mid-air collision could ruin your whole day." Even though the missions were well-coordinated and executed with a high degree of professionalism, it often appeared that confusion reigned because planes were everywhere. A-4s bore in on the flanks of the approach lanes blasting enemy gun positions and spewing protective smoke; CH-46s groped through the haze trying to find the landing zones; the hornet-like UH-1E gunships darted in from the rear in case someone was shot down; and the lone

---

(*) For comparison, as many as 16 helicopters were utilized up to four times in one day during the Super Gaggle without a loss. Prior to the conception of this technique, as many as three choppers were shot down in one day around Khe Sanh.

TA-4 circled overhead trying to keep his flock from running amuck. During the missions to 881S, the men of India and Mike, 3/26, added to the hullabaloo with a little twist of their own. When the CH-46s settled over the hill, the Marines on the ground tossed out a few dozen smoke grenades for added cover and then every man in the perimeter fired a full magazine at anything on the surrounding slopes which appeared hostile. With some 350 men hosing down the countryside at the same time, the din was terrific.

Neither the deluge of lead from 881S nor the suppressive fire of the jets and gunships kept the NVA completely quiet. The 120mm mortar crews in the Horseshoe were especially active during the resupply runs to 881S and always lobbed some rounds onto the hill in hopes of knocking down a helicopter. These tubes had been previously registered on the LZs and the smoke screens had little effect on their fire; as a result, the Marines frequently shifted landing zones.(*) The smoke did block the view of the North Vietnamese machine gunners and they were forced to fire blindly through the haze--if they dared fire at all. The choppers still took hits but nowhere near as many as before the Gaggle was initiated. The CH-46 pilots, poised precariously

----

(*)   There is an interesting possibility as to why the mortars in the Horseshoe were never silenced. Fourteen years earlier, at Dien Bien Phu, the North Vietnamese used an ingenious method to protect their heavier siege mortars from air attacks and they may well have repeated it at Khe Sanh. The mortar crews selected a site on the slope of a hill, figured the elevation and deflection necessary to hit one specific target, and then dug a small tunnel at that precise angle into the side of the hill. The mortar was emplaced at the bottom of the tunnel with connecting caves which housed the gunners. When fired, the mortar rounds traveled up the shaft, sometimes as far as 50 feet before reaching the surface. The foliage was cleared away from the mouth of the tunnel so that the rounds did not hit the over-hanging branches and detonate prematurely. Mortars emplaced in this manner were, of course, limited to only one target and, as far as the gunners in the Horseshoe were concerned, that target was 881S. When the siege was later broken and Marine units began to maneuver in the terrain surrounding the hill mass, they were never taken under fire by the 120mm mortars even though they did receive fire from smaller caliber weapons. Hill 881S, however, continued to be hit periodically by the 120mms.

above the LZs during the few agonizing seconds it took to unload their cargo, often heard the sickening smack which meant that a bullet had torn into the fuselage of their thin-skinned helos. The members of the two-man Helicopter Support Teams (HST), 3d Shore Party Battalion who were attached to the rifle companies were also prime targets. These men had to stand up while they guided the choppers into the LZs and, every few days, they had to attach bundles of cargo nets, which accumulated from previous missions, for the return trip to Dong Ha. This was dangerous for the aircrews as well as the HST men because, during the hook-up, the pilots had to hold their aircraft in a vulnerable position a few feet above the ground with the nose cocked up and the belly exposed to fire from the front. While they attached the bundles, the ground support personnel could hear the machine gun rounds zing a few inches over their heads and slap into the soft underside of the suspended helicopter. Not all the bullets and shell fragments passed overhead; on 881S, the defenders were operating with their fourth HST when the siege ended.

In spite of the seriousness of the situation, the Gaggle was not without its lighter episodes. In one instance, an HST man attached to I/3/26 hooked up an outgoing load and gave the pilot the "thumbs up" when he discovered that he had become entangled in the pile of nets. The CH-46 surged into the air with the startled Marine dangling helplessly from the bottom of the net by one foot. But for the quick reaction of his comrade on the ground who informed the pilot by radio that the chopper had taken on more than the prescribed load, the young cargo handler would have had a rather interesting trip to Dong Ha. The CH-46 crews also provided a human touch during these missions. When the Sea Knights swept over the hills, it was not uncommon to see a machine gunner on board quit his weapon for a second, nonchalantly pitch a case of soda pop out the hatch, and then quickly return to blaze away at the enemy positions. At 1st MAW Headquarters, Lieutenant Colonel Carey, who had been an infantryman in Korea before he went to flight school and who sympathized with the men on the outposts, felt that a small gesture acknowledging their continued outstanding performance was in order. Special efforts were made to obtain quantities of dry ice for packing and one day, without notice, hundreds of Dixie-cups of ice cream were delivered to the men on the hills as part of the regular resupply. This effort was dubbed Operation COOL IT. The only hitch developed on 881S where the Marines, unaware of the contents, allowed the cargo to remain in the LZ until after dark when it was safe to venture out of the trenchline.

The ice cream was a little sloppy but edible and greatly appreciated.

The introduction of the Super Gaggle was a turning point in the resupply effort. Prior to its conception, the Marines on the outposts dreaded the thought of leaving their positions to retrieve cargo--even when it included mail--because of the heavy shelling. With a dozen Skyhawks pasting the surrounding hills during each mission, this threat was alleviated to a large degree and casualties tapered off. The Company I, 3/26, commander later stated: "If it weren't for the Gaggle, most of us probably wouldn't be here today." The helicopter pilots, knowing that their jet jockey compatriots were close at hand, were also able to do their job more effectively. In the past, the transport crew chiefs occasionally had to jettison their external load prematurely when the pilot took evasive action to avoid ground fire. When this occurred, the cargo nets usually slammed into the perimeter and splattered containers all over the hilltop.(*)(131) With the Super Gaggle, the pilots had less enemy fire to contend with and did not bomb the hills with the cargo pallets as much; as a result more supplies arrived intact. In addition, the system greatly facilitated the picking up of wounded personnel.(**)

The Marine helicopters continued their flights to and from Khe Sanh throughout the siege. In spite of the obstacles, the chopper pilots crammed enough sorties into those days with flyable weather to haul 465 tons of supplies to the base during February. When the weather later cleared, this amount was increased to approximately 40 tons a day. While supporting Operation SCOTLAND, MAG-36 and MAG-16 flew 9,109 sorties, transported 14,562 passengers, and delivered 4,661 tons of cargo.(132)

(*) Of all the jettisoned loads, those containing water were the most spectacular. On one occasion, a CH-46 carrying plastic containers of water was forced to release the net about 200 feet above the ground. The containers broke open in midair and the contents cascaded on the hill below. The Company E, 2/26, commander, Captain Breeding, later recalled that it produced one of the prettiest waterfalls he'd ever seen.

(**) It is no exaggeration to say that MAG-36 helicopters played a decisive role in the battle. The maintenance of the hill outposts was imperative if Khe Sanh was to be held, and these units depended on the helicopters for survival.

Colonel Lownds was more than satisfied with the airborne pipeline which kept his cupboard full and he had quite a cupboard. The daily requirement for the 26th Marines to maintain normal operations had jumped from 60 tons in mid-January to roughly 185 tons when all five battalions were in place. While the defenders didn't live high off the hog on this amount, at no time were they desperately lacking the essentials for combat. There were periods on the hills when the Marines either stretched their rations and water or went without, but they never ran short of ammunition. Understandably, ammunition had the highest priority--even higher than food and water. A man might not be able to eat a hand grenade but neither could he defend himself very effectively with a can of fruit cocktail. This did not mean that the men of the 26th Marines went hungry. On the average, the troops at the base received two C-Ration meals a day and this fare was occasionally supplemented with juice, pastry, hot soup, or fresh fruit. The men on the hills subsisted almost entirely on C-Rations and the time between meals varied, depending on the weather. Within the compound, water was rationed only when the pump was out of commission and that was a rare occurrence. Lieutenant Colonel Heath's position on Hill 558 was flanked by two streams so 2/26 was well supplied but the Marines on the other four outposts depended on helilifts for water; it was used sparingly for drinking and cooking.(*)(133) Besides the essentials, the 26th Marines also required tons of other supplies such as fortification material, fuel, tires, barbed wire, and spare parts--to name a few. PX items were on the bottom of the bottom of the priority totem pole because, as Colonel Lownds remarked: "If you have to, you can live without those." On the other hand, mail had a priority second only to ammunition and rations. The men at Khe Sanh received over 43 tons of mail during the worst month of the siege.(134)

One portion of the airlift which affected morale as much as the arrival of mail was the swift departure of casualties. A man's efficiency was greatly improved by the knowledge that,

---

(*) During one period of extremely bad weather, the platoon from A/1/26 which held positions on Hill 950 went without re-supply for nine days and the water shortage became a major problem. Lieutenant Colonel Wilkinson authorized the platoon commander, Second Lieutenant Maxie R. Williams, to send a squad out to a small stream which was about two hours march from the perimeter. In addition to finding water, the Marines surprised a group of North Vietnamese and killed nine of the enemy. One Marine was also killed.

A CH-46 helicopter of Marine Aircraft Group-36 evacuates wounded from Hill 861A (Photo courtesy David D. Duncan)

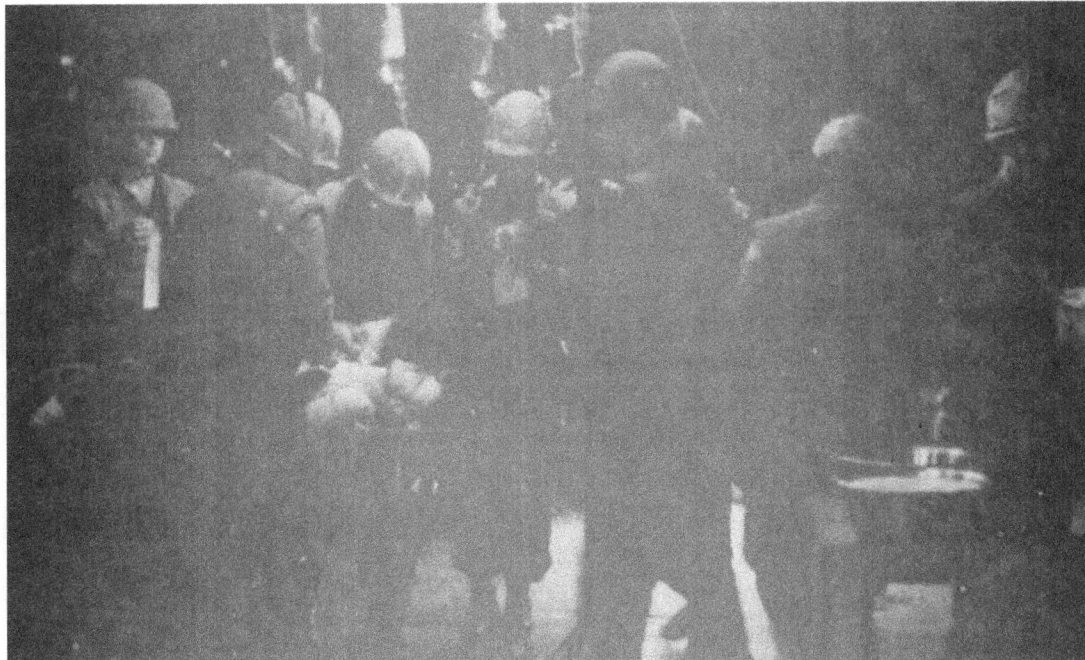

U. S. Navy doctors and corpsmen, wearing helmets and flak jackets, treat wounded at Charlie Med aid station. (Photo courtesy David D. Duncan)

if he were hit, he could expect immediate medical attention
and when necessary, a speedy evacuation.(*) Those with minor
wounds were usually treated at the various battalion aid sta-
tions and returned to duty; the more seriously injured were
taken to Company C, 3d Medical Battalion. Charley Med, as this
detachment was called, was located just south of and adjacent
to the aircraft loading ramp. There, U. S. Navy doctors and
corpsmen treated the walking wounded, performed surgery, and
prepared the litter cases for medevac. From Charley Med, it
was a short, but often nerve-racking trip to a waiting aircraft
and a hospital at Phu Bai. During the siege, the courageous
men of Charley Med, often working under heavy enemy fire,
treated and evacuated 852 wounded personnel.(135)

Thus the Marine and U. S. Air Force transport pilots, helicopter crews, loadmasters, and ground personnel kept open the
giant umbilical cord which meant life for the combat base.
Without their efforts, the story of Khe Sanh would undoubtedly
have been an abbreviated edition with a not-too-happy ending.
On the other hand, accounts of the heroism, ingenuity, and
skill demonstrated by these men would fill a book. But there
were other things besides manna falling from the heavens at
Khe Sanh and the vital role of the transports was frequently
eclipsed by the efforts of air crews who carried a much deadlier
cargo.

(*) Bad weather occasionally precluded the immediate evacuation of casualties from the hill outposts.

PART VI

SUPPORTING ARMS AND INTELLIGENCE

The amount of air and artillery support that the 26th Marines received during the defense of Khe Sanh was enormous. Few regiments ever had such an overwhelming amount of firepower at their disposal. The reason was that General Westmoreland gave SCOTLAND priority over all other operations in Vietnam. The well-publicized struggle had long since become more than just another battle; it was a symbol of Allied determination to hold the line in Vietnam. The stubborn resistance of the 26th Marines had generated an emotional impact that was felt not only in the United States but around the globe. Thanks to a small army of war correspondents and reporters, millions of people followed the battle day by day and, in essence, the military prowess of the United States was exposed to the world.

The agency at the combat base which was responsible for coordinating the vast array of supporting arms was the 26th Marines FSCC which was headed by the 1/13 commander, Lieutenant Colonel Hennelly. The FSCC, with its artillery and air representatives, was an integral part of the regimental staff and it planned and supervised the execution of all fire missions within the SCOTLAND area of operations. Subordinate to the FSCC, was the 1/13 Fire Direction Center (FDC), headed by Captain Lawrence B. Salmon, and the Khe Sanh Direct Air Support Center (DASC), under Major Charles D. Goddard. The FDC served as the brain of the artillery battalion where initial fire requests were received and transformed into numerical data for the gun crews. To speed up the process, Captain Salmon relied heavily on the Field Artillery Digital Automatic Computer or FADAC. The DASC had displaced to the KSCB on 19 January with the sole mission of handling the deluge of incoming aircraft. Requests for air support from the FSCC were channeled through the DASC to the Tactical Air Direction Center of the 1st MAW. Whenever the wing could not completely fill a quota, liaison teams within the DASC called on the other services for assistance. Once the schedule was met and the strike aircraft arrived on station, the Marine DASC, aided by an Airborne Command and Control Center (ABCCC) from Seventh Air Force, coordinated all air operations within the Khe Sanh TAOR.(*)(137)

(*)   Marine control of air support within the Khe Sanh TAOR

This mammoth air umbrella, called Operation NIAGARA, lasted from 22 January until 31 March and was truly an Allied effort. At one time or another, the Khe Sanh DASC utilized the assets of all services: 1st MAW, Seventh Air Force, Strategic Air Command, U. S. Navy Task Force 77, Vietnamese Air Force, and various U. S. Army aviation companies. The majority of the sorties, however, were flown by U. S. Marine, Navy, and Air Force crews. Their mission was to "destroy enemy forces in the SCOTLAND ...TAOR, interdict enemy supply lines and base areas,...and provide maximum tactical...air support to friendly forces." Generally, the type of strike fell into one of three categories: close air support, B-52 Arc Light strikes, or radar-controlled bombing.(*)(138)

Close air support missions were utilized against pinpoint targets in proximity of friendly troops. Along with radar-controlled bombing, this type of air strike was the most responsive to the needs of the ground commanders and the most accurate; the attack pilots, however, required reasonably good weather to be able to hit their targets. There were usually fighter/bombers overhead at Khe Sanh around the clock; if not, they could be quickly scrambled from hot pads or diverted from other missions. When the pilots arrived on station, they checked in with the DASC and were handed off to a Marine or Air Force Tactical Air Controller (Airborne) who personally directed the strike. There

---

resulted from negotiations between CG, III MAF and the Seventh Air Force. General Cushman was delegated authority for Colonel Lownds to control, through his FSCC, all supporting fire, including air strikes within a circle which encompassed the range of the regiment's 155mm howitzers. During the period 22 January-13 February, operational difficulties caused ComUSMACV to give Commander, Seventh Air Force full responsibility for the overall NIAGARA air effort through the ABCCC.

(*) Close air support in Vietnam includes all air attacks that are coordinated with the supported force. Radar-controlled bombing and B-52 strikes, in this context, can be called close air support but, for the purposes of this study, the three above mentioned categories will be considered separately. Although the delivery method is technically not a criteria, close air support in this text will refer to those missions where fixed-wing pilots, under the direction of an airborne or ground controller, visually acquire and attack a target in proximity to friendly forces.

were seven TAC(A)s assigned to the 26th Marines; the Air Force
personnel were members of the 20th Tactical Air Support Squadron
and the Marines were from Headquarters and Maintenance Squadron
36 and Marine Observation Squadron 6. At least five of these
pilots, flying 01-E Birddogs or UH-1E gunships, remained over
the battlefield during the day and maintained direct communications with both the attack aircraft and the troops on the ground.
In this manner, the TAC(A)s could rapidly employ the jets
wherever they were needed the most and the close supervision
reduced the chance of accidentally bombing friendly forces.

During the day, the air around Khe Sanh was filled with
the high-pitched shriek of jet engines: Marine, Navy, and Air
Force F-4 Phantoms; Marine and Navy A-6 Intruders, A-4 Skyhawks,
and F-8 Crusaders; Air Force F-105 Thunderchiefs and F-100 Super
Sabers. In addition to the jets, the South Vietnamese prop-
driven A-1 Skyraider, a rugged attack aircraft of Korean War
vintage, was in evidence. At times, the sky overhead resembled
a giant beehive. When a flight arrived on station, the Khe Sanh
DASC normally directed it into a holding pattern until a TAC(A)
or a Forward Air Controller on the ground was free to handle
the strike. These patterns sometimes extended up to 35,000 feet
with scores of planes gradually augering their way downward as
each preceding flight unloaded its ordnance and scooted for home.

When a TAC(A) picked out a lucrative target or was assigned
one by the FSCC, he cleared the strike aircraft into his area.
The pilots then broke up whatever formation they were in, slipped
into trail, and snaked their way through holes in the overcast--
all the while keeping a sharp eye out for helicopters. Below
the clouds, the TAC(A)s and attack pilots often had difficulty
finding each other because of the ever present haze and dust.
Even on a clear day, the camouflaged Birddogs and Hueys were
hard to spot because they blended in so nicely with the surrounding landscape. To expedite the link-up, the jet pilots
frequently used Automatic Direction Finders to get a fix on the
TAC(A)s radio transmissions. All the while, the airborne spotter
was passing on pertinent information such as target description,
elevation, run-in heading, direction of pull-off, number of
passes, direction and distance of nearest friendly troops, and
whether ground fire was expected.

When the controller and his flight made visual contact,
the real work began. The TAC(A) made a marking run during which
he either fired a smoke rocket or pitched out a colored smoke
grenade on the position he wanted hit. Once the attack pilots

Marine and Air Force TAC(A)s controlled strike aircraft from light observation aircraft called Birddogs. (USMC Photo A402048)

UH-1E Gunships of Marine Observation Squadron-6 were also used to direct close air support missions. (USMC Photo A421451)

had the smoke, the TAC(A), and the nearest friendlies in sight, they rolled in on the assigned heading and made dummy passes until the controller was satisfied that the jets were lined up on the right target. He then cleared them in for hot passes. While the jets streaked in, the controller monitored his VHF tactical net to the ground troops and gave short corrections to the attack pilots over his UHF radio. An example of an average commentary follows:

> TAC(A): Number One, from my smoke go six o'clock at 100 meters....PILOT: Roger, Ones in hot...TAC(A): I have you in sight, you're cleared to fire....TAC(A): PILOT: Ones off target...Switches Safe....TAC(A): Number Two, from One's hits come three o'clock at 50 meters...PILOT: Roger, Two's in hot....etc., etc.

The aircraft continued their race track pattern until all ordnance was expended at which time the leader announced that his flight was pulling off "high and dry."(*)

The TAC(A) would then swoop low over the smoke-shrouded target and attempt to record the results of the strike. This Battle Damage Assessment (BDA) was relayed to the departing pilots for their intelligence debriefing back at homeplate. An example of one such transmission would be:

> Your BDA follows: 5 KBA (killed by air); two bunkers, 1 automatic weapon, and 50 meters of trenchline destroyed; one secondary explosion. You have been flying in support of the 26th Marines; your controller has been SOUTHERN OSCAR. Good shooting and good afternoon, gentlemen.

While the strike pilots checked out with the Khe Sanh DASC and headed for home, the TAC(A) looked for another target and waited for another flight.(139)

One of the most unusual incidents involving the use of strike aircraft occurred near Hill 881S and the key figure in the episode was a Marine from American Samoa--Lance Corporal Molimao Niuatoa. The corporal was a bull of a man, who because of his origin and wedge-shape physique was nicknamed "Pineapple Chunk." (A second American Samoan in the company of considerably

---

(*) High and dry meant that all ordnance had been expended. Another frequently used term was "ammo minus."

smaller stature was dubbed "Pineapple Tidbit.") But it was not the muscles which distinguished Niuatoa, it was his eyes; the man had absolutely phenomenal vision. During his recruit training, this gift had enabled him to post a score of 241 out of a possible 250 on the rifle range. Besides his vision, the corporal had the patience of Job and a deep power of concentration--qualities which were essential in his job as an artillery spotter.

One day, Corporal Niuatoa, using a pair of 20-power naval binoculars, was scanning in the direction of 305 when he picked up the muzzle flash of an enemy artillery piece; he then saw the gunners hurriedly cover the weapon with a screen. As the round sputtered overhead on its way to Khe Sanh, the corporal noted the position and reported his discovery to the company commander. Referring to a map, Captain Dabney could not get anything other than a general idea of the location because the site was from 12,000 to 13,000 meters away and the terrain in that area was so mountainous that he could not pinpoint the exact contour line. Not so Corporal Niuatoa, he could see exactly where the gun was and kept his eyes glued to the binoculars. Normally, he would have adjusted on the target with marking rounds but the site was beyond the range of friendly artillery. The only way the gun could be taken out was with aircraft.

While Pineapple Chunk maintained his reference point, an 01-E Birddog aircraft arrived on the scene, and was directed to the general area of the artillery position. On the heels of the spotter craft came several flights of Marine A-4 Skyhawks armed with 500-pound bombs. Although the TAC(A) didn't know exactly where the target was, he rolled in and cranked off a smoke rocket. The puff from the 2.75-inch rocket wasn't visible to the Marines on 881S but the billowing clouds left by the 500-pound bombs of the first A-4 were. Using standard artillery terminology, Corporal Niuatoa adjusted: "Left 2,000, add 1,000." The corrections were passed to the TAC(A) who fired another rocket, on which an A-4 pilot placed another string of bombs. Gradually, the bracket was closed until a Skyhawk in the fourth flight scored a direct hit and the gun position erupted in a series of secondary explosions.(140)

The NVA troops, however, were not always on the receiving end; they frequently dished it out. In addition to numerous helicopters shot down around the combat base, several of the speedier jets were also knocked out of the sky. During one

Marine F-4B Phantom delivers Snakeye bombs on enemy
trenches. Large tail fins retard the descent of the
bombs. (Photo courtesy David D. Duncan)

Corporal Robert J. Arrotta (center), controlled over 200
airstrikes from Hill 881S. (Photo courtesy Major William
H. Dabney)

close air support mission, an A-4 flown by Major William E. Loftus of Marine Attack Squadron 311 received heavy battle damage and the pilot realized that he could not make it to the coast. Not wanting to end up in "Indian Country," he nursed his crippled Skyhawk toward Khe Sanh and ejected right over the base. As the smoking A-4 knifed into the lush jungle growth and erupted in a brilliant orange fireball, Major Loftus floated down and landed in an outer ring of barbed wire just outside the Company B, 1/26 perimeter. Lieutenant Dillon, the 2d Platoon commander, took several men out and helped extricate the major who had become hopelessly entangled in his parachute shroud lines and the barbed wire. After being freed, Major Loftus grinned and told the lieutenant: "If you weren't so damn ugly, I'd kiss you." After a quick medical check-up, the major climbed aboard a helicopter and returned to his squadron at Chu Lai for another plane and another day.(141)

One of the closest escapes, however, occurred to the south-west of the base. In late January, Lieutenant Colonel Harry T. Hagaman, Commanding Officer of Marine Fighter Attack Squadron 323, and his Radar Intercept Officer, Captain Dennis F. Brandon, were leading a flight of F-4B Phantoms against what the TAC(A) described as a "suspected" antiaircraft position. The enemy gunners confirmed their presence during the first pass. As Lieutenant Colonel Hagaman's F-4B, armed with napalm and 250-pound Snakeyes, skimmed low over the treetops, the North Vietnamese cut loose and laced the belly of his plane with a stitch of 50 caliber shells. The aircraft shuddered under the impact and burst into flames. Captain Brandon, a backseat veteran with over 300 combat missions, knew instantly when he heard the series of ominous "thuds" that the Phantom had been mortally wounded; he quickly pulled his face curtain and ejected. Lieu-tenant Colonel Hagaman stayed with the bucking Phantom momentarily in a vain effort to stabilize the aircraft by using his rudders. The delay almost cost the pilot his life because the F-4B began to tumble end-over-end barely 100 feet above the ground. Sud-denly the world outside became a spinning blur of blue and green. The second time that he saw green--indicating that the aircraft was inverted--Lieutenant Colonel Hagaman started to pull his alternate ejection handle which was located between his knees. In the second that it took the escape mechanism to function, the Phantom flipped upright and the ejection cartridges blasted the pilot from the flaming cockpit. Seconds later, the plane cartwheeled into the ground and exploded. The pilot was so low when he "punched out" that the chute had scarcely deployed when his feet touched the ground. Both crewmen hid in the tall elephant grass within earshot of the North Vietnamese who were searching for them. Within minutes, rescue helicopters lumbered on the scene and, while the downed crew's wingman made dummy passes to discourage the enemy soldiers, the choppers darted in and plucked the shaken, but otherwise uninjured, Marines to safety.(*)(142)

If there was anything that could top that performance, it was the spectacular air shows provided daily by B-52 Stratofortresses of the 4133d Provisional Heavy Bombardment Wing, based at Andersen Air Force Base, Guam, and the 4258th Strategic Bombardment Wing in Thailand. The B-52 pilots did not count on finesse as much as they did on sheer power because each Stratofortress carried a 27-ton payload of 108 mixed 500- and 750-pound bombs. Since these giants had the means to virtually move mountains, the Arc Light strikes were used on area targets such as troop concentrations, marshalling points, supply depots, and bunker sites. The result of the enemy build-up around the base was an enormous number of targets located in dispersed but common areas and such complexes were ideal for heavy bombers. These targets were programmed into computers aboard the aircraft and the strikes were conducted from altitudes above 30,000 feet. To the bomber crews, it was an impersonal type of warfare because, from above the overcast, they rarely even saw their bombs explode. The bombs did not have to be seen to be felt.(143)

When several flights of B-52s worked over a target, the results were awesome. The exploding bombs churned up strips of the terrain several thousand meters long and the ground for miles around literally shook from the blasts. Many enemy casualties were sustained from the concussion alone. One entry from a captured North Vietnamese diary read: "18 February: The heavy bombing of the jets and B-52 explosions are so strong that our lungs hurt." In some instances, NVA soldiers were found after an Arc Light strike wandering around in a daze with blood streaming from their noses and mouths.(**) Often the

---

(*) Both crews suffered sore backs from the ejection but no other injury. Lieutenant Colonel Hagaman became the third CO in a row from VMFA-323 to leave an F-4B via the ejection route. Captain Brandon returned to action and eventually compiled 400 combat missions--a first for Marine Radar Intercept Officers.

(**) To catch stunned survivors above ground, the 1/13 batteries frequently put massed artillery fire into the target area 10 to 15 minutes after the bombers departed.

internal hemorrhaging induced by the concussion was so severe
that it resulted in death. Quite understandably, such missions
could not be unleashed too close to the Marines.(144)

In the early stages of the conflict, Arc Light strikes
were not authorized within a prescribed distance of friendly
lines. The same rule had applied during the heavy fighting at
Con Thien the year before and the NVA had taken advantage of
the buffer zone by moving troops and supplies in as close to
the Marine base as possible to avoid the bomber raids. They
tried the same thing at Khe Sanh. When American airborne observers noted enemy bunker complexes cropping up near the KSCB,
the no-bomb line was moved in to about half of the original
distance. At first the regimental commander was afraid that
the resulting concussion would collapse his own bunkers and
trenches; as it turned out, the enemy fortifications were the
only ones which suffered. The first few B-52 raids inside the
old line touched off scores of secondary explosions and undoubtedly snapped the North Vietnamese out of their sense of
security. The closer strikes also served as a morale booster
for the defenders who flocked from their bunkers to watch, what
the Marines called, "Number One on the hit parade."(145)

According to the regimental Target Intelligence Officer
(TIO), Captain Mirza M. Baig, the B-52 was an accurate weapons
system which the FSCC employed around Khe Sanh much the same
as the other supporting arms. About 95 percent of the Arc Light
missions were targeted at the 26th Marines headquarters.(*)
Requests were submitted to the 3d Marine Division Air Officer
15 hours prior to the drop at a rate of 8 strikes every 24 hours.
Up to three hours before the strike, the TIO, upon direction,
could divert the bombers to new unscheduled targets, but after
that the Stratofortresses were restricted to their original
target. The response time was later trimmed even more by using
cells of three B-52s which left Guam and Thailand every three
hours; this put the bombers over Khe Sanh every hour and a half.
In spite of this streamlining, the B-52s were never as responsive

---

(*) General Westmoreland gave his constant personal attention
to the targeting of these strikes and while most of the targets
were generated by the 26th Marines Headquarters, General
Westmoreland personally approved the requests. Based on intelligence he also directed or diverted B-52 raids from Saigon.
To keep right on top of this aspect of the battle, the general
slept at night in his Combat Operations Center during the siege.

or flexible as the droves of fighter/bombers which were overhead constantly. Nevertheless, the devastating power and
psychological effect produced by the Stratofortresses, coupled
with the surprise factor, made them an extremely valuable
adjunct.(*)(146)

The type of strike which most impressed the regimental
commander, however, was the ground-controlled radar bombing.
Although these raids lacked the punch of an Arc Light strike,
they were as accurate and flexible as dive-bombing attacks and
could be conducted in the worst weather. In fact, the technique
was designed especially to cope with the inherent bad weather
which accompanied the monsoons in Southeast Asia when attack
aircraft could not get below an overcast to hit the target.

The controlling agency at Khe Sanh for these strikes was
Air Support Radar Team - Bravo (ASRT-B), Marine Air Support
Squadron 3 which had moved from Chu Lai on 16 January. The
ground controllers operated from a heavily reinforced van which
housed their sensistive computer equipment and used the TPQ-10
radar to guide aircraft to their target; thus, the missions
were called TPQs.(**)(147) The radar emitted a pencil-shaped
beam which detected and locked on to the aircraft. Using target coordinates provided by the FSCC, the controller programmed
the enemy position, ballistic characteristics of the bombs,
current winds, and other pertinent data into a computer which
was connected to the radar. The computer also received inputs
from the radar and, in turn, provided corrections in airspeed,
altitude, and heading which the operator passed on to the pilot.
The controller closely monitored his set and, at a predetermined
release point, called a "Mark" to the pilot who "pickled" his
bombs.(***) In specially-equipped aircraft, such as the A-4

(*)   The 26th Marines Command Chronology does not list sorties
but strikes which were made up of several aircraft and 430
strikes were recorded.

(**) The van, as well as crew living quarters, was emplaced
underground and was heavily sandbagged. The sturdiness of the
bunker was an important factor because of the heavy shelling.
One enemy round scored a direct hit on top of the bunker with
no damage to the fragile equipment. The computer van remained
operational throughout the siege.

(***) The term "pickled" is slang used by pilots which means
to drop their ordnance.

Skyhawk and the A-6 Intruder, the bombs could be released automatically from the ground. One ground controller could handle a single plane, a section (two planes), or a division (four planes) on the same pass as long as the pilots flew in a tight formation and the radar did not break lock. One of the controllers' favorite aircraft was the A-6 because it packed such a heavy wallop; a single Intruder usually carried 28 500-pounders. Any fighter/bomber, however, could be used as long as it carried low-drag ordnance and the pilot could make a smooth run.(148)

Even though most TPQs were conducted from around 14,000 feet, the accuracy of ASRT-B was phenomenal. When new personnel arrived at Khe Sanh, they were given several check drops on a nearby hill to test their proficiency before the newcomers were allowed to conduct strikes near friendly troops. The first drop was always within 40 meters of the target and, after they adjusted there was virtually no error. Calibration drops were also conducted twice weekly to ensure the accuracy of the equipment. One member of the FSCC stated that, if he were in a foxhole and under attack, he would have no qualms about calling an ASRT-B controlled TPQ within 35 meters of his position. The rule of thumb which the FSCC generally applied when determining a safe distance for normal operations, however, was one meter from the friendlies for every pound of conventional ordnance being delivered. Thus, for TPQs, a 250-pound bomb would not normally be dropped within 250 meters of Allied troops, a 500-pounder within 500 meters, and so on. This criteria was not established because the men on the ground lacked confidence in the system but because of the large fragmentation pattern produced by the bombs. Besides, anything inside the prescribed radius could be handled just as effectively by artillery, mortars, and direct fire weapons. In an emergency, the regimental commander would have undoubtedly lifted the restriction. Concerning the quality of support he received from ASRT-B, Colonel Lownds said, "Anything but the highest praise would not be enough."(149)

In addition to its accuracy, the TPQ system was extremely flexible. A strike could be programmed and executed within 10 or 12 minutes utilizing any available aircraft. Most of the missions were at night when it was inefficient and dangerous to conduct dive-bombing strikes. As a matter of routine, two Marine and three Air Force flights were scheduled every hour unless an emergency developed. On 18 February, ASRT-B set a new squadron record for a single 24-hour period by controlling aircraft which delivered 486 tons of ordnance on 105 separate

B-52 Stratofortresses flew strikes daily in support of the 26th Marines. (Photo courtesy USAF)

A-6 Intruder, under TPQ control, provides precision bombing around Khe Sanh despite poor weather. (USMC Photo A422000)

targets. After that, the record was approached frequently but never broken. During the siege, ASRT-B controlled 4,989 TPQs in support of the 26th Marines.(150)

Beginning on 20 February, ASRT-B also assisted with supply drops whenever the Khe Sanh MATCU was inoperable. Normally, the controllers could have guided the transport pilots to an exact release point but, at Khe Sanh, the C-130s had to fly directly over the station and the TPQ-10 would break lock. (*)(151) Therefore, the ASRT personnel used the same technique as the MATCU controllers and called a "Mark" when the Hercules was over the eastern threshold and the pilots completed the runs with Doppler navigation and stop watches. The only problem was that, when the ASRT conducted supply drops, it was drawn away from the primary mission of handling TPQs.(152)

While air support was vital to the defense of the base, Colonel Lownds felt that his artillery played an equally important role. When the fighting first broke out, the colonel surmised that the side which managed to keep its artillery intact would win the battle. The Marine artillery emerged almost unscathed. Many incoming rounds landed within the battery positions, however, very few actually hit the gun pits and throughout the operation only three artillery pieces at the base were destroyed; one was a 155mm howitzer parked alongside the loading ramp awaiting airlift to Dong Ha.(**) Generally the pieces, were tucked away inside heavily sandbagged revetments and, while the crews were often showered with fragments, it would have taken a direct hit, squarely on top of the weapon, to knock out a howitzer. Fortunately for the Marine gunners, the North Vietnamese scored only one such a hit which led the regimental commander to the conclusion: "Either they were amazingly inaccurate or we were amazingly lucky."(153)

The enemy's failure to silence Lieutenant Colonel Hennelly's batteries was a big point in favor of the Marines. While American news reporters gave wide coverage to the number of shells falling on the base, they frequently neglected to mention that 1/13 answered each enemy round with 10 of its own. Throughout

---

(*) When a TPQ-10 broke lock, the radar beam strayed from the aircraft and inputs to the computer were interrupted. The operator also lost visual contact on the radar screen.

(**) One 105mm howitzer on 881S was also destroyed.

the battle, 1/13 cranked out 158,891 mixed rounds in direct support of the 26th Marines. The methods employed by the FSCC were reminiscent of those used in World War I. Time On Target (TOT) by massed batteries, Harassment and Interdiction (H&I) by battery volley instead of a single piece, artillery boxes, rolling barrages, and battery zones were a few techniques adopted by the FSCC which more than lived up to its motto: "Be Generous."(*)

Since the enemy did most of his manuevering under the cover of darkness, that was when the Marine and Army batteries were the most active. Captain Baig, who wore one hat--Target Intelligence Officer--in the S-2 section and another--Target Information Officer--in the FSCC later described a good night's work:

An average night's pattern of pre-planned fires was as follows: Combined TOTs from 9 batteries (4-6); separate battalion TOTs (Army 4-6, Marine 10-15); battery multiple volley individual missions (40-50); battery H&Is (20-30). Normal 1 gun, 1 round H&Is were not used; this type of fire was of little value. Marine and Army artillery were employed in target areas and at ranges to reduce to a minimum check fires caused by the arrival of TPQ and reconnaissance aircraft. Later, as we learned finesse, air was given the targets south of the base and west of the maximum range of the 175mm guns; 1/13 was given any targets whose range required a maximum ordinate of less than 14,000 feet (altitude of TPQ run); and the 175mm guns were assigned targets to the north, northwest, and east of the base. Such were the pre-planned fires.(155)

In addition to volume, reaction time was a key factor. Unless friendly aircraft in the target area necessitated a check fire, artillery response was immediate--no matter what the weather. To test the proficiency of the Fire Direction Center and the gun crews, Colonel Lownds periodically walked into the

---

(*) Not every artillery round that left Khe Sanh was high explosive. During March, Lieutenant Colonel Hennelly's battalion had accumulated more ammunition than it could safely store. Since the ammo would not fit in the berms and presented a hazard above ground, the decision was made to fire it all. This excess included some 90-odd rounds of green smoke. On 17 March--St. Patrick's Day--the Marines fired all the green smoke rounds on known enemy positions to honor the patron saint of the Fighting Irish.

A 105mm howitzer of 1/13 lashes out at NVA troops surrounding Khe Sanh. The artillery battalion was in direct
support of the 26th Marines. (USMC Photo A190832)

The 175mm guns of the 2d Battalion, 94th Artillery, USA
were in general support of the Khe Sanh garrison. This
gun was located at Camp J. J. Carroll. (USMC Photo
A190709)

FSCC bunker, pointed to a spot on the huge map which adorned the wall and directed Lieutenant Colonel Hennelly to hit it. The coordinates were quickly sent to the FDC where they were either fed into the FADAC computer or worked out manually and the firing data was then passed on to the gun crew. After adjusting the tube, the gunners slammed a round home and sent it on its way. The entire process usually took less than 40 seconds. This "instant artillery" constantly hampered enemy movement within the TAOR and helped break up numerous attacks.(156)

The defensive fire plan adopted by the FSCC was separate from and not to be confused with the final protective fires employed by the defenders who manned the perimeter. The artillery batteries were used to prevent the enemy assault forces from reaching the wire and to cut off the lead elements from reinforcements. The fact that the North Vietnamese usually attacked with their battalions in column made it somewhat easier for the FSCC to isolate the assault elements from the reserves. When the enemy launched his attack, the FSCC placed a three-sided artillery box around the lead battalion; three batteries of 1/13 executed this mission. The fourth battery then closed the remaining side, which faced the friendly positions, with a barrage that rolled from one end of the box to the other--much like a piston within its cylinder. The NVA force in the box could not escape and could not avoid the rolling barrage. Those North Vietnamese who spilled out of the open end of the box were subjected to the final protective fires of the Marines along the perimeter.

At the same time 1/13 worked over the assault force, the FSCC put a secondary box into effect for the benefit of the back-up units. The Army 175mm batteries were responsible for two sides which were about 500 meters outside the primary box. On order, the gunners rolled their barrages in toward the sides of the primary box and back out again. The third side was sealed by continuous flights of aircraft under the control of the TPQ-10 radar. Whenever B-52s could be diverted in time, Arc Light strikes were used to saturate the approach routes to the battle area.(157)

Another key factor in the defense of Khe Sanh was the manner in which Lieutenant Colonel Hennelly's FSCC coordinated their air effort with the artillery so that the two components were complimentary. One prime example was the Mini-Arc Light which was devised by the Assistant Fire Support Coordinator, Captain Kenneth O. W. Steen and the TIO, Captain Baig. As the name implies, this technique was used against an area target the same as a B-52 strike, only the former could be organized and employed much quicker. When intelligence reports indicated that NVA units were in a certain region, the FSCC plotted a 500 by 1,000-meter block in the center of the suspected area or across a likely route of march. Two A-6 Intruders, each armed with 28 500-pound bombs, were called on station for a TPQ and the batteries at Khe Sanh, Camp Carroll, and the Rockpile were alerted for a fire mission. Thirty seconds before the two A-6s dropped, the 175mm batteries, concentrating their fire on one half of the block, salvoed the first of approximately 60 rounds. At the same time the A-6s rippled their load down the middle of the block, the 1/13 batteries opened up on the second half with around 200 155mm, 105mm, and 4.2-inch rounds. The trajectory and flight time of all ordnance were computed so that the bombs and initial artillery shells hit at the same instant. The saturation of the target area was such that any enemy soldiers caught in the zone during the bombardment simply ceased to exist.(158)

During the second week in February, a special Mini-Arc Light was directed against a major NVA headquarters. Two members of the 26th Marines S-2, Majors Robert B. Coolidge and Jerry E. Hudson, learned from their various sources that a force-wide meeting of NVA commanders and their staffs would occur in an abandoned schoolhouse near the Laotian border. A beefed-up Mini was prepared to welcome the delegates. For this strike, the target block was reduced to 500 by 300 meters around the schoolhouse which would take in, as one of the planners stated, "the hangers-on and other idlers who usually congregate around large staffs." Twenty minutes after the meeting was scheduled to start, the trap was sprung. Two Marine A-6 Intruders and four F-4B Phantoms unloaded 152 500-pound bombs into the block in concert with the opening volleys of eight artillery batteries (total of 350 artillery rounds).(159) The target was obliterated, but whether or not this unusual ambush netted any NVA brass-hats was never ascertained.

The Micro-Arc Light was executed in the same manner as the Mini except smaller amounts of ordnance were used and the block was cut down to 500 by 500 meters. Any aircraft on station would suffice, preferably ones armed with 12 to 16 500-pounders. Artillery fire was reduced to 30 rounds from the 175mm guns and 100 mixed rounds from Lieutenant Colonel Hennelly's battalion. The advantage of the Micro was that it could be put into effect within 10 minutes while it took roughly 45 minutes to plan and execute the Mini. On an average night, three to four Minis and six to eight Micros were executed, usually to the south and southeast of the base; both were extremely effective.(160)

The massive firepower supporting the Marines would have been almost useless had they not known where and when to employ it. The 26th Marines intelligence section was responsible for this facet of the operation and these people had more than a passing knowledge of the enemy's past strategy. At Dien Bien Phu and Con Thien, the Communists had followed a fairly predictable pattern--not unlike the classic siege of the 18th Century. There were three distinct phases involved in this type of campaign: arrival on the scene and encirclement of the garrison, construction of siege works and support facilities, T-ing the sapheads and final assault. After investing the base, the North Vietnamese first established numerous forward logistic bases within a few thousand meters of the base. Under the cover of darkness, the enemy soldiers dug a series of shallow trenches, interlaced with supply bunkers, leading from these points toward the American positions. The first trenches began to appear at Khe Sanh around 23 February and the heaviest concentration was to the south and southeast. Once in close, the main trenches branched off into ones which paralleled the Marines lines; these secondary trenches, which from the air looked like long fingers reaching greedily toward the base, were the ones from which the NVA assault troops intended to attack.(161)

At first, the defenders tried to prevent the enemy from moving in too close to the base. The routes into the valley were saturated; artillery H&I fire and frequent air strikes were employed but such tactics only tended to slow down the enemy and force him to bypass certain routes--they did not stop him. Constant, massed artillery would have effectively blocked infiltration but that alternative was, from a logistics standpoint, impossible. The S-2 personnel recommended that the best way to counter the enemy was to allow the North Vietnamese to close and pursue their siege tactics and then, to borrow a phrase used by General "Chesty" Puller (then a colonel) on 28 November 1950 when his regiment was surrounded near the Chosin Reservoir in Korea, "that simplifies our problem of finding these people and killing them."(162)

The S-2 section utilized a multitude of sources to develop an accurate picture of the enemy's activity around the base. While much of this information was self-generated, the 26th

Marines received substantial intelligence support from the MACV, III MAF, and 3d Marine Division Headquarters. Ground and aerial observers, photo reconnaissance, infrared imagery, target lists of higher headquarters, crater analysis, shell/flash reports, and agent reports were all tools of the intelligence community at Khe Sanh. By comparing this information with the knowledge of enemy doctrine as applied in past situations, the S-2 staff was able to accurately estimate the intentions of the NVA on a day-to-day basis.

One good example of how this intelligence produced hard results occurred in late February. From their various inputs, the two men who were responsible for the earlier attack on the NVA staff conference, Majors Coolidge and Hudson, pinpointed the exact location of 12 artillery positions and 2 major ammunition depots. These targets were concentrated in two main areas to the south of the base. Air strikes were called in on the enemy positions and, after the planes departed, the whole area erupted in secondary explosions which lasted for the next 40 minutes. Two weeks later, these officers repeated a similar performance in another area.(163)

The activities of the intelligence community at Khe Sanh and higher headquarters were vital to the conduct of the battle. Almost every major attack against the 26th Marines was picked up well in advance by the S-2 section. Whenever enemy activity was detected, the information was passed to the FSCC and this was the signal for Colonel Lownds to put his defensive fire plan into effect. The base was placed on Red Alert, the primary and secondary boxes fired, and saturation air strikes were employed. This method of cutting off the attack force by massed fires, once the S-2 section had provided a warning, proved to be a decisive factor in thwarting the major enemy thrusts which came late in February.(164)

PART VII

THE TURNING POINT

While the supporting arms continued to whittle away at
the enemy's strength, the defensive posture of the 26th Marines
grew more formidable with each passing day. By the end of
February, the Americans and South Vietnamese had erected some
510 bunkers, dug miles of trenchline, and laid hundreds of
minefields and trip flares. Each sector was guarded by a maze
of double-apron, tanglefoot, and concertina barbed wire obstacles.(*) The Marines also had sophisticated anti-infiltration
equipment such as the Night Observation Device, the PPS-6
ground-surveillance radar, and the Starlight Scope; all of
which could detect infiltrators along the wire during night-
time and other periods of reduced visibility.(165) Wherever
these apparatus were employed, the number of enemy killed along
the perimeters increased and the number of probes decreased.

In addition to the standard issue, the men improvised
many of their own jerry-rigged gadgets. Drawing from his
childhood experiences on the farm, Colonel Lownds devised a
type of electric fence which was employed along some of the
company fronts in the main perimeter. The plan was simple;
the Marines figured out which strands of barbed wire the enemy
would more than likely cut to penetrate those obstacles and
they attached trip wire in a circuit. Flashlight batteries
were the power source and the network of wires tied into a
central switchboard located in each company CP. When a North
Vietnamese soldier clipped the barbed wire, he short-circuited
the system and one of the warning lights on at the switchboard
went out. A few grenades in the right place or a broadside
from a Claymore mine and the snooper usually became another
grim statistic.

On the hill outposts, the _fougasse_ was used extensively.
The Marines dug holes along the slopes which faced the enemy

(*) Tanglefoot, as the name implies, is a barbed wire entangle-
ment that is stretched low to the ground and is usually used
between larger barriers. Concertina comes in rolls which are
laid side by side or on top of each other. Double-apron obstacles
are simply barbed wire fences in depth.

and embedded barrels or cans of mixed gasoline and diesel fuel. The detonator for this volatile concoction was usually a grenade, a blasting cap, or a pound of C-4 plastic explosive taped to the container. The triggering device was a wire leading back up the hill to the Marine positions. When attacked, the defender simply jerked the wire and detonated the lethal munitions.(166)

The Scout Sniper Platoon attached to the 26th Marines provided another kind of deterrent. At least one team of these hand-picked, specially-trained sharpshooters was assigned to each company. Using commercial, bolt-action rifles with high-powered scopes, the snipers preyed on individual NVA soldiers who carelessly exposed themselves around the fringes of the perimeter. Patience was a must in this business and the marks-men often waited for days until their quarry appeared. When the snipers finally got a chance to practice their deadly art, the results were almost unbelievable. As though they were firing for record on a rifle range, they calculated the wind, adjusted their slings, took steady positions, and slowly squeezed off their shots. Many North Vietnamese who felt safe beyond 1,000 meters of the Marine positions never received a chance to ponder their mistake. The psychological impact was also a factor. One can imagine the eerie feeling experienced by an NVA soldier who had just seen a comrade "zapped" and never heard the report of the rifle that did the trick.(167)

By no stretch of the imagination did the 26th Marines have a monopoly on good snipers. The NVA marksmen, armed with rifles and scopes which were comparable to those of their American counterparts, lurked around the edges of the perimeters--especially the hill outposts--and waited for a target. Although none of this deadly business could be categorized as humorous, there was one sniper incident on Hill 881S which could not help but evoke a chuckle. The men of Company I had been cursed with the presence of a particularly accurate sniper who was located in the brush to the south of their perimeter. The rifleman scored frequently and had wounded 10 Marines in the period of about a week, all of whom were medevaced. In addition to being a hazard, the sniper was also a general nuisance. A man moving from one place to another within the perimeter was always hurried on his way by slugs which kicked up dirt at his heels or buzzed past his head like angry hornets. Thus, the Marines were con-stantly waiting for the culprit to expose himself and one day a glint off the telescopic sight proved to be his undoing. The Marines marked his position and, on Captain Dabney's order,

Men of 1/26 lay wire along Blue Sector. Dong Tri Mountain is in the background. (Photo courtesy David D. Duncan)

Sniper attached to Company E, 2/26 on Hill 861A waits for a target. (Photo courtesy David D. Duncan)

lugged a 106mm recoilless rifle from the northern side of the hill, sighted in, and blew the sniper away--tree and all. The victory was short lived because his successor proved equally as effective. More Marines were hit. The second rifleman lasted about as long as the first before he suffered the same fate at the hands of the 106mm gunners.

His replacement, however, was a complete wash-out. Expending between 20 and 30 rounds a day, the misfit flailed away for over a week without hitting anyone. In the process, he too gave himself away. After the Marines had manhandled the 106 into position for the third time, and were sighting in, one private, after deep thought, approached the company commander with a proposition: "Skipper, if we get him, they'll just replace him with someone who might be able to shoot. He hasn't hit anyone so why not leave him there until he does." It was so ordered. The sniper's ineptitude had saved his life and he blasted away for the rest of the battle and never touched a soul.(*)(168)

The incident with the snipers pointed out the advantage of having 106mm recoilless rifles on the hills. Unlike the artillery pieces at Khe Sanh, the 106mms were used in a direct fire role and because of their extremely flat trajectory, they could be employed when attack aircraft were in the target area. Another feature which endeared these weapons to the Marines was their extraordinary accuracy. The recoilless rifles were used with great finesse, especially against the well-camouflaged enemy gun positions which ringed the outposts. In most cases, it required minute adjustments to put a round squarely on target and knock out these emplacements. This was evident in one instance when a 106mm on 881S was used to silence an NVA 12.7mm machine gun which had been spraying Marine helicopters.

The automatic weapon was situated inside the mouth of a small tunnel which had been cut deep into the side of a hill located north of the Company I, 3/26, perimeter. The tiny aperture, which faced south, restricted the gunner's fields of fire but that was no drawback because he only concentrated on

---

(*) To rub salt into the wound, the Marines devised a red flag--Maggies Drawers--like the ones used on rifle ranges to signal that the shooter had missed the entire target, and waved it every time the sniper fired.

the resupply choppers as they hovered over the Marine positions. On the other hand, the small opening prevented the gun from being knocked out by anything except a direct hit from the front. Once the men on 881S had pinpointed the heavily camouflaged site, they went to work with their 106mm. Out of necessity, their firing routine was erratic; the gunners cranked off a round, dived for cover when enemy mortars responded, jumped up, adjusted the weapon, and fired again. While spotters guided them with such unorthodox jargon as "Right a tad," or "Up a hair," the gunners repeated the process and slowly closed in on the enemy position. Finally, one glowing round disappeared completely into the side of the hill and a split second later there was a muffled explosion from deep within. Smoke belched out the mouth of the tunnel and the NVA machine gun was no more. This performance was repeated several times during the battle with the same results.(169)

The three 105mm howitzers on 881S were also used extensively in the direct fire role and were especially useful against targets of opportunity. The ever-present fog around the hill reduced the number of such targets but on one occasion a momentary break in the weather yielded an extremely lucrative prize. When the fog suddenly lifted, an alert Company I machine gunner spotted a 20-man column of North Vietnamese slowly climbing Hill 758 which was due south of 881S. They were carrying what appeared to be several mortar tubes. The Marine immediately opened fire and even though the range was 1,200 meters he managed to hit several of the enemy soldiers. Instead of scattering, the remaining NVA troopers clustered around their fallen comrades and this proved to be a fatal error. The C/1/13 gunners attached to Company I sprang to the 105mm howitzer on the south side of the hill, quickly knocked aside the parapet, and depressed the tube for a downhill shot. Using a combination of point detonating and VT fuzes which were set to explode 50 feet above the ground, the gunners slammed a dozen rounds of direct fire into the midst of the tightly packed enemy soldiers. By the time the fog closed in again, there was no sign of life on the opposite slope. The action was so brief, that the first report received at the 3/26 CP was a laconic message from Captain Dabney that 20 North Vietnamese had been sighted, engaged, and killed.

There were also innovations inside the compound. Ever since 21 January, the NVA gunners had concentrated their fire on the base ammunition dumps. Originally there were two large caches but the main one was totally destroyed on the opening day of the battle. After that, Colonel Lownds decentralized his stores in several widely-scattered berms which were large, 12-foot-deep trenches, gouged out of the ground by bulldozers. One end of the berm was sloping so that 2½ ton trucks could be driven down a corridor between two flanking stacks of ammunition which lined the sides of the trench. This arrangement greatly facilitated loading because the Marines could stand on top of the stacks and pass rounds onto the bed of the truck which was at their level. The driver then backed out of the berm and took the ammunition to the distribution points of the various units. The ammunition was not only dispersed, it was also segregated according to type. This way, if a berm of artillery high-explosive shells was hit, fire fighters were not hampered by tear gas or white phosphorous fumes. On three occasions, ammunition stores were hit but the resulting devastation never reached the proportion of that on the 21st.(170)

Although the berms were prime targets, the ASRT, MATCU, FDC, 26th Marines communications center, and other units which depended on sophisticated and delicate equipment suffered from the heavy shelling. Consequently, they all had one common problem--maintenance. The normal difficulties associated with keeping the various radars, radios, antennae, generators, and cooling components in an "up" status were complicated by the constant incoming, the dust, and the limited supply of replacement items. The vans and bunkers were heavily sandbagged but antennae and some communication lines were exposed and frequently knocked out by enemy rounds.(*)(171) The speed with which the vital installations were returned to operation served as a tribute to the technicians who maintained the equipment under the most adverse conditions imaginable. In one instance, a 122mm rocket exploded a scant seven meters from the ASRT-B van and sheared off most of the radio antennae. Thanks to several trouble shooters who braved the intense barrage and repaired the damage, the station was back on the air within 20 minutes.(**) Such performances were routine. The ASRT normally

---

(*)   To keep the North Vietnamese from zeroing in on his communication bunkers, Colonel Lownds ordered that fake antennae be placed on every structure at Khe Sanh--including the four-holers.

(**)   The ASRT-B radar antennae sustained over 200 hits from shell fragments but continued to function near maximum efficiency throughout the siege.

operated 23 hours a day and shut down one hour for maintenance.
The MATCU, which was essential for ground-controlled approaches
and paradrops, was kept operable 95 percent of the time.(172)

Major John A. Shepherd, Communications Officer of the
26th Marines, was responsible for the vast nework which enabled the ground commanders to keep abreast of the situation
and in touch with their units. The major praised the accomplishments of his men, stating that they "provided support in winning
every battle, firing every round of artillery, controlling
every air strike, and providing the means to receive every
bean and bullet." There were six radio relay teams which kept
open 52 channels between Khe Sanh and the outside world. In
addition, there were five external teletype nets in operation
24-hours a day. Radio relay provided voice and teletype links
to agencies at Dong Ha and Da Nang. For classified information,
there were two secure voice circuits operating full time. One
net linked the Combat Operations Center of the 26th Marines to
that of the 3d Marine Division at Dong Ha. The other, the
Regimental Tactical Net, enabled Colonel Lownds to disseminate
hot information to his battalion commanders.

To protect it against the artillery, mortar, and rocket
attacks, all communication equipment was either underground or
heavily sandbagged. Major Shepherd moved his communications
center into a shelter which was made from 4 conex boxes, 16
feet underground.(*) This nerve center housed the teletype
equipment and switchboards which provided service for 65 on-
base subscribers and 40 external radio relay voice circuits.
In spite of the protective measures, the antenna and internal
wire system sustained damage on a daily basis. Following every
barrage, wiremen tracked down cuts and spliced them and repaired
damaged antennae so that the various nets were back in operation within minutes. The maintenance and repair of the elec-
tronic devices used for perimeter security placed an additional
burden on the communicators.(173)

While trucks and forklifts were not exactly delicate equipment, the base motor transport personnel had their share of
problems. These vehicles were used constantly. During the
summer and fall of 1967, they were used to haul rock for the
repair of the runway. Throughout the siege, the drivers

(*)   A conex box is a large metal container primarily used to
sea-lift cargo.

carried ammunition from the berms to the distribution points
and supplies from the drop zone to the combat base. Many of
the trucks were in bad shape and mechanics worked around the
clock to keep them rolling. The biggest headache was caused
by flat tires, of which the constant shelling produced an
abundance; the drivers became paste and patch experts of the
highest order. More often than not, these men were caught out
in the open when the enemy decided to pound the base. Since
their cargo usually contained high explosives, the drivers had
good reason to be apprehensive. Some simply bailed out of the
cabs during the attacks and dived for cover; others, performing
a wild imitation of the Grand Prix, raced for revetments.
Needless to say, the base speed limit of five miles per hour
was frequently violated.(174)

When there wasn't any work to do, many Marines created
some and the threat of enemy tunnels provided a powerful moti-
vation. When the word spread that the enemy might try to dig
under the base, the tunnel ferrets went to work. Many of the
defenders became fascinated with the prospects of uncovering a
"mole" and their antics were near comical. It was not uncommon
to see a man crawling around in front of his position, patting
the ground with the flat side of a shovel, and listening for
hollow spots. Others drove metal stakes into the ground and
listened with stethoscopes by the hour for tell-tale signs of
digging. If they heard something, the next step was to dig a
large hole in front of the enemy so that he would tunnel himself
into a trap. Some self-appointed water witches walked around
with divining rods and waited for the downward tug which meant
that they had discovered a subterranean intruder. When the
news media got into the act and publicized the possibility of
tunnels, the regimental commander began receiving scores of
letters from around the world with "If I were you" themes.
One American planter who lived in Sao Paulo, Brazil, wrote and
suggested that the Marines purchase commercial sensors like
the ones he used to detect bugs which fed on the roots of his
trees. Another suggested that the defenders strap hand grenades
onto rats and turn them loose in the tunnels.(175)

Unknown to the Marines at the time, the enemy never tried
to tunnel under the base. The KSCB sat atop a plateau, and
the slopes were wrinkled with deep ravines. Colonel Lownds
later surmised that the enemy would have had to go so deep to
keep from breaking the surface that such excavations were im-
practical. The men of Company K, 3/26 did, however, discover
one tunnel leading toward Hill 861 and called in air strikes

against it; at the base itself, the North Vietnamese limited their digging to trenches.(176)

Unlike the phantom tunnels, the trenches were very real and served as a constant reminder of the enemy's intentions. These networks were quite understandably a source of concern to the defenders who watched with fascination and no small apprehension as the trenchlines drew closer and closer each day. Working at night or under the cover of fog, the North Vietnamese often moved their lines forward as much as 200-300 meters at a time. There were several methods used to counter the trenches with artillery and tactical air strikes being the most prevalent. Lieutenant Colonel Hennelly's batteries provided constant fires during the night especially to the east and southeast where the heaviest enemy siegeworks were concentrated. The VT-fuzed ammunition with its deadly airbursts no doubt hampered the enemy efforts considerably. During the day, attack aircraft hit the trenches with every type of aerial ordnance from 20mm cannon fire to 2,000-pound bombs. At night, TPQs were run to within about 250 meters of the wire while Mini and Micro Arc Lights were targeted from 500 to 1,500 meters.(177)

In addition, the Marines along the perimeters concocted their own schemes which added to the displeasure of the enemy. During the day, Lieutenant Colonel Wilkinson's men registered on the close-in trenches with their M-79 grenade launchers; these shotgun-like weapons fired a 40mm projectile to a maximum range of about 375 meters and produced a frag pattern approximately 5 to 10 meters in diameter. At night when the North Vietnamese were digging, the Marines periodically lobbed these rounds into the trenches and disrupted the sappers.(178)

In spite of the harassment, the NVA launched several attacks against the base from the trenchlines during the last 10 days in February. At 1245, 21 February, the North Vietnamese fired 350 mortar, rocket, recoilless rifle, and artillery rounds into the eastern sector and followed up with a company-sized probe against the 37th ARVN Ranger Battalion. The enemy troops, however, did not attempt to close with the South Vietnamese and, after a distant fire fight, withdrew at about 1500. Although no body count was ascertained, the Rangers estimated that 1/13 artillery and their own defensive fires had claimed from 20 to 25 of the enemy. Six Marines from 1/26 and 18 Rangers were wounded during the encounter.(179)

On 23 February, the base received the worse shellacking

of the siege. In one eight-hour period, the installation was
rocked by 1,307 rounds--a total which surpassed the daily high
received at Con Thien in 1967. Many of the rounds came from
the 130mm and 152mm artillery pieces in Laos. The runway took
several hits but the Seabee and Marine working parties filled
the craters and quickly replaced the damaged strips of runway
matting. At 1600, the barrage touched off a fire at one of the
supply points and 1,620 rounds of 90mm and 106mm ammunition were
destroyed. Cumulative friendly casualties for the day were 10
killed, 21 medevaced, and 30 wounded but returned to duty.(180)

Two days later the Marines suffered one of their most
serious setbacks. On the morning of the 25th, the 1st and 3d
Squads, 3d Platoon, B/1/26 departed Grey Sector on a patrol to
the south of the base; the patrol leader was a second lieutenant.
The two squads were reinforced by an 81mm mortar FO, an S-2
representative, a Kit Carson Scout, one rocket team, and a
machine gun section (two guns).(*) Each man carried 500 rounds
of ammunition and six grenades; each machine gun team had 1,800
rounds. Their mission was to sweep to the south along a well-
defined route and attempt to locate an enemy mortar which had
been harassing the Marines. The patrol leader was assigned
three checkpoints from which he was to radio his position and
progress to the company commander, Captain Pipes. The lieutenant was under strict orders to follow the planned route and
keep within sight of the base as much as possible.(181)

Around 0900, the two squads reached their first checkpoint;
the lieutenant made the required radio report and the Marines
started on the second leg of their trek. Unknown to Captain
Pipes, the patrol had deviated from course and was actually
about 600 meters south of its scheduled route. Shortly after
his first transmission, the lieutenant spotted three NVA
soldiers walking along a road which branched off Route 9 and
ran northwest into the FOB-3 compound. The North Vietnamese
were apparently trying to suck the Americans into a trap--a
trick as old as war itself. In spite of warnings from the Kit
Carson Scout, the young patrol leader took the bait and pursued
the three men; the decision was to cost him his life.(182)

The Marines moved south across the road, chased the North
Vietnamese and ran head-on into an ambush. A heavily reinforced

---

(*) Kit Carson Scouts were enemy ralliers who scouted for
the Allies.

NVA company was entrenched just south of the road in a crescent-shaped bunker complex, the tips of which curved to the north. When the trap was sprung, the patrol was caught squarely in the center and, in essence, was double-enveloped by stationary positions. At first the Marines opened up and gained the advantage but the enemy fire gradually built to an overwhelming crescendo and the patrol became pinned down. When the lieutenant realized the full implications of his predicament, he dispatched the 1st Squad to flank the NVA emplacements from the west. The maneuver might have worked but the squad leader did not hook out far enough to the west before turning back in on the enemy positions. Instead of hitting the tender flank, the 1st Squad walked into more blistering, frontal fire. When the lieutenant was unable to raise the squad leader on the radio, he sent one of his few unwounded men, Hospitalman 3d Class Frank V. Calzia, a U. S. Navy corpsman, to find out what had happened. The corpsman returned later and reported that every man in the 1st Squad, except one, was dead.(183)

Captain Pipes immediately realized that his men were in trouble and, upon direction of higher authority, sent the 2d Platoon to the aid of the patrol. The cunning North Vietnamese anticipated such a move, however, and positioned a blocking force in the path of the relief column. The two separated Marine units were engaged in heavy fighting for about four hours before the remnants of the patrol could break contact and withdraw through the positions of the 2d Platoon. Marine tanks rumbled into the southern portion of the compound but supporting fires were restricted by ground fog and the proximity of the combatants. As he pulled back, the patrol leader was hit in both femoral arteries and bled to death before reaching the perimeter. His radioman, Corporal Rolland R. Ball, a full-blooded Sioux Indian, carried the lieutenant's body back to the base. Friendly casualties during the day were 1 killed, 25 missing and presumed dead, 13 medevacs, and 8 wounded but returned to duty; the bodies of the missing men were all recovered. Enemy losses were undetermined. The action on the 25th sobered the men of Company B and there was one predominant thought in their minds. Captain Pipes probably understated the feelings of his men when he said: "We are anxious to repay the loss." Before the siege ended, Company B did just that.(184)

The flurry of activity to the east and south of the base led General Tompkins and Colonel Lownds to believe that the major enemy thrust was imminent. Recalling the accuracy of the North Vietnamese lieutenant's previous predictions, they felt

sure that the attack would come from the east. From various
other reports, they knew that large NVA units were massing
around a deserted plantation to the south and an old French
fort near the junction of Route 9 and the two roads which tied
in with the KSCB. Although the North Vietnamese had not secured the hill outposts according to the first phase of their
plan, time was running out. Each day, the skies over Khe Sanh
cleared a little more as one of the enemy's greatest allies,
the monsoons, slowly abandoned him. If American airpower, unhindered by the weather, were ever fully brought into play, the
enemy's task would have been next to impossible. The NVA
launched a heavy attack against the base on 29 February; whether
it was in fact the main prong of the Communist offensive, his-
torians may never know for sure.(185)

Largely because of the quick response by the FSCC and the
overwhelming firepower at its disposal, the enemy attack never
got up a full head of steam. Early in the evening of 29 February, current intelligence showed that the enemy was on the
move. Each succeeding report indicated that the North Vietnamese
were heading toward the eastern perimeter. The FSCC sprang
into action and called on all assets to saturate the enemy's
route of march. Massed artillery, TPQs, as well as Mini and
Micro Arc Lights were targeted in blocks to the east, southeast,
and south. Flights of B-52s, diverted from other targets,
arrived overhead in two and a half hours and added to the carnage
before the enemy troops had moved completely through the killing
zone.(186)

At 2130, a battalion from the 304th NVA Division launched
the first attack against the 37th ARVN Ranger Battalion. The
South Vietnamese responded with their final protective fires;
1/13 contributed thousands of conventional and special artillery
rounds while strike aircraft streaked in and raked the attacking
force. The enemy pulled back without even breaching the outer
defenses. The first assault was followed by one at 2330 and
another at 0315 (1 March); both were similarly stifled short
of the wire. The North Vietnamese finally called it quits and
withdrew with those bodies which they could retrieve. When
the Rangers investigated the next morning, they found 78 dead
NVA soldiers huddled in three successive assault trenches a few
hundred meters from the perimeter. Some were in a kneeling
position as if they had been killed just before going over the
top. Many had been peppered by the artillery airbursts and
were covered with small holes. Crude devices made from bamboo
strips and laced with blocks of TNT lay beside many of the

bodies. These were obviously to be used as bangalore torpedoes but the sappers never had the chance. The slaughter along the perimeter, however, was nothing compared to the losses sustained by the NVA reserves.(187)

While the S-2 personnel could never ascertain the exact number of enemy killed, they felt reasonably certain that an entire NVA regiment had been virtually wiped out. The eastern approach was saturated with tons of high explosives; the road junction, the plantation, the old French Fort, and all bottle-necks along the enemy's route were heavily hit. Montagnard tribesmen, who inhabit the surrounding hills, later reported finding from 200 to 500 North Vietnamese bodies at a time stacked in rows along the trails and roads leading to the base. It was obvious that they had been caught while on the march and mangled by air raids and piston-like artillery concentrations. While many of the defenders at the KSCB never fired a shot, what was believed to be the long-awaited enemy onslaught came and passed with a whimper instead of a roar.(188)

Even though the North Vietnamese continued to probe through-out March, it was obvious that they had shot their bolt on the night of 29 February/1 March. The NVA never mustered another large ground attack against the base; the battle had reached a turning point. Having had their fingers burned too often, the North Vietnamese settled into a wait-and-see strategy. They continued to pound the base with artillery but exerted no major ground effort; instead they lurked in the hills and waited for patrols which ventured too far from the perimeter.(189)

The waiting game proved to be just as disastrous for the enemy as had his previous strategy. The month of March was marked by clear skies over Khe Sanh and there were only five days during which weather hampered flight operations. While the overcast had never interfered with Arc Light strikes or TPQs, the retreat of the monsoons was a blessing for the attack pilots and fighter/bombers swarmed into the valley like locusts. The number of close air support sorties in March almost doubled the amount flown the previous month. Any enemy movement with-in the TAOR during the day invariably drew a flight of sleek jets, prop-driven A-1 Skyraiders, or helicopter gunships with-in minutes. The trenches and bunker complexes inside the B-52 line were also worked over daily to insure that the NVA stayed at arm's length. What's more, the unrestricted visibility en-abled the TAC(A)s and airborne observers to ferret out and call in artillery on the enemy gun positions which had been hammering the base. For the most part, 1/13 had been limited to intelligence-generated concentrations during February, but the good weather in March provided Lieutenant Colonel Hennelly's men with something they could sink their teeth into--observed targets. Enemy gunners no longer enjoyed a reprieve and each round they fired was an invitation to instant retaliation. With Birddogs or Hueys overhead, the enemy seldom even fired and this was no small consolation to the men at the base. The clear skies and accurate supporting fires were a potent combination and the number of confirmed enemy dead recorded in March increased approximately 80 percent over February.(190)

The enemy's plight at Khe Sanh was echoed, albeit in veiled terms by his propaganda broadcasts. The Radio Hanoi, English-speaking announcer, Hanoi Hanna--the Communist's anemic version of Tokyo Rose--gradually shifted her theme from, "We will crush Khe Sanh" to "Ho Chi Minh would be unhappy if we wasted our time on only 6,000 Marines." The Communists also attempted to sell the line that 20,000 North Vietnamese had "tied down" the 26th Marines. Such rationale smacked of sour grapes. This illogical reasoning would be similar to a defeated football coach saying that he didn't really want to win the game, only keep the other team "tied down" for an hour or so. At the KSCB itself, there were a few feeble attempts to sway the defenders. On 10 March, an incoming mortar round released about 200 propaganda leaflets. The following day, an NVA loudspeaker blared a message to the 37th ARVN Ranger Battalion which invited the South Vietnamese to "join their brothers from the North in driving out the Americans." There were no takers. The psychological effort was just one more indication that the enemy was hurting.(191)

About mid-March, the 26th Marines S-2 began noting an exodus of major NVA units from the Khe Sanh TAOR. Most of these reports came from mountain tribesmen who provided valuable information on enemy troop dispositions throughout the siege. The 325C NVA Division Headquarters was one of the first to pull out toward Laos, followed by elements of the 95C and 101D Regiments which also relocated to the west. About the same time, the 304th NVA Division withdrew several thousand meters to the southwest. The enemy still retained enough troops around the base to maintain pressure and thus the shelling and probes continued.(192)

Closely correlated with the enemy's retrograde movement was another large influx of refugees into the KSCB. Most were

Montagnards who had inhabited the smaller villages surrounding the base and unfortunately had become the pawns of war. When the fighting first broke out, the Allies advised them to evacuate their homes and move overland to Cam Lo or else they would be exposed to fire from both sides. During the period 23-28 January, 1,050 Vietnamese and tribesmen with their families were air evacuated to Da Nang and then on to Quang Tri City. About the same time, some 1,800 tribesmen completed an overland trek from Khe Sanh to Cam Lo by way of the the Ba Long Valley. Later an additional 3,000 or more attempted to reach Cam Lo, but during the journey, the North Vietnamese intercepted this group and directed them back into the Khe Sanh area. Presumably, the NVA used the Montagnards to screen troop movements and confuse American intelligence. The next surge of refugees into the combat base occurred in early February following the attack on Lang Vei. On 7 March, the tribesmen again started to filter into the base. They were screened, interrogated, and processed for evacuation in the FOB-3 compound. As many as 661 were airlifted to eastern Quang Tri Province in a single day and the total for March was 1,432.(193)

Although the enemy had scaled down his forces, the heavy incoming continued to plague the Marines. On the average, the base received about 150 rounds a day during March. During the course of a normal day, the preponderance of fire was from the 82mm mortars but on peak days the greatest number of rounds was from the heavier artillery. On 23 March, the KSCB received its heaviest daily saturation of the month--1,109 rounds. Of these, over 30 percent were from the enemy's big guns in Laos. In addition to the indirect fire, the Marines took a sprinkling of recoilless rifle shells; but these weapons were easy to spot because of their large back blast and thus were vulnerable to air attack and counterbattery fire.(194)

During March, the defenders, on order of General Cushman, began to push out from the perimeter. On 8 March, the ARVN Rangers conducted a series of sweeps east of the runway. The first patrol made no contact but the next two became heavily engaged with an NVA force of unknown size. The Rangers attacked and poured into the enemy trenches, got eye-ball to eye-ball with "their brothers from the North" and killed 26. On the 24th, a patrol from Company A, 1/9, made contact with two NVA platoons which were dug in approximately 1,500 meters northwest of Lieutenant Colonel Mitchell's main perimeter. The Marines attacked the enemy emplacements and in a four-hour battle killed 31 North Vietnamese. During the fighting, a UH-1E helicopter of VMO-6 was shot down while supporting the Marines but the crewmen were rescued.(*) Friendly casualties were five killed, four medevaced, and two with minor wounds. The largest encounter, however, came on 30 March when Company B, 1/26, received a chance to settle an old score. The target area was the same complex, approximately 850 meters south of the perimeter, where the B/1/26 patrol had been ambushed on 25 February.(195)

The attack had been planned by the battalion commander, Lieutenant Colonel Frederick J. McEwan (who relieved Lieutenant Colonel Wilkinson on 1 March) and his operations officer, Major Charles E. Davis III, with careful attention to every detail. In fact, the 1/26 staff had been working on this attack for a month. The sweep was also closely coordinated with the FSCC to ensure that the maximum supporting arms were available. To support Company B, Lieutenant Colonel Hennelly's staff worked out a variation of the defensive fire plan with nine batteries participating. Marine artillery (1/13) formed the primary box and rolling barrage while the Army 175mms and TPQ-10 controlled aircraft were responsible for the sides of the secondary box. The latter fell on the high ground adjacent to the objective which might influence the battle. The plan called for Captain Pipes to move his unit into the primary box and follow approximately 75 meters in trace of the rolling barrage. As the company advanced, the entire cylinder also advanced. Outside the primary box, the sides of the secondary would open and close over the terrain like a giant accordian. One extremely important factor was that the artillery fire would not necessarily alert the enemy of the impending attack because the same technique had been used so frequently in that area. The element of surprise still belonged to the Marines.

At 0800, Captain Pipes' men swept out of a draw and, under the cover of heavy fog, crossed the access road which ran from the Route 9 junction to the FOB-3 compound. This jumping off point had been secured by one platoon during the night. To their front and flanks, waves of exploding artillery shells churned up the terrain. At the same time, four 106mm recoilless rifles and six .50 caliber and M-60 machine guns provided overhead fire; a type of support "which would have warmed the heart of 'Manila John' Basilone."(**) The crescent-shaped defenses,

_____

(*)   The pilot was badly burned in the crash and died that night.

(**) Gunnery Sergeant John Basilone was a Medal of Honor winner

manned by an NVA battalion, were roughly 100 meters southeast of the road and extended along a 700 meter front. The enemy troops occupied heavily fortified bunkers, trenches, and fighting holes. Although the objective was indeed formidable, Company B was not to be denied that day.(196)

After about 10 minutes of continuous supporting fire, Company B moved swiftly into final assault positions and Captain Pipes directed the FSCC to collapse the two artillery boxes. The fire was shifted to cut off any enemy reinforcements from reaching the battle area and to suppress NVA artillery and mortars. As if on cue, the dense fog suddenly lifted; the last thing that many enemy soldiers saw that morning was two Marine assault platoons with fixed bayonets only a few yards in front of their positions. The surprise was complete. Pipes' men poured into the trenches and swarmed over the startled defenders before they could react. While one element laid down a base of fire with small arms and machine guns, Marines armed with flame-throwers, grenades, and satchel charges rushed through the trenches to sear and blast enemy emplacements. The men of Company B carried out their grisly work for over three hours and, by noon, the trenchworks had become a smoking tomb for 115 North Vietnamese.

The only effective resistance during the battle was enemy mortar fire. Eventually, the NVA placed about 100 rounds on the attacking force. One of these scored a direct hit on the company CP and killed the radio man, the artillery FO, and the 81mm mortar FO. The company commander was also hit. A mortar fragment passed through Captain Pipes' arm and lodged in the side of his chest about two inches from his heart. Pipes not only survived, he continued to direct the attack.

With the loss of his two forward observers, the captain had to handle the coordination of supporting arms by himself. Fortunately, Lieutenant Colonel McEwan and Major Davis had made allowances for such a possibility. During the planning phase, they plotted general fire zones in the objective area and assigned each one a call sign (e.g. Apples, Oranges, Grapes, etc.) Captain Pipes knew where these zones were located and whenever

---

in World War II. During an action at Edson's Ridge on Guadalcanal, Basilone's machine gun section fired over 26,000 rounds in one night and helped break up a fanatical Japanese attack. Manila John was later killed on Iwo Jima.

he wanted to hit a target he simply told the FSCC, "Fire Apples" or "Fire Oranges." In short order, the designated zone was saturated with mortar and artillery rounds. Pipes utilized this technique throughout the rest of the battle.(197)

Once the Marines had consolidated the objective, they collected their casualties which included nine dead and returned to the perimeter. As Company B retired, the primary and secondary boxes closed back in around the Marines and walked them home. During the battle, the raiding force was shielded by some 2,600 artillery shells and 1,000 mortar rounds. On the return trip, NVA artillery tracked the column; ironically, one casualty during the withdrawal was an NVA prisoner who was killed by his own fire. Lieutenant Colonel McEwan later described the operation as a "classic raid." He attributed the success to the detailed planning, the coordination with the FSCC, and Captain Pipes' precise execution which "adhered to the tactical fundamentals and principles of war."(*) For his part, the captain was later awarded the Silver Star and the entire company received a warm congratulatory message from General Westmoreland. The debt had been paid in full.(198)

This purge to the south of the base marked the last significant encounter of SCOTLAND and, at 0800 on 31 March, the operation was officially terminated. The operational control of the 26th Marines was passed to the U. S. Army 1st Air Cavalry Division (1st ACD), commanded by Major General John J. Tolson, III, and Operation PEGASUS commenced. The Army division, along with the 1st Marines and the 3d ARVN Airborne Task Force started the push from Ca Lu to reopen Route 9, relieve the pressure on the KSCB, and destroy remnants of the NVA units in the Khe Sanh TAOR. In effect, the siege was over. Cumulative friendly casualties for SCOTLAND, which began on 1 November 1967 were 205 friendly KIA, 852 medevaced, and 816 minor wounded. The extent of NVA losses was never determined and more than likely

---

(*) Another interesting point was that the attack was largely carried out by inexperienced troops. During the siege, Company B suffered considerable casualties and most of the replacements were fresh from the States. Major Davis later commented that the conduct of these Marines during the operation spoke highly of the type of training that they received before arriving in Vietnam. This ability to adapt quickly plus the high quality of small unit leadership was, in Davis' opinion, a key factor in the Marine victory.

never will be. The Marines counted 1,602 enemy bodies along the perimeters but the total number of North Vietnamese dead was probably between 10,000 and 15,000. The enemy always carried off his dead when possible and many others undoubtedly died in the surrounding hills and were not found by anyone. There was little doubt that the heart of two crack NVA divisions had been ripped out at Khe Sanh. The full impact of the suffering endured by the enemy, however, did not become evident until the Marine, Army, and ARVN troops began mopping up operations around the base.(*)(199)

(*)   The breakdown of fixed-wing tactical sorties under Operation NIAGARA follows: Marine-7,078, Seventh Air Force-9,684, and U. S. Navy-5,167. These figures were derived from 1st MAW Command Chronologies and Project CHECO, Southeast Asia Report. The two sources do not agree on Marine sorties (Project CHECO credits USMC aircraft with 6,385); 1st MAW records in this case have been cited. Statistics for B-52 strikes and Marine helicopter operations have been previously incorporated in the text.

PART VIII

THE BREAKOUT

The blueprints for a major Allied drive into the Khe Sanh
Plateau had been on the drawing boards at III MAF Headquarters
in the embryo stage since late January. The 1st ACD was slated
for the campaign since that division had displaced from Bong
Son, in II Corps, and arrived at Phu Bai on 22 January. Three
days after he assumed operational control of the new division,
General Cushman directed General Tolson to prepare a contingency
plan for the relief of Khe Sanh. This action eventually resulted in Operation PEGASUS but there was a series of events
which delayed its start until April. The first was the dis-
ruptive Communist TET Offensive and the resulting Battle of
Hue City which raged until 25 February. Throughout February
and early March, the 1st ACD was busily engaged in and around
the old imperial capital. Logistics was another consideration.
General Westmoreland had initiated a supply build-up in I Corps
during December 1967 but III MAF did not yet have sufficient
stock levels to support an operation the size of PEGASUS, especially while the heavy fighting still continued in Hue.
Finally, the poor weather prevented large-scale helicopter
operations in the Khe Sanh area.(200)

An alteration of the command structure in I Corps also in-
directly affected the proposed operation. Until the early part
of 1968, the three divisions in I Corps (1st MarDiv, 3d MarDiv,
and the U. S. Army Americal Division) were under the direct
control of General Cushman, CG, III MAF. General Westmoreland,
however, was convinced that a critical, if not the most critical,
phase of the war was taking shape in I Corps and had begun to
pump reinforcements into the two northern provinces. These included the 1st ACD and the 101st Airborne Division. To keep
closer tabs on the action in the north, General Westmoreland
also established a forward echelon of his MACV Headquarters,
under the Deputy, ComUSMACV, General Creighton W. Abrams, at
Camp Hochmuth, Phu Bai on 9 February. There was little formal
change in the command structure; General Abrams simply acted
as an agent for ComUSMACV in an advisor/coordinator role. On
10 March, however, the structure did change; MACV Forward was
converted to Provisional Corps, Vietnam (PCV) and placed under
the operational control of General Cushman, CG, III MAF. PCV's
new commander, Lieutenant General William B. Rosson, U. S. Army,

132

assumed control of all American combat forces operating in the
northern two provinces, less the southern portion of Thua Thien.
At that time the three major U. S. units in the area were the
3d MarDiv, the 1st ACD, and the 101st Airborne Division. In addition, the reinforced ARVN 1st Division was operating in this
region. In essence, PCV was established to provide closer supervision over growing U. S. forces and coordination with the Vietnamese units in the northern area.(201)

As the operations around Hue tapered off, General Cushman,
on 29 February, directed General Tolson to take the plans for
PEGASUS back off the shelf. During the first week in March,
General Tolson met in Da Nang with Generals Cushman and Abrams
for a discussion of the operation.(*) The mission was threefold: relieve the Khe Sanh Combat base, reopen Route 9 from
Ca Lu to Khe Sanh, and eradicate any NVA elements within the
area of operations. In addition to the three brigades of the
1st ACD, General Tolson was to assume operational control of
the 26th Marines, the 1st Marines, and the 3d ARVN Airborne
Task Force. D-day was tentatively set for 1 April--depending
on the weather. With the basic directives, General Tolson returned to Camp Evans, and settled down to detailed planning with his division staff. During the next few weeks, there
were numerous planning and coordination meetings with III MAF,
PCV, the 3d Marine Division, 1st Marine Aircraft Wing, Seventh
Air Force, and representatives of the attached units.(202)

The logistics portion of the plan hinged around construction
of a base and airfield near Ca Lu which could accommodate C-7
Caribou transports and later C-123s. Before work could be
initiated, elements of the 3d MarDiv had to secure and repair
the stretch of Route 9 between Ca Lu and the Rockpile so that
supplies, fuel, ammunition, and construction material could be
stockpiled. Once this was accomplished, a joint task force of
engineers--the 11th Engineer Battalion, Fleet Marine Force, the
1st ACD's 8th Engineer Battalion, and Navy Mobile Construction
Battalion 5--began construction of an airfield, parking ramps,
logistical facilities, and defensive positions. By the time the
lead assault elements were ready to jump off in the attack, the
installation was 83 percent completed. The base was dubbed
Landing Zone (LZ) Stud.

(*) It was around this time that PCV was formed and General
Abrams departed I Corps. General Rosson then became a key
figure in the planning of the operation.

On 25 March, D-6, the 1st Squadron, 9th Cavalry (1/9 CavSqd), operating from LZ Stud, began extensive reconnaissance in the PEGASUS area of operations to pave the way for the initial air assaults. The mission of the unit was "to find the enemy, destroy his antiaircraft capability, acquire hard intelligence for exploitation, and locate and prepare suitable landing zones." Since General Tolson had little concrete information on exact enemy locations, the activities of the 1/9 CavSqd were essential to the operation. The squadron fanned out from LZ Stud in ever increasing concentric circles under the cover of tactical air, B-52 strikes, and the 8-inch and 105mm batteries which had been moved to Ca Lu. During this phase, the air cavalrymen called in 632 tactical air strikes, 49 specially fuzed construction sorties (Daisy Cutters), and 12 Arc Light strikes on enemy antiaircraft positions, troop concentrations, and future landing zones.(203)

As a prelude to PEGASUS, the 3d MarDiv launched a regimental-size, diversionary attack in eastern Quang Tri Province. On 30 March, Task Force KILO, comprised of the 2d Battalion, 4th Marines; the U. S. Army 3d Squadron, 5th Cavalry; and the 3d Battalion, 1st ARVN Regiment pushed northward from Dong Ha on a search and destroy sweep through the Gio Linh coastal plain area between the Cua Viet River and the DMZ. In addition, a company from the 101st Airborne Division was used as a reconnaissance force and to convey a picture of greater weight and diversity of attack. Although the foray was primarily designed to confuse the NVA and draw attention away from the mailed fist which was poised at Ca Lu, the Allies of Task Force KILO killed 150 North Vietnamese during the first day.(204)

At 0700 on D-day (1 April), two battalions controlled by the 1st Marines (2/1 and 2/3), which had moved from Phu Bai to LZ Stud several days before, spearheaded the attack to the west. Meeting only light resistance, 2/1 wheeled to the north of Route 9 and secured its objective while 2/3 swept through and consolidated the area to the south of the road. With both flanks screened by the infantry, the 11th Engineer Battalion began the mammoth task of renovating Route 9. Later in the day, elements of the 3d Brigade (Bde) 1st ACD leapfrogged by helicopter to positions midway between Ca Lu and Khe Sanh. The 1st and 2d Squadrons, 7th Cavalry swarmed into LZ Mike which encompassed Hill 248, approximately 7,500 meters east of the KSCB. This high ground to the south of Route 9 was cradled on three sides by branches of the Quang Tri River. To the north some 3,000 meters, the 5th Battalion, 7th Cavalry air-assaulted the southern slope of Dong Chio Mountain which was designated LZ Cates. This stretch was particularly critical because the road was sandwiched between the Quang Tri River on the south and the nearly perpendicular cliffs which towered menacingly over Route 9 to the north. Following the initial waves, the 3d Brigade Headquarters displaced to LZ Cates and established a CP. By 1650, the Flying Horsemen were in place and continued to expand both zones while 105mm howitzers of the 1st Battalion, 21st Artillery, were helilifted in for direct support. Throughout the PEGASUS area of operations, the Americans established defensive perimeters and passed the night with little or no contact.(205)

While the combat engineers continued their steady movement along Route 9, additional elements of the airmobile armada were thrown into the action. On D plus two, the 2d Brigade, 1st ACD which had been staging at Ca Lu conducted a vertical envelopment into LZ Tom and LZ Wharton which were roughly 6,000 and 8,500 meters southeast of Khe Sanh. The air assault went smoothly even though the zones were shelled by NVA gunners. By the end of the day, all 2d Brigade units were in position along with three batteries of the 1st Battalion, 77th Artillery. In the meantime, the 3d Brigade and the 1st Marines expanded their TAORs along Route 9.(206)

On 4 April, General Tolson began to put the squeeze on enemy elements to the south of the KSCB. Moving northeast from LZ Wharton, the 1/5 CavSqd attacked the old French fort near the junction of Route 9. At the same time, the 26th Marines, which had been attached to the 1st ACD since 31 March, began the long awaited breakout from the base. At 0600, three companies of Lieutenant Colonel John J. H. Cahill's 1/9 (relieved Lieutenant Colonel Mitchell on 1 April) moved out of the rock quarry perimeter and advanced on Hill 471 which was 2,500 meters due south of the airstrip. The hill was a key terrain feature since it overlooked the road junction and that segment of Route 9 which snaked to the southwest. The area was also occupied by major elements of the 304th NVA Division. After heavy prep fires, the Marines stormed up the slope in the face of light enemy fire and secured their objective at 1720.(*) Thirty North Vietnamese

---

(*) Although the rifle companies encountered only slight resistance during the assault, the Company A command group, while advancing toward the objective, took a direct hit from an enemy mortar. The Air Officer, Captain Walter C. Jones, III was killed as was one radio operator; the battalion Operations Officer,

bodies were strewn over the hilltop.

The men of 1/9, however, were in for a long night. Later that night, the enemy lashed out at the hill with 192 mortar and artillery rounds. The barrage was undoubtedly designed to soften up the Marines for a counterattack the next morning. The North Vietnamese might as well have saved their ammunition and their counterattack.(207)

At 0515, the 7th Battalion, 66th Regiment, 304th NVA Division, charged up Hill 471 in a vain attempt to knock 1/9 from the crest. The 66th Regiment was definitely a hard-luck outfit; it had been bloodied at Khe Sanh Village on 21 January and again during the abortive attack against the 37th ARVN Ranger Battalion, on 29 February/1 March. The enemy's string of bad luck remained unbroken on the morning of 5 April. Lieutenant Colonel Cahill's Marines stood their ground, poured withering fire into the onrushing enemy troops, and, with the aid of artillery and tactical air strikes, smashed the North Vietnamese attack. During the one-sided exchange, one Marine was killed and 19 wounded; the 66th Regiment left 122 dead on the slopes. This fight was one of the major highlights of Operation PEGASUS.(*)(208)

The surge of Allied units into the previously uncontested domain of the 304th NVA Division continued for the next few days.(**) On the afternoon of the 5th, the last element of the 1st ACD--the 1st Brigade--departed Ca Lu aboard droves of helicopters and swooped into LZ Snapper, 7,500 meters south of the base. The following morning, the 2d Battalion, 12th Cavalry (2d Brigade) moved northeast from LZ Wharton and relieved Lieutenant Colonel Cahill's battalion on Hill 471. After relief was effected,

---

Major Ted R. Henderson, was seriously wounded and evacuated. The Battalion Commander, Lieutenant Colonel Cahill and his Artillery Officer, First Lieutenant John K. LeBlond, Jr. were also wounded at that time but were able to continue.

(*) In addition to the Marine killed during the attack, nine were killed by enemy shelling the night before. A total of 57 Marines were medevaced.

(**) The 325C NVA Division had long since departed the area and left the 304th to continue pressure on the 26th Marines. Some elements of the 304th swung to the north of the base and replaced units of the 325C.

1/9 initiated a drive toward Hill 689 some 4,500 meters to the northwest. On the opposite side of the KSCB, the 5th Battalion, 7th Cavalry (1st Brigade) conducted a landing just 500 meters north of the Blue Sector wire. The 2d and 3d Battalions, 26th Marines fanned out to the north and northwest of their hill outposts. Company G, 2/26 bumped into an NVA company that afternoon and killed 48 of the enemy.

The initial relief of the combat base occurred at 1350 on 6 April when the lead company of the 3d ARVN Airborne Task Force was airlifted to Khe Sanh and linked up with the 37th Rangers. This move was primarily intended as a morale booster for the 37th. Two days later, after 2/7 CavSqd had completed the sweep along Route 9 and linked up with the 26th Marines, the official relief took place. At 0800 on 8 April, the 3d Brigade airlifted its CP to the base and became the new landlord. Relieved of its duties along the perimeter, Lieutenant Colonel McEwan's 1/26 saddled up and attacked to the west that day but made little contact.(209)

Traditionally, the lifting of a siege has been the occasion for great emotional outbursts, bands, and stirring oration; in this regard, the relief of Khe Sanh was somewhat of a disappointment. General Tolson intended for the link-up to be "as business like as possible with a minimum of fanfare" so that he could get the Marines on the offensive again. A few newsmen at the base snapped pictures of Marines shaking hands with the Cavalrymen but the men usually shrugged indifferently afterwards and went about their business. The defenders generally looked on the proceedings with sort of a "ho-hum" attitude, perhaps they felt that they had not been rescued from anything. In fact, they were right; the enemy threat had been squelched weeks before PEGASUS had gotten off the ground. "I've been at Khe Sanh for nine months," the regimental commander stated, "and if they keep me supplied, I could stay here another nine months." No doubt most men were glad they did not have to remain because the stand at Khe Sanh had not been "all peaches and cream," but, as far as the defenders being snatched out of the jaws of destruction --it just did not happen that way.(210)

With the arrival of the 3d ARVN Airborne Task Force, all maneuver elements involved in PEGASUS were on the Khe Sanh Plateau. On the 8th, the three South Vietnamese battalions (minus one company) leapfrogged from Quang Tri to LZ Stud and then conducted a helicopter assault into LZ Snake about 2,000 meters southwest of the base. In effect, the encirclement was complete; only, this time, pressure was being applied in the opposite direction. As the Allied oil slick spread over the valley, the Americans and South Vietnamese uncovered ghastly evidence of how badly the NVA had been beaten. The various units found hundreds of North Vietnamese in shallow graves; hundreds more lay where they fell. A total of 557 individual weapons, 207 crew-served weapons, and 2 antiaircraft pieces were either captured or destroyed. In addition, 17 vehicles, ranging from PT-76 tanks to motor scooters, and tons of ammunition, food, radios, and individual equipment were discovered. The mountains of captured or abandoned enemy stores indicated that either Operation PEGASUS had caught the NVA completely flat-footed or the remnants of the two enemy divisions were in no shape to cart off their equipment and supplies.(211)

Even though the rest of the operation centered around completing work on Route 9 and sifting through the debris of battle, there were several contacts with the retreating enemy. On 8 April, the ARVN forces turned back an NVA counterattack west of the base and killed 78 in the process. The same day, the 1st Battalion, 9th Marines, assaulted and seized Hill 689 with no opposition but discovered 37 NVA killed during a fight the previous night. Air and artillery also hammered away at the NVA; on one occasion, a U. S. Army airborne observer spotted 100 North Vietnamese in the open and called in artillery fire which accounted for 30 of the enemy. While the NVA pulled away to the west, the engineer task force crept toward the base from the opposite direction, and at 1600 on 11 April, Route 9 was officially declared open. The engineers had repaired 14 kilometers of road, replaced 9 vital bridges, and constructed 17 bypasses; General Westmoreland applauded their feat as "herculean."(212)(See Maps 8 and 9).

The day before the road was completed, General Tolson received a visit from the PCV commander, General Rosson, which resulted in an alteration of Operation PEGASUS. General Rosson directed his division commander to begin extracting units to Quang Tri and Camp Evans in preparation for an assault into the A Shau Valley (Operation DELAWARE). General Tolson anticipated that the operation would last much longer and had initially planned to expand his sweeps far to the south, north, and northwest. In addition, the 1st Marines was slated for air assaults into a valley west of the Rockpile. The A Shau Valley, however, was a major enemy base area and logistics complex which supported his operations in Thua Thien and Quang Nam provinces. To launch a mobile strike into this region and destroy the enemy's base

138

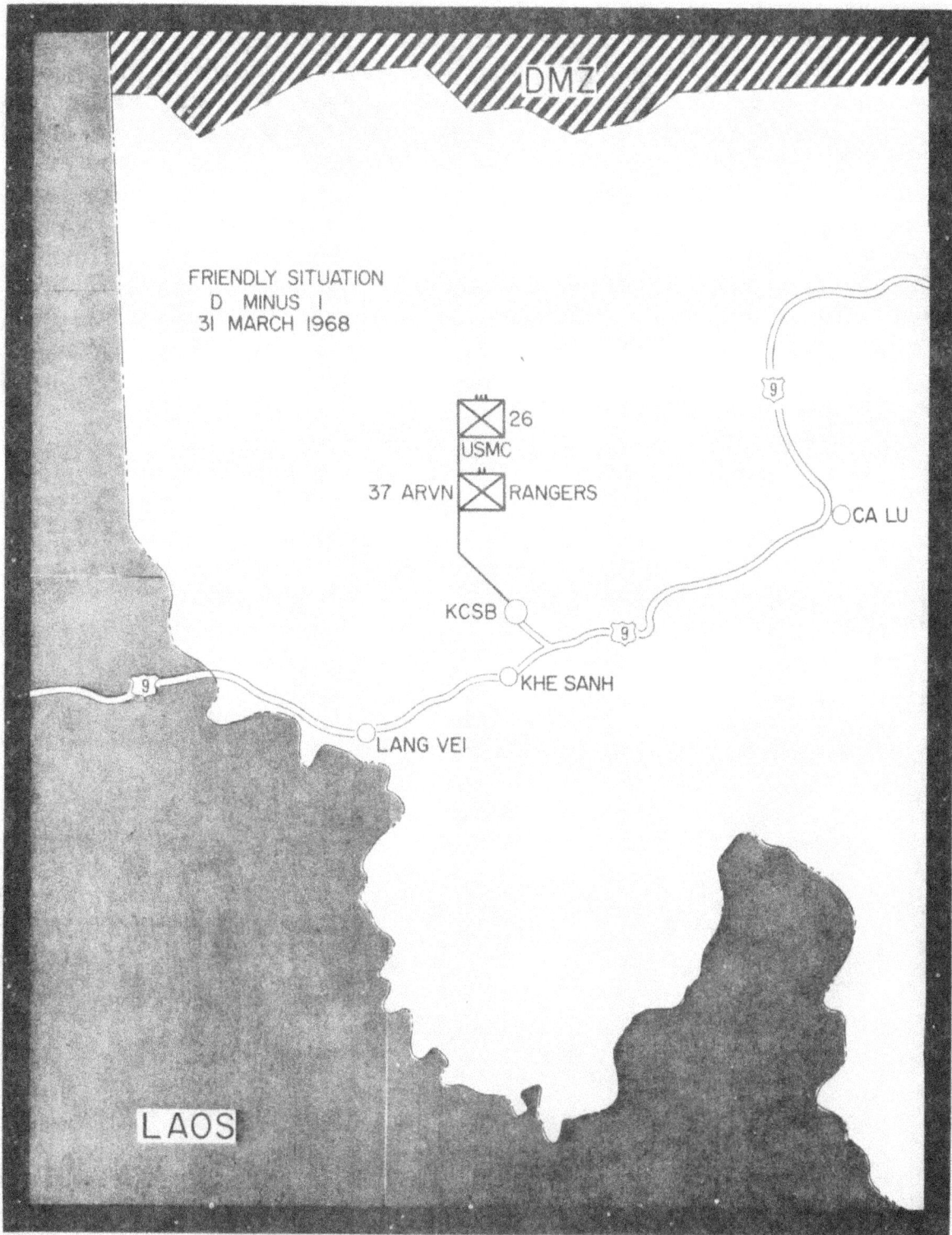

FRIENDLY SITUATION
D MINUS I
31 MARCH 1968

DMZ

9

CA LU

26
USMC

37 ARVN RANGERS

KCSB

9

KHE SANH

9

LANG VEI

LAOS

MAP 8

OPERATION PEGASUS

K.W.WHITE

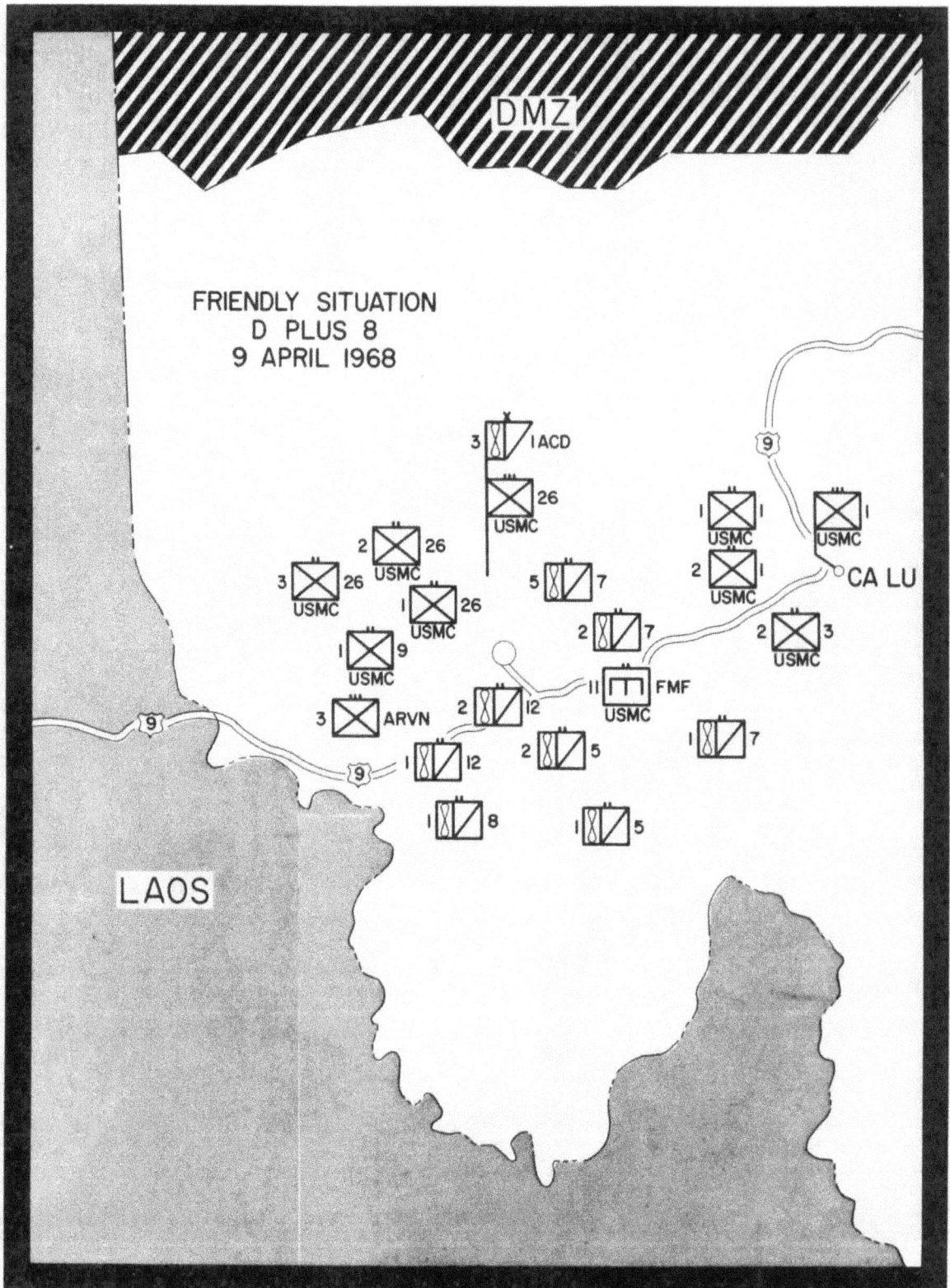

FRIENDLY SITUATION
D PLUS 8
9 APRIL 1968

DMZ

LAOS

CA LU

OPERATION PEGASUS

MAP9   K.W. WHITE

140

had been a major MACV objective of long standing. Support of this operation had been one of the reasons for the troop and logistical buildup in the northern area which had begun the previous December. The weather in the A Shau Valley was now ideal for airmobile operations and General Westmoreland was anxious to get DELAWARE underway before the end of April. The following day, the 11th, all air assaults were cancelled and General Tolson began to withdraw elements from Khe Sanh. The 1st Brigade, less one battalion, was airlifted to Quang Tri City and the 37th ARVN Ranger Battalion, which had fought so valiantly, was pulled out and sent to Da Nang. Two days later, the division command post and elements of the 3d Brigade departed for Camp Evans.(213)

Another noteworthy departure was that of Colonel Lownds. The colonel, who did his job well enough to earn the nation's second highest award--the Navy Cross--turned over the reins of the 26th Marines to Colonel Bruce F. Meyers on 12 April. The new commander wasted no time; he planned and executed the attack which in effect, ended the Battle for Khe Sanh. It was scheduled for 14 April--Easter Sunday.

Ironically, the last engagement took place between Hills 881S and 881N precisely where, on 20 January, the whole affair had begun. The 3d Battalion, 26th Marines which had started the fight was also on hand to finish it. Ever since the 4th, Lieutenant Colonel John C. Studt's battalion (relieved Lieutenant Colonel Alderman on 15 March) had been sweeping to the north and northwest of Hill 881S and, on several occasions, had taken fire from 881N. The enemy troops still clung tenaciously to that piece of real estate from which they had directed rocket fire against Khe Sanh and antiaircraft fire against the helicopters resupplying the Marines on 881S. Lieutenant Colonel Studt's mission was to secure the terrain between the two hills, then attack and seize 881N.(214)

Since the enemy gunners had zeroed in on the slopes of 881S with their mortars, Lieutenant Colonel Studt moved his attacking elements into position the night of the 13th. The assault companies of 3/26 slipped out of the defensive wire under the cover of darkness and moved down the forward slope of the hill along routes which were protected by security patrols. As he watched the Marines file by, the battalion's operations officer, Major Caulfield, could not help but be concerned about them. Most of the men had spent the past two and a half months in a foxhole or trench; they had received minimum rations and a maximum of enemy shelling. All were tired and dirty; some suffered from large body sores because the water received by these men had gone into their bodies and not on them. Even though they were Marines, the major wondered how they would perform the next morning. At 0800, he received his answer.(215)

The attack, which the troops referred to as their "Easter Egg Hunt," was preceded by a deluge of supporting fire. Colonel Meyers, who flew to 881S by helicopter, observed the attack and personally ensured that sufficient supporting arms were employed. In addition to the artillery of 1/13 at Khe Sanh and the 175mm bases, 155mm and 8-inch batteries of the 1st ACD at LZ Stud were called on to help cave in the enemy bunkers. Strike aircraft worked over the hill with bombs, rockets, and napalm. The Marines who remained on 881S also provided heavy support. Besides the 60mm and 81mm mortars, these men had pooled all eight of the battalion's 106 recoilless rifles, the two remaining 105mm howitzers, and six .50 caliber machine guns which had been salvaged from downed helicopters or stripped off of trucks at the base. As the assault troops advanced, the weapons on 881S provided direct overhead fire which sometimes preceded the front ranks by no more than 50 meters. As usual, the recoilless rifles were extremely effective. One observer later remarked that when the lead elements approached a treeline, no chances were taken; the 106 gunners fired a broadside and the treeline was simply blown away.(216)

Because of the weight and speed of the attack, the enemy was never able to recover. Moving behind a wall of steel, the battalion clawed its way through the defenses between the two hills and prepared for the final push. Major Caulfield, who had worried about the Marines' weakened condition the night before, soon found the opposite was true--he was having trouble holding them back. At one point, a group of NVA soldiers who had been hammered senseless by the prep fires, broke from their positions and fled into the open. An airborne spotter directed the companies to hold up while he called in air and artillery. Scanning the front lines, Major Caulfield noticed that a handful of Marines with fixed bayonets were in hot pursuit of the enemy. The major contacted the company commander by radio and told him to collar his troops. The reply was, "Sir, I can't stop them...." Neither could the enemy.(217)

The men of 3/26 stormed the hill, swarmed over the crest, and killed anyone who stood in their way. At 1428, the objective was secured and the men signaled their victory in traditional

Marine Corps fashion, as Colonel Meyers later described:

> On Sunday, 14 April (Easter), I helicoptered to
> 881S and with Captain Bill Dabney, Company Commander of
> I/3/26, personally watched the U. S. Colors (which had
> been fortuitously carried in a squad leader's pack)
> hoisted again over 881N. This was the signal (visual)
> that Lieutenant Colonel John Studt's assault had been
> completed. I watched the jungle utility-clad Marine
> "shinny-up" a shrapnel torn tree whose limbs had been
> sheared from the intensive prep fires, and affix the
> Stars and Stripes.(218)

With the enemy either dead or gone, the hill again lost its
value. Terrain wasn't so important in the fluid Vietnam war,
but people were and, in that respect, Lieutenant Colonel Studt's
men had completed a very successful operation--106 North Vietnamese were dead. In addition to the enemy dead on the objective, air strikes and artillery fire had completely blanketed
three large groups of NVA fleeing from the hill but because of
the dense vegetation and the approaching darkness, no bodies
were recovered. Two slightly shot-up North Vietnamese, one of
them an officer, were captured and flown back to Khe Sanh in
Colonel Meyers' helicopter. Considering the strength of the
enemy defenses, Marine casualties were surprisingly light--6
killed and 19 medevaced. Lieutenant Colonel Studt stated:
"...stand off plastering with supporting arms...prior to each
assault was the key factor here."(219)

That night the battalion commander and his operations
officer stood at the gate on 881S and slapped the men on the
back as they trooped back into the perimeter. One Marine, a
tall, lanky, slow-talking Kentuckian, held out a captured rifle
for Lieutenant Colonel Studt's inspection--it was filthy. During
the attack, the Marine had come face to face with the owner;
both men raised their rifles simultaneously and pulled the trigger
but only the M-16 barked out--the enemy's rifle jammed. The
survivor's explanation was simply, "I cleaned my weapon last
night, he didn't."(220)

The next morning at 0800, PCV terminated PEGASUS. The
operation was very successful and all objectives were achieved;
Route 9 was open, the enemy had been routed, and the base itself
was relieved. The North Vietnamese had lost another 1,304
killed and 21 captured, while 41 U. S. Army troops, 51 Marines,
and 33 South Vietnamese died. Air support again had played an

important role. There were 45 B-52 Arc Light strikes and 1,625 tactical sorties conducted during PEGASUS. Of the latter number, 650 sorties were flown by Marines, 463 by the U. S. Air Force, 436 by carrier-based Task Force 77, and 77 by the U. S. Army and VNAF. From 31 March to 8 April, U. S. Air Force C-130 and C-123 aircraft delivered 843 tons of supplies to Khe Sanh by paradrop and the low altitude extraction system. On 9 April, the strip was reopened to C-130s and the supply level at the KSCB began to grow large enough so that the 1st ACD could draw from the 26th Marines stockpile.(221)

With the termination of PEGASUS, the 3d Marine Division again assumed responsibility of the Khe Sanh area. Task Force GLICK, comprised of the 26th Marines, the 1st Marines, and the 2d Brigade(-), 1st ACD, launched Operation SCOTLAND II at 0801, 15 April. The 26th Marines, however, did not remain in the operation very long. Three days later, the new commanding officer and two of his battalions were transferred to Quang Tri Base and, for the men who had taken 77 days of the best the NVA could offer, the defense of Khe Sanh was over.(*)(222)

(*) The 2d Battalion, 26th Marines did not return to Quang Tri with the regiment but was transferred to the operational control of the 4th Marines at Camp Carroll. General Tompkins saw to it that each man who returned from Khe Sanh immediately received a hot shower, a clean uniform, and a big steak dinner. As an added touch, the 3d Marine Division band was on hand, and greeted each arrival with a stirring rendition of the "Marines Hymn."

144

PART IX

EPILOGUE

On 23 May 1968, several members of the 26th Marines who
had fought at Khe Sanh had a reunion of sorts in Washington,
D. C. and the surroundings were a far cry from the dirt and
grime of the combat base. The "CP" belonged to the President
of the United States, Lyndon B. Johnson. In the Cabinet Room
of the White House, the Commander in Chief paused to honor the
men of the 26th Marines and awarded the Presidential Unit
Citation to the regiment. Colonel Lownds, whose large handle-
bar mustache had been shaved off at the direction of "the
highest possible authority"--his wife, and Sergeant Major
Agrippa W. Smith, senior enlisted man at the KSCB, were on
hand to receive the award. While it was fitting that the 26th
Marines be cited as a unit, the President also praised the
South Vietnamese, U. S. Army, U. S. Navy, U. S. Air Force, and
Marine aviation and support units which contributed so gallantly
to the defense of the installation.(223)

In some quarters, however, there were still grumblings
over the Khe Sanh issue. During the siege, there had been a
virtual storm of protest from critics who opposed the Adminis-
tration's decision to hold the base. These doomsday prophets
suffered from what some military experts referred to as the
"Dien Bien Phu Syndrome." Many noted intellectuals were in the
van of this group and throughout the battle they could not be
convinced that air and artillery support would provide the margin
of difference; they warned that the tiny base would suffer the
same fate which had been meted out to the French garrison 14
years earlier.(224)

There are several reasons why Khe Sanh did not become
another Dien Bien Phu. The first and most obvious being that
the Americans possessed the overwhelming supporting arms which
were not available to the French. Contrary to the predictions
of many critics, air and artillery were decisive and more than
made up for the numerical superiority of the enemy. Over
100,000 tons of bombs and 150,000 artillery rounds were delivered
--and delivered intelligently--by the Americans during the siege.
Much of the credit goes to the regimental commander and his staff
who knew how to coordinate their different sources of firepower
to achieve maximum results. The NVA learned this during the

145

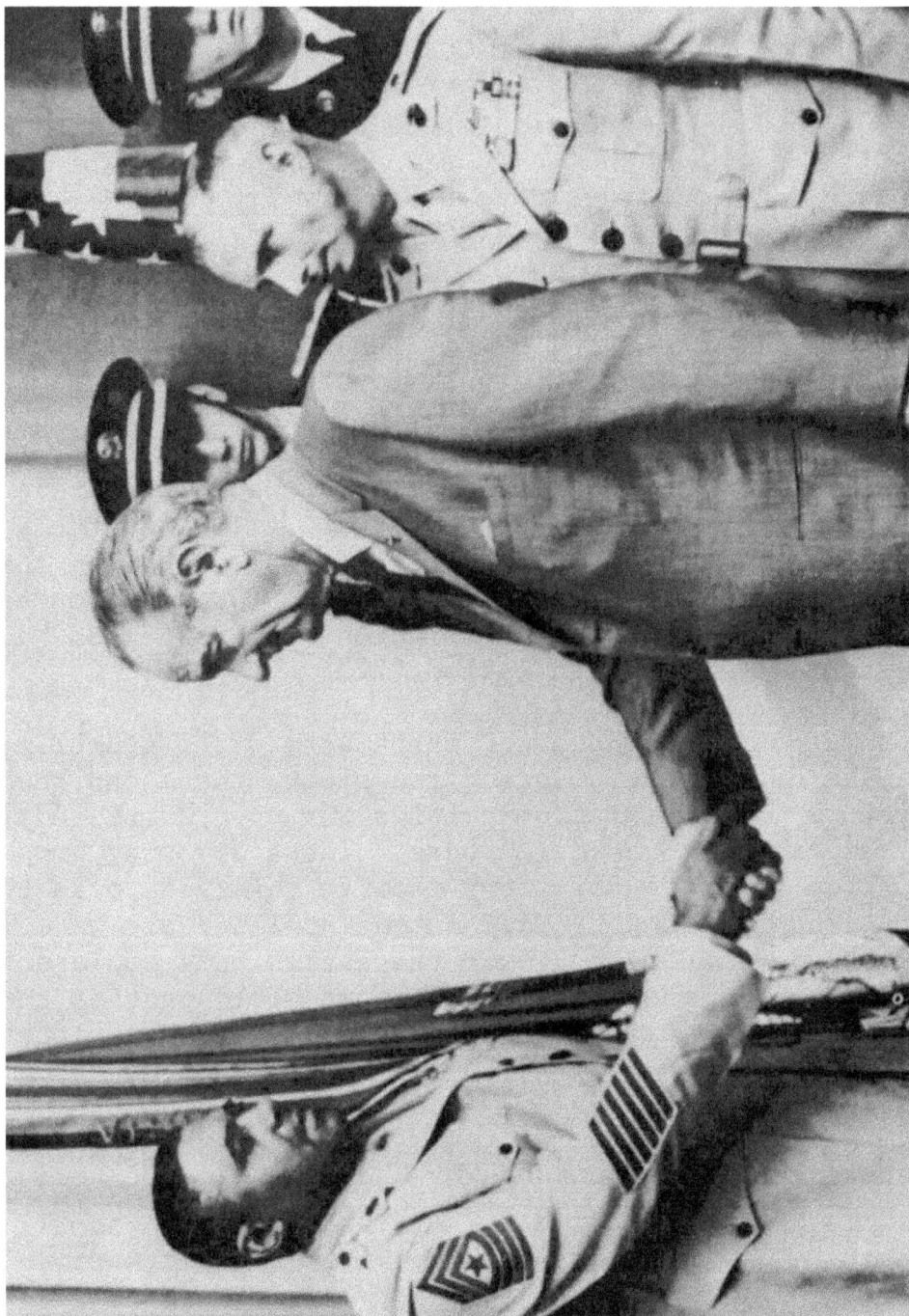

During the presentation of the Presidential Unit Citation to the 26th Marines, President Lyndon B. Johnson (C) congratulates Sergeant Major Agrippa W. Smith (L) while Colonel David E. Lownds (R) looks on.

146

five major attacks against the base and hill outposts.

The ability to keep Khe Sanh resupplied was another major factor. The NVA encirclement did not coincide with the monsoon season by accident. With Route 9 interdicted, the fate of the garrison hinged on the success or failure of the airlift and apparently the North Vietnamese anticipated that it would fail. The fact that the airlift was successful in the face of heavy enemy fire and the foulest weather imaginable is indeed a tribute to the aircrews and recovery personnel but the resupply effort went much deeper than just delivering the goods. The Force Logistics Command at Da Nang augmented by U. S. Army sources at Cam Ranh Bay was responsible for the mountain of supplies and material which sustained the 26th Marines. An excerpt from the works of Winston Churchill which was selected as the motto of the Force Logistics Command best describes the vital role these logistics agencies played: "Victory is the beautiful colored flower. Supply is the stem without which it could never have blossomed."(225)

Another important facet of the defense was the close supervision and leadership provided by the senior commanders, namely CG, 3d MarDiv, CG, III MAF, and ComUSMACV. Since much of the supporting arms and all of the logistical support was handled by agencies external to the 26th Marines, constant coordination among these three headquarters was imperative. General Tompkins was the pivotal figure of the triumvirate. During his daily trips to the base, the general learned first hand what the regimental commander needed; he not only saw that Colonel Lownds received adequate support but he insured that the defenders made the most of their resources. In so doing he exposed himself to heavy enemy antiaircraft, artillery, and mortar fire as did General Cushman during his periodic visits to Khe Sanh. Commenting on the strong role played by the 3d Marine Division commander, General Cushman later said, "General Tompkins made or approved every major decision during the battle."(226)

The real hero of Khe Sanh, however, was on the opposite end of the rank scale--the individual fighting man. For 77 days the defenders waited in the trenchlines while the bulk of the credit and publicity went to the artillery, fighter/bombers, and B-52s. On several occasions the supporting arms could not prevent major enemy assaults from reaching the wire; at this point, it was the Marines or ARVN Rangers, armed with rifles, grenades, and bayonets, who stopped the North Vietnamese--often in bitter hand-to-hand combat. Without exception, the battalion commanders were lavish in their praise of the young Americans and South Vietnamese who held the perimeter and denied the enemy a much-needed victory. In spite of the inherent hardships which accompanied the siege and the incessant shelling, the defenders were always itching for a fight. The most overused expression during the battle was, "I wish they (North Vietnamese) would hurry up and come so we can get this thing over with." When asked by a reporter if the NVA troops could take Khe Sanh, one officer answered, "Hell no, those 19-year-old Marines won't let them."(*)(227)

Finally, much of the credit for the American success at Khe Sanh belongs to the NVA. The North Vietnamese obliged the 26th Marines by standing toe to toe in a slugging contest during which they were outgunned and outfought; in effect, the enemy destroyed himself. If there was one salient feature which resulted in the enemy's defeat it might well be his rigid adherence to a siege strategy in the face of certain failure. Even when it became obvious that the Americans were aware of their master plan, the North Vietnamese doggedly pursued their siege tactics without alteration. The extremely lucrative target presented by the massed NVA forces which ringed the base was one of the main reasons the garrison was maintained. Thus, the question may be legitimately asked, "Who besieged whom?"(228)

To a lesser degree, there was a controversy over who or what had won the battle. Proponents of air power and strategic bombing were the most vocal; they felt that the B-52 had been the most decisive instrument of defense. While the Strato-fortress was a valuable asset and, without doubt played a major role, any attempt to single out one supporting arm as the ultimate weapon in the battle would be futile. The B-52 was but one part of an intricate defensive fire plan. The bombers struck targets beyond 1,100 meters of the base; tactical air and artillery took up the slack to within about 250 meters and the organic weaponry of the defenders provided close-in fires. The system was balanced and effective but, if any part were eliminated, the defenders would have paid a much higher price in casualties. Both General Tompkins and Colonel Lownds were unstinting in

---

(*) Many of these young men exhibited a maturity beyond their years. One message, scrawled on the back of a C-ration carton by an anonymous Marine, was found after the siege. It read: "Life has a special flavor to those who fight for it that the sheltered never know."

their praise of all supporting arms, as well as the logistical
effort; they stressed, and stressed heavily, that the defense
of Khe Sanh was a joint endeavor. The highly successful results
were achieved through the contributions of all U. S. Services
and the South Vietnamese. While the Marines had been unable to
find an infantryman who could carry a 27-ton payload, neither
had the U. S. Air Force come up with a B-52 which could man a
foxhole. Both, in their own way, were essential.(229)

The Khe Sanh story again became news in late June 1968
and the old controversy over strategy was rekindled. Prior to
leaving his post as ComUSMACV on 11 June, General Westmoreland
visited PCV Headquarters in I Corps and approved the recommenda-
tions of Generals Cushman and Rosson to raze the KSCB and withdraw all Allied forces to the Ca Lu area. While General
Westmoreland made the decision prior to his departure, he did
not close the base at that time, because mopping-up operations
were being conducted around Khe Sanh. In addition, large
amounts of supplies had been stockpiled there and the general
deemed it more economical to maintain the base while these
stocks were consumed in support of the operations rather than
backhaul them to Ca Lu. For these reasons, he left the choice
concerning the optimum time to dismantle the installation up to
his successor, General Abrams. When bulldozers finally began
to level the bunkers and structures which had housed the 26th
Marines throughout the siege, the American people wondered why
the base had been so tenaciously defended if it was to be
eventually abandoned. Had American blood been shed in vain?
Critics of the hold-out policy argued that, in the final analysis,
they had been right and those who decided to defend the base
had been wrong. Such rationale pinpointed the inability of
many Americans to break away from the techniques employed in
past wars and recognize the pecularities of the conflict in
Vietnam.

There were several reasons for the deactivation of the KSCB
since, for all practical purposes, the base had outlived its
usefulness. The rationale endorsed by General Cushman and
General Rosson was threefold. First, the enemy had reduced his
forces and changed his modus operandi in the Khe Sanh area.
Secondly, the NVA artillery in Laos had accurately targeted the
base and access road which compounded the casualty and resupply
problems. Finally and most important, General Cushman had sufficient assets in June to pursue the mobile offensive strategy
which he had advocated strongly for such a long time. Two U. S.
Army divisions (i.e. 1st ACD and the 101st Airborne) with their

inherent helicopter resources had been shifted to III MAF and, during March and April,the tremendous logistics burden associated with the introduction of these 50,000 men into northern I Corps had been alleviated. Since he had sufficient maneuver elements to go on the offense in western Quang Tri Province, General Cushman no longer needed five battalions buttoned up in Khe Sanh.(230)

An additional consideration for the abandonment of the base was President Johnson's announcement on 31 March that the U. S. would end air strikes in North Vietnam.(*) While the decision was a major step toward peace, it also enabled thousands of NVA support personnel who were responsible for road repair in North Vietnam to move further south. These workers constructed a network of infiltration arteries which bypassed the combat base and the continued policy of positioning static Allied defense installations in the path of these routes would have been inefficient and undesirable. In this regard, the best defense was a highly mobile offense and while a forward operating base for such operations was essential, the LZ Stud/Ca Lu area was much better suited than Khe Sanh.(231)

By the time PEGASUS was over, LZ Stud was in full operation. The airstrip was extended to accommodate C-123s, a Force Logistics Area was established, and local defenses were strengthened. The base was outside the range of the North Vietnamese 130mm and 152mm guns in Laos and the stretch of Route 9 from Ca Lu to the Rockpile and eventually Dong Ha was easier to keep open. Thus, two factors--enemy shelling and resupply problems--which had negated the effectiveness of Khe Sanh as a base of operations were absent at LZ Stud.

While not physically located on the Khe Sanh Plateau, the forces at LZ Stud controlled it. Two forward fire bases were established in the vicinity of the old combat base from which extensive patrolling was conducted. Ground patrols were supplemented by air surveillance. Whenever contact with the enemy was made, lighting-fast helicopter assaults were launched from LZ Stud and were supported by the artillery of the forward fire bases, tactical aircraft, and Huey gunships. The enemy was attacked by these mobile forces whenever and wherever he appeared.

(*)   The attacks were halted except in the area north of the demilitarized zone where the continuing enemy buildup directly threatened Allied forward positions and where the movements of their troops and supplies clearly related to that threat.

When a major NVA unit was encountered, sufficient reinforcements were also injected by helicopter. So, the only thing that changed on the Khe Sanh Plateau, besides the face of the combat base, was the style and tempo of operations.(232)

The new strategy by no means diminished the accomplishments of the men who had held Khe Sanh; it was simply a continuation of the battle in another form. When the leaders in Hanoi finally accepted President Johnson's peace overtures and consented to meet with U. S. representatives in Paris, there was one thing that the North Vietnamese negotiators did not possess--the battle standard of the 26th Marines. An editorial in the Washington Star provided an appropriate tribute to the men of Khe Sanh:

To be sure, Khe Sanh will be a subject of controversy for a long time, but this much about it is indisputable: It has won a large place in the history of the Vietnam war as an inspiring example of American and Allied valor. One day, in fact, the victory over the siege may be judged a decisive turning point that finally convinced the enemy he could not win.(233)

APPENDIX A

BIBLIOGRAPHICAL NOTES AND FOOTNOTES

Explanatory Note: Unless otherwise noted the material in this monograph is derived from Admiral Ulysses S. G. Sharp, USN, and General William C. Westmoreland, USA, Report On The War In Vietnam, hereafter Sharp and Westmoreland, Report On The War; Maj John J. Cahill, USMC, and Jack Shulimson, "History of U. S. Marine Corps Operations in Vietnam, Jan-Jun65"; FMFPac, Operations of U. S. Marine Forces Vietnam, Mar67-Apr68, hereafter FMFPac Marine Opns in Vietnam; FMFPac, U. S. Marine Corps Forces in Vietnam Mar65-Sep67 Historical Summary, Volume I: Narrative, hereafter FMFPac HistSum; III MAF Command Chronologies Apr67-Apr68, hereafter III MAF CmdChron; 3d Marine Division Command Chronologies, Apr67-Apr68, hereafter 3d MarDiv CmdChron; 1st Marine Aircraft Wing Command Chronologies, Apr67-Apr68, hereafter 1st MAW CmdChron; 26th Marines Command Chronologies, Apr67-Apr68, hereafter 26th Marines CmdChron; 1/26 Command Chronologies, Apr67-Apr68, hereafter 1/26 CmdChron; 2/26 Command Chronologies, Jan68-Apr68, hereafter 2/26 CmdChron; 3/26 Command Chronologies, Jun67-Apr68, hereafter 3/26 CmdChron; 3d Marines Khe Sanh Operations After Action Report, 9Jun67, hereafter 3d Marines Khe Sanh AAR; VMGR-152 Command Chronologies Jan68-Apr68, hereafter VMGR-152 CmdChron; Marine Corps Command Center, Status of Forces, Apr68, hereafter MCCC Status of Forces; Defense Intelligence Bulletins Dec67-Apr68, hereafter DIA IntBul; Six Month Evaluation Report, prepared by HQ, MACV 31May68; Presentation of LtGen Robert E. Cushman, Jr., USMC, in 1968 General Officers Symposium Book, HQMC, dtd 15Jul68; CG, FMFPac msg to CMC dtd 200327Z Mar68; Combat Operations After Action Report, Operation PEGASUS (C), hereafter PEGASUS AAR; Gen William C. Westmoreland ltr to CMC dtd 14Dec68, Subj: Review of the draft manuscript "The Battle of Khe Sanh Apr67-Apr68," hereafter Westmoreland Comments; LtGen Lewis W. Walt Interviews with HistBr dtd 17Dec67 and 14Jan69; LtGen Robert E. Cushman, Jr., USMC, ltr to Deputy Assistant Chief of Staff, G-3, HQMC, dtd 26Dec68, Subj: "The Battle of Khe Sanh, Apr67-Apr68," hereafter Cushman Comments; LtGen Herman Nickerson, USMC, memo to Assistant Chief of Staff, G-3, HQMC, dtd Dec68, Subj: Review of draft manuscript, "The Battle of Khe Sanh Apr67-Apr68," hereafter Nickerson Comments; LtGen William B. Rosson, USA, ltr to CMC dtd 18Dec68, Subj: "The Battle of Khe Sanh, Apr67-Apr68," hereafter Rosson Comments; LtGen John J. Tolson, III, USA, ltr to CMC dtd 21Jan69,

Subj: "The Battle of Khe Sanh," hereafter Tolson Comments;
MajGen Norman J. Anderson, USMC, ltr to HistBr, G-3 Division,
HQMC, dtd 2Jan69, Subj: Khe Sanh Historical Monograph, here-
after Anderson Comments; MajGen Louis Metzger, USMC, memo to
Assistant Chief of Staff, G-3, HQMC, dtd 23Dec68, Subj: "The
Battle of Khe Sanh, Apr67-Apr68," hereafter Metzger Comments;
MajGen John R. Chaisson comments on draft manuscript, "The
Battle of Khe Sanh, Apr67-Apr68," hereafter Chaisson Comments;
Interview with MajGen Rathvon McC. Tompkins, USMC, dtd 26Aug68
No. 3088 (Oral History Collection, HistBr, HQMC), hereafter
Tompkins Interview; Deputy Chief of Staff (Air) comments on
draft manuscript, "The Battle of Khe Sanh," dtd 9Dec68, here-
after DCS/Air Comments; BGen Robert P. Keller, USMC, ltr to
Deputy Assistant Chief of Staff, G-3 Division, HQMC, dtd 17Dec68,
Subj: "The Battle of Khe Sanh," hereafter Keller Comments;
BGen Harry C. Olson, USMC, ltr to HistBr, G-3 Division, HQMC,
dtd 13Jan69, Subj: "The Battle of Khe Sanh," hereafter Olson
Comments; BGen Carl W. Hoffman, USMC, ltr to CMC (Code AO3D)
dtd 22Dec68, Subj: "The Battle of Khe Sanh," hereafter Hoffman
Comments; Chief, USAF Historical Division Liaison Office ltr to
HistBr, G-3 Division, HQMC, dtd 18Dec68, Subj: Review of
Historical Study, "The Battle of Khe Sanh"; Chief, Historical
Studies Branch, USAF Historical Division ltr to HistBr, G-3
Division, HQMC, dtd 22Jan69, Subj: Review of Historical Study,
"The Battle of Khe Sanh"; Chief, Project CORONA HARVEST ltr to
HistBr, G-3 Division, HQMC, dtd 15Jan69, Subj: Review of Draft
Manuscript, "The Battle of Khe Sanh," hereafter Air Force
Historical Comments; Interview with Col David E. Lownds, USMC,
dtd Jul68, No. 801 674/4 (Oral History Collection, HistBr, HQMC),
hereafter Lownds Jul Interview; Col David E. Lownds, USMC, Inter-
view with HistBr dtd 13Sep68, hereafter Lownds Sep Interview;
Col Frank E. Wilson, USMC, ltr to HistBr, G-3 Division, HQMC,
dtd 6Jan69, Subj: Review of "The Battle of Khe Sanh," here-
after Wilson Comments; Col Bruce F. Meyers, USMC, ltr to HistBr,
G-3 Division, HQMC, dtd 16Dec68, Subj: "The Battle of Khe Sanh"
hereafter Meyers Comments; Interview with Col Franklin N. Pippin,
USMC, dtd 24Jun68, No. 2907 (Oral History Collection, HistBr,
HQMC); Interview with Col Johnnie C. Vance, Jr., USMC, dtd
20Jun68, No. 2909 (Oral History Collection, HistBr, HQMC); Col
Robert D. Brown, USAF, ltr to HQMC (AO3D) dtd 8Jan69, Subj:
"The Battle of Khe Sanh" hereafter Brown Comments; Col Robert
E. Brofft, USAF, ltr to HQMC (AO3D) dtd 8Jan69, Subj: Monograph,
"The Battle of Khe Sanh," hereafter Brofft Comments; LtCol John
F. Mitchell, USMC, ltr to HistBr, G-3 Division, HQMC, dtd 31Jan69,
Subj: Comments on "The Battle of Khe Sanh," hereafter Mitchell
Comments; LtCol Harry L. Alderman, USMC, ltr to HistBr, G-3

Division, HQMC, Subj: "The Battle of Khe Sanh" hereafter
Alderman Comments; LtCol James B. Wilkinson, USMC, ltr to
HistBr, G-3 Division, HQMC, dtd Dec68, Subj: Response to HQMC
ltr AO3D-rem S807 373 of 6Dec68, "The Battle of Khe Sanh,"
hereafter Wilkinson Comments; LtCol John A. Hennelly, USMC,
comments on draft manuscript, "The Battle of Khe Sanh" of
15Feb69, hereafter Hennelly Comments; Interview with LtCol
Edward J. A. Castagna, USMC, dtd Mar68, No. 2621 (Oral History
Collection, HistBr, HQMC); LtCol Francis J. Heath, Jr., USMC,
comments on draft manuscript, "The Battle of Khe Sanh, Apr67-
Apr68," hereafter Heath Comments; LtCol Frederick J. McEwan,
USMC, ltr to HistBr, G-3 Division, HQMC, dtd 30Dec68, Subj:
Comments on "The Battle of Khe Sanh Apr67-Apr68," hereafter
McEwan Comments; LtCol Johnny O. Gregerson, USMC, ltr to HistBr,
G-3, HQMC dtd 3Jan69, Subj: Review of a draft copy of the
historical monograph: "The Battle of Khe Sanh, Apr67-Apr68,"
hereafter Gregerson Comments; LtCol John C. Studt, USMC, ltr to
HistBr, G-3, HQMC dtd 24Dec68, Subj: "The Battle of Khe Sanh"
manuscript, hereafter Studt Comments; Interview with LtCol Harry
T. Hagaman, USMC, dtd 2Mar68, No. 2548 (Oral History Collection,
HistBr, HQMC); LtCol William J. White, USMC, comments on draft
manuscript, "The Battle of Khe Sanh, Apr67-Apr68" n.d., here-
after White Comments: Interview with Maj William J. Sullivan,
USMC, dtd 26Apr68, No. 2621 (Oral History Collection, HistBr,
HQMC); Maj John A. Shepherd,USMC, ltr to HistBr, G-3 Division,
HQMC, dtd 2Jan69, Subj: "The Battle of Khe Sanh, Apr67-Apr68"
hereafter Shepherd Comments; Taped comments of Maj Matthew P.
Caulfield, USMC, on the draft manuscript, "The Battle of Khe
Sanh, Apr67-Apr68" dtd 2Jan69, hereafter Caulfield Comments;
Interview with Maj Matthew P. Caulfield, USMC, dtd 10Feb68,
No. 2535 (Oral History Collection, HistBr, HQMC); Maj Wayne M.
Wills, USMC, ltr to HistBr, G-3, HQMC, dtd 2Jan69, Subj:
Historical Monograph, "The Battle of Khe Sanh, Apr67-Apr68,"
hereafter Wills Comments; Maj Harper L. Bohr, USMC, ltr to
HistBr, G-3, HQMC, dtd 18Dec68, Subj: Comments concerning
"The Battle of Khe Sanh" hereafter Bohr Comments; Maj Jerry E.
Hudson, USMC, ltr to HistBr, G-3, HQMC, dtd 2Jan69, Subj: Re-
view of Historical Monograph of Khe Sanh, hereafter Hudson
Comments; Maj Mirza M. Baig, USMC, ltr to HistBr, G-3 Division,
HQMC dtd 23Dec68, Subj: Comments on draft manuscript, "The
Battle of Khe Sanh, Apr67-Apr68" hereafter Baig Comments; Maj
William H. Dabney, USMC, comments on draft manuscript nd, "The
Battle of Khe Sanh, Apr67-Apr68" hereafter Dabney Comments; Maj
William H. Dabney, USMC, Interview with HistBr dtd 10Jan69;
Maj Earl G. Breeding, USMC, comments on draft manuscript dtd
22Dec68, "The Battle of Khe Sanh, Apr67-Apr68," hereafter

Breeding Comments; Interview with Capt Earl G. Breeding, dtd
Jul68, No. 2121 (Oral History Collection, HistBr, HQMC); Maj
Kenneth W. Pipes, USMC ltr to HistBr, G-3 Division, HQMC, n.d.,
Subj: Khe Sanh Manuscript, hereafter Pipes Comments; Interview
with Capt Kenneth W. Pipes, USMC, dtd Mar68, No. 2621 (Oral
History Collection, HistBr, HQMC); 1stLt James M. Alexander,
USMC, ltr to HistBr, G-3 Division, HQMC, n.d., Subj: "The Battle
of Khe Sanh, Apr67-Apr68" hereafter Alexander Comments; Inter-
view with 1stLt James M. Alexander, USMC, dtd 26Apr68, No. 2621
(Oral History Collection, HistBr, HQMC); Interview with 1stLt
William L. Everhart, USMC, dtd 10Feb68, No. 2535 (Oral History
Collection, HistBr, HQMC); Interview with Sgt Timothy B. Keady,
USMC, dtd Mar68, No. 2621 (Oral History Collection, HistBr, HQMC);
Interview with HM3 Frank V. Calzia, USN, dtd Mar68, No. 2621
(Oral History Collection, HistBr, HQMC); LCpl Michael A. Barry,
USMC, Interview with HistBr dtd 17Feb69; Cornelius D. Sullivan,
et al., The Vietnam War: Its Conduct and Higher Direction
(Washington, D. C.: The Center For Strategic Studies, Georgetown
University, 1968) (U), hereafter Sullivan, et al., The Vietnam
War; Bernard B. Fall, The Two Viet-Nams (New York: Frederick
A. Praeger, 1965 ed.) (U); Colonel Robert D. Heinl, Jr., USMC,
Soldiers of the Sea (Annapolis: United States Naval Institute
1962 ed.) (U); Capt Ken Kashiwahara, USAF, "Lifeline to Khe
Sanh," The Airman, v. XII, no. 7 (Jul68) (U), hereafter
Kashiwahara, "Lifeline to Khe Sanh"; Washington Star, 25May68,
p. 13 (Early Bird) (U); Washington Star, 9Jun68, p. 1-E (Early
Bird); Baltimore Sun, 25May68, p. 2 (Early Bird) (U). All
documentary material cited is located in the HistBr, G-3 Division,
HQMC and, unless otherwise noted, carries an overall classifi-
cation of Secret.

(1)   Major John J. Cahill, USMC and Jack Shulimson, "History of U. S. Marine Corps Operations in Vietnam, Jan-Jun65," pp. 67, 68, 126 (S).

(2)   FMFPac, Marine Opns in Vietnam, Jun67, pp. 5-12 (S).

(3)   Ibid.

(4)   3d MarDiv CmdChron, Oct68, p. 11 (S).

(5)   FMFPac, Marine Opns in Vietnam, Mar67, p. 15 (S).

(6)   3d Marines Khe Sanh AAR, p. 7 (S); Bernard B. Fall, The Two Viet-Nams (New York: Frederick A. Praeger 1965 ed.), p. 3.

(7)   Westmoreland Comments.

(8)   3d Marines, Khe Sanh AAR, p. 12 (S).

(9)   Lieutenant General Lewis W. Walt Interview with Historical Branch dtd 17Dec68 and 14Jan69 (S).

(10)   3d Marines Khe Sanh AAR, pp. 7-30 (S).

(11)   Ibid

(12)   Ibid., pp. 32-33 (S).

(13)   FMFPac Marine Opns in Vietnam, May67, p. 11 (S).

(14)   Ibid., pp. 7-10, 19 (S).

(15)   FMFPac HistSum, pp. 7-17 (S).

(16)   FMFPac Marine Opns in Vietnam, Jul67, pp. 9-13 (S).

(17)   Ibid.

(18)   FMFPac Marine Opns in Vietnam Sep67, pp. 52-73 (S); 3d MarDiv ComdChron, Sep67, p. 25 (S); Chaisson Comments; Personal observations of the author.

(19)   Westmoreland Comments; Metzger Comments.

(20)   FMFPac, Marine Opns in Vietnam, Oct67, pp. 24-36 (S).

(21)   Metzger Comments.

(22)   26th Marines CmdChron, May67, p. 4 (S).

(23)   Ibid.

(24)   26th Marines CmdChron, Jun67, p. 4 (S).

(25)   Ibid., Jul67, p. 4 (S).

(26)   Col Lownds tape No. 801 674/4 (S); 26th Marines CmdChron,
        Aug67, p. 4 (S); Metzger Comments.

(27)   Wilkinson Comments.

(28)   Col Lownds Tape No. 801 674/4 (S); 26th Marines CmdChron,
        Aug67, p. 4 (S); Brown Comments.

(29)   26th Marines CmdChron, Nov67, p. 4 (S).

(30)   Cushman Comments; Hoffman Comments.

(31)   26th Marines CmdChron, Dec67, p. 4 (S).

(32)   Alderman Comments.

(33)   Bohr Comments.

(34)   Hudson Comments.

(35)   FMFPac Marine Opns in Vietnam, Jan 68, pp. 8, 9; III
        MAF CmdChron, Jan and Feb68 (S); 26th Marines CmdChron,
        Feb68, p. 60 (S); Lownds Sep Interview (S).

(36)   Lownds Sep Interview (S); 3/26 CmdChron, Jan68, p. 10
        (S); Caulfield Comments.

(37)   Lownds Sep Interview (S); 26th Marines CmdChron, Jan68,
        p. 4 (S).

(38)   3/26 CmdChron, Jan68, p. 3 (S).

(39)   2/26 CmdChron, Jan68, p. 2 (S).

(40)   Ibid.; Breeding Comments; Caulfield Comments.

(41) 26th Marines CmdChron, Jan68, pp. 3, 4 (S); Lownds Sep Interview (S).

(42) FMFPac Marine Opns in Vietnam, Jan68, p. 10 (S).

(43) 26th Marines CmdChron, Jan68, pp. 3, 4 (S); 3/26 CmdChron, Jan68, p. 3 (S); Alderman Comments; Dabney Comments; Caulfield Comments.

(44) Ibid.

(45) Dabney Comments.

(46) Ibid.; 26th CmdChron, Jan68, pp. 3, 4 (S); 3/26 CmdChron, Jan68, p. 3 (S); Alderman Comments; Dabney Comments.

(47) Ibid.

(48) Cushman Comments; Tompkins Interview (S); Lownds Sep Interview (S); Wilkinson Comments; Pipes Comments; 26th Marines CmdChron, Jan68, p. 5 (S).

(49) Caulfield Comments.

(50) Alderman Comments.

(51) Caulfield Comments.

(52) Ibid.

(53) 3/26 CmdChron, Jan 68, p. 3 (S); Caulfield Comments.

(54) Lownds Sep Interview (S); Interview with Major Matthew P. Caulfield, USMC dtd 10Feb68, No. 2535 (Oral History Collection, HistBr, HQMC) (S); Caulfield Comments.

(55) Dabney Comments; Caulfield Comments.

(56) Ibid.; 26th Marines CmdChron, Jan68, p. 4 (S); Lownds Sep Interview; White Comments.

(57) Pipes Comments.

(58) Wilkinson Comments.

(59) 26th Marines CmdChron, Jan68, p. 4 (S); Hudson Comments.

(60) Interview with First Lieutenant William L. Everhart,
      dtd 10Feb68 No. 2535 (Oral History Collection, HistBr,
      HQMC) (S); Hennelly Comments.

(61) 26th Marines CmdChron, Jan68, p. 9 (S); FMFPac Marine
      Opns in Vietnam, Jan68, p. 11 (S); Tompkins Interview
      (S); Hudson Comments.

(62) Lownds Sep Interview (S).

(63) 26th Marines CmdChron, Jan68, p. 9 (S).

(64) Cushman Comments.

(65) Ibid.; Westmoreland Comments.

(66) Westmoreland Comments.

(67) Ibid.; Sharp and Westmoreland, Report on The War, p. 163.

(68) 26th Marines CmdChron, Jan68, pp. 4, 11 (S); Lownds
      Sep Interview (S).

(69) Lownds Sep Interview (S); Baig Comments.

(70) Wilkinson Comments.

(71) 26th Marines CmdChron, Jan68, p. 4 (S); Lownds Sep
      Interview; Wilkinson Comments.

(72) 26th Marines CmdChron, Jan68, pp. 3, 4 (S); III MAF
      CmdChron, Jan68, pp. 3-10 (S).

(73) Sharp and Westmoreland, Report on The War, p. 158.

(74) Presentation of Lieutenant General Robert E. Cushman,
      Jr., USMC, in 1968 General Officers Symposium Book,
      dtd 15Jul68 (S).

(75) Sullivan, et al., The Vietnam War, pp. 101-104.

(76) Ibid., Sharp and Westmoreland, Report on The War, p. 235.

(77) Ibid.

(78) Sullivan, et al., The Vietnam War, p. 99.

(79) Ibid.

(80) Lownds Jul Interview (S).

(81) Ibid.

(82) Ibid.; CG FMFPac msg to CMC, dtd 200327Z Mar68 (S).

(83) Lownds Jul and Sep Interviews (S).

(84) Dabney Comments.

(85) Ibid.

(86) Ibid.

(87) Ibid.; Caulfield Comments.

(88) Dabney Comments.

(89) Lownds Jul Interview (S).

(90) Mitchell Comments.

(91) Lownds Jul and Sep Interviews (S); Tompkins Interview (S).

(92) Ibid.; Mitchell Comments.

(93) 26th Marines CmdChron, Feb68, p. 8 (S); Interview with Captain Earl G. Breeding, USMC, dtd Jul68, No. 2121 (Oral History Collection, HistBr, HQMC) (S): Breeding Comments.

(94) Ibid.

(95) Ibid.

(96) Ibid.; Dabney Comments.

(97) Ibid.

(98) White Comments.

(99) 26th Marines CmdChron, Feb68, pp. 8-10 (S); Tompkins Interview (S).

(100) Ibid.; Lownds Jul Interview (S); Hennelly Comments.

(101) Hennelly Comments.

(102) Hudson Comments.

(103) Wilkinson Comments.

(104) Lownds Sep Interview; Caulfield Comments.

(105) Anderson Comments.

(106) Westmoreland Comments; White Comments; 26th Marines
       CmdChron, Feb68, pp. 4-8 (S).

(107) DIA IntBul.

(108) 26th Marines CmdChron, Feb68, pp. 8, 48 (S); Mitchell
       Comments.

(109) Ibid.

(110) Lance Corporal Michael A. Barry Interview with HistBr,
       dtd 17Feb69.

(111) Ibid.

(112) 26th Marines CmdChron, Feb68, pp. 8, 48, 49 (S);
       Mitchell Comments.

(113) 26th Marines CmdChron, Feb68, p. 49 (S).

(114) Ibid., p. 51 (S).

(115) Air Force Historical Comments; 1st MAW CmdChron, Feb68,
       p. 8 (S).

(116) Wilkinson Comments; White Comments.

(117) 26th Marines CmdChron, Feb68, p. 51 (S); Kashiwahara,
       "Lifeline to Khe Sanh".

(118) Ibid.; Lownds Sep Interview (S).

(119) VMGR-152 CmdChron, Feb68, p. 4 (S); Gregerson Comments.

(120) Kashiwahara, "Lifeline to Khe Sanh"; Meyers Comments; Brown Comments; Air Force Historical Comments.

(121) Ibid.; Lownds Jul Interview (S).

(122) Ibid.

(123) Information provided by the Marine Corps Command Center on 19Feb68.

(124) Ibid.

(125) 1st MAW CmdChron, Jan, Feb, Mar68 (S); Wilson Comments.

(126) Ibid.

(127) Dabney Comments.

(128) Ibid.

(129) Wilson Comments.

(130) DCS/Air Comments.

(131) Breeding Comments.

(132) See 1st MAW CmdChron, Jan, Feb, Mar68 (S); CG FMFPac msg to CMC dtd 200327Z Mar68 (S).

(133) Wilkinson Comments.

(134) CG FMFPac Msg to CMC dtd 200327Z Mar68 (S); Lownds Jul Interview (S).

(135) See 26th Marines CmdChron, Jan, Feb, and Mar68 (S).

(136) Lownds Sep Interview (S).

(137) 26th Marines CmdChron, Jan, Feb, and Mar68 (S); Lownds Sep Interview; Interview with Major William J. Sullivan, USMC, dtd 26Apr68, No. 2621 (Oral History Collection, HistBr, HQMC) (S); Hennelly Comments; Gregerson Comments; Air Force Historical Comments.

(138) 1st MAW CmdChron, Jan and Feb68 (S).

(139)   Ibid., Debrief Sheets (S).

(140)   Dabney Comments.

(141)   1st MAW CmdChron, Feb 68, p. 2-2 (S); Pipes Comments.

(142)   Interview with Lieutenant Colonel Harry T. Hagaman,
        USMC, dtd 2Mar68, No. 2548 (Oral History Collection,
        HistBr, HQMC) (C).

(143)   Information supplied by U. S. Air Force Public Informa-
        tion Office, 16Oct68 (U); Chaisson Comments; Air Force
        Historical Comments; Brofft Comments.

(144)   Tompkins Interview (S).

(145)   Ibid.; Lownds Sep Interview (S); Kashiwahara, "Lifeline
        to Khe Sanh."

(146)   Air Force Historical Comments; 26th Marines CmdChron,
        Jan, Feb and Mar68 (S); Tompkins Interview, Baig Comments.

(147)   Gregerson Comments.

(148)   Lownds Jul Interview (S); Interview with Major William
        J. Sullivan, USMC, dtd 26Apr68, No. 2621 (Oral History
        Collection, HistBr, HQMC) (S); Gregerson Comments.

(149)   Lownds Sep Interview (S); Interview with First Lieu-
        tenant James M. Alexander, USMC, dtd 26Apr68, No. 2621
        (Oral History Collection, HistBr, HQMC) (S). Hennelly
        Comments.

(150)   Interview with Major William J. Sullivan, USMC, dtd
        26Apr68, No. 2621 (Oral History Collection, HistBr,
        HQMC) (S); Interview with First Lieutenant James M.
        Alexander, USMC, dtd 26Apr68, No. 2621 (Oral History
        Collection, HistBr, HQMC) (S); 26th Marines CmdChron,
        Jan, Feb and Mar 68 (S); Gregerson Comments.

(151)   Ibid.

(152)   Ibid.

(153)   Lownds Interview; Hennelly Comments.

(154)   Hennelly Comments.

(155)   Baig Comments.

(156)   Hennelly Comments.

(157)   Ibid.; 26th Marines CmdChron, Jan, Feb and Mar68 (S);
        Baig Comments.

(158)   Ibid.

(159)   Baig Comments.

(160)   Ibid.

(161)   Ibid.

(162)   Ibid.; Interview with Lieutenant Colonel Edward J. A.
        Castagna, USMC, dtd Mar68, No. 2621 (Oral History
        Collection, HistBr, HQMC) (S); Colonel Robert D. Heinl,
        Jr., USMC, Soldiers of the Sea (Annapolis: United States
        Naval Institute 1962 ed.) p. 563.

(163)   Baig Comments.

(164)   Six Month Evaluation Report, HQ USMACV, 31May68 (S);
        Interview with Colonel Franklin N. Pippin, USMC, dtd
        24Jun68, No. 2907 (Oral History Collection, HistBr,
        HQMC) (S).

(165)   1/26 CmdChron, Jan and Feb68 (S); CG FMFPac msg to CMC
        dtd 200327Z Mar68 (S); Information provided by Research,
        Development, and Study Division, HQMC, 8Nov68 (U);
        Lownds Jul Interview (S).

(166)   26th Marines CmdChron, Jan and Feb68 (S); Lownds Jul
        and Sep Interviews (S).

(167)   26th Marines CmdChron, Jan, Feb and Mar68 (S).

(168)   Dabney Comments.

(169)   Ibid.

(170)   Lownds Sep Interview (S); Interview with Sergeant Timothy
        B. Keady, USMC, dtd Mar68, No. 2621 (Oral History
        Collection, HistBr, HQMC) (S).

(171) Baltimore Sun, 25 May, p. 2 (Early Bird) (U).

(172) Interview with First Lieutenant James M. Alexander, USMC,
       dtd 26Apr68, No. 2621 (Oral History Collection, HistBr,
       HQMC) (S); Interview with Major William J. Sullivan,
       USMC, dtd 26Apr68, No. 2621 (Oral History Collection,
       HistBr, HQMC) (S); Interview with Colonel Johnnie C.
       Vance, Jr., USMC, dtd 20Jun68, No. 2909 (Oral History
       Collection, HistBr, HQMC) (S); Interview with Major John
       A. Shepherd, USMC, dtd 26Apr68, No. 2621 (Oral History
       Collection, HistBr, HQMC) (S).

(173) Shepherd Comments.

(174) Lownds Sep Interview (S).

(175) Lownds Jul Interview (S).

(176) Ibid.; Tompkins Interview (S).

(177) Keller Comments.

(178) Wilkinson Comments.

(179) 26th Marines CmdChron, Feb68, Encl 1 (S).

(180) Ibid.

(181) Lownds Sep Interview (S); Interview with HM3 Class
       Frank V. Calzia, dtd Mar68, No. 2621 (Oral History
       Collection, HistBr, HQMC) (S).

(182) Ibid.; Interview with Captain Kenneth W. Pipes, USMC,
       dtd Mar68, No. 2621 (Oral History Collection, HistBr,
       HQMC) (S).

(183) Ibid.

(184) Ibid.; 26th Marines CmdChron, Feb68, Encl 1 (S).

(185) Lownds Jul and Sep Interviews (S).

(186) Ibid.; 26th Marines CmdChron, Mar68, p. 4 (S); Baig
       Comments.

(187) 26th Marines CmdChron, Mar68, pp. 3, 4 (S); Wilkinson
       Comments.

(188) Ibid.; Lownds Sep Interview.

(189) 26th Marines CmdChron, Mar68, p. 8 (S).

(190) Ibid., pp. 11, 12.

(191) Ibid., p. 7.

(192) Ibid., pp. 7, 8.

(193) Ibid., p. 6.

(194) Ibid., p. 10 (S)

(195) Ibid.; White Comments.

(196) Ibid.; McEwan Comments; Pipes Comments.

(197) 26th Marines CmdChron, Mar68, pp. 9, 10, and Encl 1.

(198) Ibid.; Baig Comments.

(199) MCCC, Status of Forces, Apr 68 (S); Lownds Sep Interview (S); PEGASUS AAR, pp. 1-4.

(200) PEGASUS AAR, Encl 1 (C); Westmoreland Comments; Cushman Comments.

(201) Ibid.

(202) Tolson Comments.

(203) Ibid.

(204) PEGASUS AAR, Encl 1 (C); Rosson Comments.

(205) Ibid.

(206) Ibid.

(207) Ibid.; Lownds Jul and Sep Interviews (S).

(208) PEGASUS AAR, Encl 1 (C).

(209) Ibid.

(210)   Ibid.; Lownds Jul and Sep Interviews (S); Tolson Comments.

(211)   PEGASUS AAR, pp. 13, 14 (C).

(212)   Ibid., Encl 1.

(213)   Ibid.

(214)   3/26 CmdChron, Apr68, p. 4 (S); Studt Comments; Meyers Comments.

(215)   Ibid.; Caulfield Comments.

(216)   Ibid.; Dabney Comments.

(217)   Caulfield Comments.

(218)   Meyers Comments.

(219)   3/26 CmdChron, Apr68, p. 4 (S); Meyers Comments; Studt Comments.

(220)   Caulfield Comments

(221)   PEGASUS AAR.

(222)   Ibid.; 26th Marines CmdChron, Apr68, p. 4 (S); Caulfield Comments.

(223)   Baltimore Sun, 25May68, p. 2 (Early Bird) (U); Washington Star, 25May68, p. 13 (Early Bird) (U).

(224)   Ibid.

(225)   Olson Comments.

(226)   Cushman Comments.

(227)   Alderman Comments; Caulfield Comments.

(228)   Baig Comments.

(229)   Tompkins Interview; Lownds Jul and Sep Interviews (S).

(230) Westmoreland Comments; Cushman Comments; Rosson Comments.

(231) Ibid.

(232) Ibid.

(233) Washington Star, 9Jun68, p. 1-E (Early Bird) (U).

APPENDIX B

GLOSSARY

AAR	After Action Report
ABCCC	Airborne Command and Control Center
A-4 Skyhawk	A single-seat, lightweight, jet attack bomber in service with Navy and Marine Corps squadrons. Built by Douglas.
AN/PRC-25	U. S.-built, short-range, portable, frequency-modulated radio set used to provide two-way communication in the 30 megacycle to 75.95 megacycle band.
AN/TPQ-10	U. S.-built, ground-based radar system used to guide aircraft on bombing missions.
A-1 Skyraider	U. S.-built, prop-driven, attack aircraft built by Douglas.
Arc Light	Operational name for B-52 strikes in South Vietnam.
ARVN	Army of The Republic of Vietnam.
A-6A Intruder	U. S. Navy and Marine Corps twin-engine, low-altitude, jet attack bomber specifically designed to deliver ordnance on targets completely obscured by weather or darkness. Carries a heavier and more varied load than any other U. S. naval attack aircraft. Built by Grumman.
ASRT	Air Support Radar Team
BDA	Battle Damage Assessment
Bde	Brigade
B-52 Stratofortress	USAF eight-engine, swept-wing heavy jet bomber. Built by Boeing.
BLT	Battalion Landing Team

CAC	Combined Action Company
CACO	Combined Action Company Oscar
CavSqd (e.g. 1/9)	1st Squadron, 9th Cavalry
C-4	Plastic explosives
CG, 1st MarDiv	Commanding General, 1st Marine Division
CG, FMFPac	Commanding General, Fleet Marine Force, Pacific
CG, 3d MarDiv	Commanding General, 3d Marine Division
CG, III MAF	Commanding General, III Marine Amphibious Force
ChiCom	Chinese Communist
CH-53A Sea Stallion	U. S.-built, single-rotor, heavy assault transport helicopter powered by two shaft-turbine engines with an average payload of 12,800 pounds. Full-sized rear opening with built-in ramp permits loading of 105mm howitzer and carriage. External sling will accommodate a 155mm howitzer (towed). Carries crew of 3 plus 38 combat troops or 24 litters. Built by Sikorsky.
CH-46D Sea Knight	U. S.-built, medium transport, twin-turbine, tandem rotor helicopter with an average payload of 4,800 pounds. Has rear loading ramp and external sling mount. Carries crew of 3 plus 25 combat troops or 15 litters and 2 attendants. Built by Boeing.
CIDG	Civilian Irregular Defense Group
Claymore	U. S.-built, directional antipersonnel land mine employed above ground and normally in an upright position.
CMC	Commandant of the Marine Corps

CmdChron	Command Chronology
CO	Commanding Officer
ComUSMACV	Commander, U. S. Military Assistance Command, Vietnam
CP	Command Post
CS	Designation for tear gas
DASC	Direct Air Support Center
D-Day	Day scheduled for the commencement of an operation.
DIA IntBul	Defense Intelligence Agency Intelligence Bulletin
DMZ	Demilitarized Zone
EC-121 Super Constellation	USAF and USN four-engine, prop-driven, long-range, heavy transport modified with special equipment for radar early warning patrols and electronic warfare duty. Built by Lockheed.
FADAC	Field Artillery Digital Automatic Computer
FDC	Fire Direction Center
F-8 Crusader	U. S. Navy and Marine Corps supersonic, single-seat, single-engine, jet fighter with afterburner. Primarily used in South Vietnam in an attack role. Carries air-to-air and air-to-ground ordnance. Built by LTV Vought Aeronautics.
F-4B Phantom II	U. S. Navy and Marine Corps twin-engine, two-seat, supersonic fighter/attack jet with afterburners; has dual role of interceptor and bomber. Of all U. S. naval attack aircraft, F-4B carries second largest payload. Built by McDonnell.
F-4C	U. S. Air Force model of the Phantom II.

1st ACD	1st Air Cavalry Division
1st MarDiv	1st Marine Division
1st MAW	1st Marine Aircraft Wing
FOB-3	Forward Operating Base 3
F-100 Super Sabre	Single-engine, jet (with afterburner) sweptwing, supersonic fighter-bomber; in production since 1953, the F-100 was the first supersonic operational fighter developed for the U. S. Air Force. Carries air-to-air and air-to-ground ordnance. Built by North American.
F-105 Thunderchief	U. S. Air Force supersonic, single-seat, single-engine, jet fighter/bomber with afterburner. Built by Republic.
FMFPac	Fleet Marine Force, Pacific
FO	Forward Observer
FSCC	Fire Support Coordination Center
GCA	Ground Controlled Approach
GPES	Ground Proximity Extraction System
Grenade Launcher, M-79	U. S.-built, single-shot, break-open, breech-loaded shoulder weapon which fires 40mm projectiles and weighs approximately 6.5 pounds when loaded; it has a sustained rate of aimed fire of 5-7 rounds per minute and an effective range of 375 meters.
Gun, 100mm M1944	Soviet-built, dual purpose field and anti-tank gun introduced toward the close of World War II; it weighs 7,628 pounds, is 30.9 feet in length and has a muzzle velocity of 900 meters per second. Maximum range is 21,000 meters and maximum rate of fire is 8-10 rounds per minute. Is recognizable by long tube, double-barrel muzzle brake, dual wheels, and sloping shield.

Gun, 130mm	Soviet-built fieldpiece which utilizes either a limber for transport or is self-propelled. Towed weapon weighs 19,000 pounds, is 38 feet in length, and has a muzzle velocity of 930 meters per second. Maximum range is 27,000 meters and maximum rate of fire is 6-7 rounds per minute. Tube has a multi-perforated muzzle brake.
Gun, 175mm	U. S.-built, self-propelled gun which weighs 62,100 pounds and fires a 147-pound projectile to a maximum range of 32,800 meters. Maximum rate of fire is 1/2 round per minute.
Hand Grenade, Fragmentation M-26	U. S.-manufactured, hand-thrown bomb, which weighs approximately one pound, and contains an explosive charge in a body that shatters into small fragments; it has an effective range of 40 meters.
H&I	Harassment and Interdiction
H&S Co	Headquarters and Service Company
HistBr	Historical Branch
HMM	Marine Medium Helicopter Squadron
Howitzer, 105mm M2A1	U. S.-built, towed, general purpose light artillery piece; the weapon is mounted on a carriage equipped with split box trails and pneumatic tires. On-carriage sighting and fire control equipment are used both for direct and indirect fire. The piece weighs 4,980 pounds, is 19.75 feet in length, has a muzzle velocity of 470 meters per second, and a maximum range of 11,155 meters. Maximum rate of fire is 4 rounds per minute.
Howitzer, 155mm M1	U. S.-built, towed, medium artillery piece mounted on a two-wheel, split-trail carriage with detachable spades. The howitzer is fired from a three-point suspension, with the trails spread and the carriage resting

upon an integral firing jack, the wheels being clear of the ground. The piece weighs 12,700 pounds, is 24 feet long, has a muzzle velocity of 560 meters per second and a maximum range of 15,080 meters. Maximum rate of fire is 3 rounds per minute.

Howitzer, 8-inch M-110	U. S.-built, self-propelled heavy artillery piece; 37 feet long tracked carriage is identical to that of 175mm gun. M-110 has a maximum range of 16,930 meters and a rate of fire of 1/2 round per minute.
HQMC	Headquarters, United States Marine Corps
IFR	Instrument Flight Rules
KBA	Killed By Air
KIA	Killed In Action
KSCB	Khe Sanh Combat Base
LAPES	Low Altitude Proximity Extraction System
LSA	Logistics Support Area
LZ	Landing Zone
MACV	Military Assistance Command, Vietnam
MAG	Marine Aircraft Group
Machine Gun, .50 Caliber	U. S.-built, belt-fed, recoil-operated, air-cooled automatic weapon, which weighs approximately 80 pounds without mount or ammunition; it has a sustained rate of fire of 100 rounds per minute and an effective range of 1,450 meters.
Machine Gun, M-60	U. S.-built, belt-fed, gas-operated, air-cooled, 7.62mm automatic weapon, which weighs approximately 23 pounds without mount or ammunition; it has a sustained rate of fire of 100 rounds per minute and an effective range of 1,100 meters.

_____ Marines	Designation of Marine regiment
MATCU	Marine Air Traffic Control Unit
Medevac	Medical evacuation
Mortar, 60mm	U. S.-built, smooth-bore, muzzle-loaded, single-shot, high-angle of fire weapon, which weighs 45.2 pounds when assembled and fires an assortment of high explosive and pyrotechnic rounds; it has a maximum rate of fire of 30 rounds per minute and sustained rate of fire of 18 rounds per minute; the effective range is 2,000 meters.
Mortar, 81mm	U. S.-built, smooth-bore, muzzle-loaded, single-shot, high angle of fire weapon, which weighs approximately 115 pounds when assembled and fires an assortment of high explosive and pyrotechnic rounds; it has a sustained rate of fire of 2 rounds per minute and an effective range of 2,200-3,650 meters, depending upon the ammunition used.
Mortar, 82mm	Soviet-built, smooth-bore, muzzle-loaded, single-shot, high-angle of fire weapon which weighs approximately 123 pounds when assembled and fires high explosive and pyrotechnic rounds; it has a maximum rate of fire of 25 rounds per minute and a maximum range of 3,040 meters.
Mortar, 120mm	Soviet-or Chinese Communist-built, smooth-bore, drop or trigger fired, single-shot, high-angle of fire weapon, which weighs approximately 606 pounds when assembled and fires high explosive and pyrotechnic rounds; it has a maximum rate of fire of 15 rounds per minute and a maximum range of 5,700 meters.
Mortar, 4.2 inch M2	U. S.-built, 107mm, rifled, muzzle-loaded, drop-fired weapon consisting of tube, base-plate and standard; weapon weighs 330 pounds, is 4 feet in length, and has a

maximum range of 4,020 meters. Rate of fire is 20 rounds per minute and utilizes both high explosive and pyrotechnic ammunition. (Five M2s were employed at KSCB)

Mortar, 4.2-inch M98 Howtar	U. S.-built, 107mm, rifled, muzzle-loaded, mortar; a towed weapon, the howtar is mounted on a carriage with two pneumatic tires. Tube and carriage weigh 1,289 pounds; maximum range is 5,500 meters. (Two Howtars were employed at KSCB)
M-16	U. S.-built, magazine-fed, 5.62mm gas-operated, air-cooled shoulder weapon designed for either semiautomatic or full automatic fire; fully loaded weighs 7.6 pounds, fires a maximum rate of 150-200 rounds per minute, and has a maximum effective range of 460 meters.
9th MAB	9th Marine Amphibious Brigade
9th MEB	9th Marine Expeditionary Brigade
NVA	North Vietnamese Army
01-E	U. S.-built, single engine, two-seat, prop-driven light observation aircraft built by Cessna.
Ontos	U. S.-built, lightly-armored tracked vehicle armed with six coaxially mounted 106mm recoilless rifles. Originally designed as a tank killer, the Ontos is primarily used in Vietnam to support the infantry.
PCV	Provisional Corps, Vietnam
PF	Popular Forces
PMDL	Provisional Military Demarcation Line
RC-292	U. S.-built, elevated, wide-band, modified ground-plane antenna designed to operate

with and increase the distance range of various radio sets.

Recoilless Rifle, 106mm, M40A1	U. S.-built, single-shot, recoilless, breech-loaded weapon which weighs 438 pounds when assembled and mounted for firing; it has a sustained rate of fire of 6 rounds per minute and an effective range of 1,365 meters. The weapon can be singly or Ontos mounted.
RF	Regional Forces
RLT	Regimental Landing Team
Rocket, 122mm	A Soviet-built, four-piece, fin-stabilized, 9-foot long rocket weighing 125 pounds; maximum range is approximately 17,000 meters. Launcher tube and mount weigh 121 pounds and are 8.1 feet in length.
RPG-2	A Soviet- and Chinese Communist-built antitank grenade launcher; a smooth-bore, muzzle-loaded, shoulder-fired, recoilless weapon which fires a 40mm spin-stabilized round. The weapon weighs 6.3 pounds, is 3.2 feet in length, has a muzzle velocity of 84 meters per second, and an effective range of 100 meters. Maximum rate of fire is 4-6 rounds per minute utilizing High Explosive Antitank ammunition.
SLF	Special Landing Force
S-2	Intelligence section or officer
TA-4	Two-seat trainer model of the A-4 Skyhawk
TAC(A)	Tactical Air Controller (Airborne)
TAFDS	Tactical Airfield Fuel Dispensing System
Tank, PT-76	Soviet-built, 15.4-ton, amphibious tank with a crew of 3; primary armament is turret mounted 76mm gun and maximum thickness of armor is 0.6 inches.

Tank, M-48	U. S.-built 50.7-ton tank with a crew of 4; primary armament is turret-mounted 90mm gun with one .30 caliber and one .50 caliber machine gun. Can be configured with water fording equipment. Maximum road speed of 32 miles per hour and an average range of 195 miles.
TAOR	Tactical Area Of Responsibility
TET	Vietnamese Lunar New Year
3d MarDiv	3d Marine Division
III MAF	III Marine Amphibious Force
TIO	Target Intelligence/Information Officer
TOT	Time On Target
UHF	Ultra High Frequency
UH-1E Huey Gunship	A single-engine, Marine, light attack/transport helicopter noted for its maneuverability and firepower; carries a crew of three with seven combat troops or three litters, two sitting casualties and a medical attendant, or 3,000 pounds of cargo. It is armed with air to ground rocket packs and fuselage mounted, electrically fired machine guns.
UH-34D Sea Horse	A single-engine, Marine, medium transport helicopter with a crew of three; carries 16-18 combat troops or 8 litters or a normal 5,000 pound payload.
USAF	United States Air Force
USA	United States Army
USMC	United States Marine Corps
USN	United States Navy
VC	Viet Cong

VFR	Visual Flight Rules
VHF	Very High Frequency
Viet Minh	The Vietnamese contraction for Viet Nam, Doc Lap Nong Minh Hoi, a Communist-led coalition of nationalist groups which actively opposed the Japanese in World War II and the French in the early years of the Indo-China War.
VMA	Marine Attack Squadron
VMFA	Marine Fighter/Attack Squadron
VMGR	Marine Aerial Refueler Transport Squadron
VMO	Marine Observation Squadron
VNAF	Vietnamese Air Force
VT	Variable Timed fuze for artillery shell which causes airburst over target area.

APPENDIX C

CHRONOLOGY

1962

Aug   U. S. Army Special Forces establish CIDG camp at Khe Sanh.

1966

Apr   1/1 sweeps Khe Sanh plateau during Operation VIRGINIA.

Oct   1/3 occupies KSCB; CIDG displaces to Lang Vei.

1967

Feb   1/3 replaced by single company, E/2/9.

15 Mar   Company B, 1/9, replaces E/2/9 as resident defense company.

20 Apr   Combat assets at KSCB pass   to operational control of Col Lanigan's 3d Marines which commences Operation PRAIRIE IV.

24 Apr   B/1/9 patrol engages large enemy force north of Hill 861 and prematurely triggers attack on Khe Sanh; "Hill Fights" begin.

25 Apr   2/3 and 3/3 airlifted to KSCB to counter enemy drive.

28 Apr   After heavy prep fires, LtCol DeLong's 2/3 assaults and seizes first objective--Hill 861.

2 May   LtCol Wilder's 3/3 seizes Hill 881S after four days of heavy fighting.

3 May   2/3 repulses strong enemy counterattack south of 881N.

5 May   2/3 secures final objective--Hill 881N.

11-13 May	"Hill Fights" terminate with 940 NVA and 155 Marine KIA. 3d Marines shuttled to Dong Ha as 26th Marines (FWD) and 1/26 move into Khe Sanh.
13 May	Col Padley, CO 26th Marines (FWD), relieves Col Lanigan as Senior Officer Present at Khe Sanh. Elements of 1/26 occupy combat base, Hills 881S, 861, and 950. Operation CROCKETT commences.
13 Jun	Due to increasing enemy contacts, LtCol Hoch's 3/26 airlifted to KSCB.
16 Jul	Operation CROCKETT terminates with 204 NVA and 52 Marines KIA.
17 Jul	Operation ARDMORE begins.
12 Aug	Col Lownds relieves Col Padley as CO, 26th Marines.
13 Aug	Due to lack of significant contact around Khe Sanh, Company K and L, 3/26, transferred to 9th Marines and Operation KINGFISHER.
17 Aug	Khe Sanh airfield closed to normal traffic for repair of runway.
3 Sep	Remainder of 3/26 withdrawn to eastern Quang Tri Province.
27 Oct	Air strip reopened to C-123 aircraft.
31 Oct	Operation ARDMORE terminated with 113 NVA and 10 Marines KIA.
1 Nov	Operation SCOTLAND I begins.
28 Nov	MajGen Tompkins assumes command of 3d MarDiv.
13 Dec	LtCol Alderman's 3/26 returns to Khe Sanh because of increased enemy activity in Khe Sanh TAOR.
21 Dec	3/26 conducts five-day sweep west of base and uncovers evidence of enemy buildup around KSCB.

2 Jan   Five NVA officers killed near western edge of main perimeter.

Intelligence reports indicate influx of two NVA divisions, and possibly a third, into Khe Sanh TAOR.

16-17 Jan   LtCol Heath's 2/26 transferred to operational control of 26th Marines and arrive KSCB; 2/26 occupies Hill 558 north of base.

ASRT-B of MASS-3 displaces from Chu Lai to Khe Sanh to handle ground controlled radar bombing missions.

17 Jan   Team from Company B, 3d Reconnaissance Battalion ambushed near Hill 881N.

19 Jan   While searching ambush site, patrol from I/3/26 comes under fire from estimated 25 NVA troops and withdraws under cover of supporting arms. Two platoons from M/3/26 helilifted to Hill 881S as reinforcements for I/3/26 which prepares for sweep toward 881N the next day.

20 Jan   Capt Dabney's I/3/26 attacks and, with the aid of air and artillery, badly mauls NVA battalion entrenched on southern slopes of 881N; 7 Marines and 103 North Vietnamese KIA.

On strength of testimony of captured NVA lieutenant that enemy attack is imminent, I/3/26 is withdrawn to 881S and base placed on Red Alert.

DASC of MASS-3 displaces to Khe Sanh.

20-21 Jan   Estimated NVA battalion attacks K/3/26 on Hill 861. After penetrating southwestern portion of Marines' perimeter, the enemy is repulsed leaving 47 dead; NVA reserves are hit by heavy air strikes and artillery fire.

21 Jan	KSCB comes under heavy mortar, artillery, and rocket attack which destroys main ammunition dump. NVA battalion attacks and partially overruns Khe Sanh village before CAC and RF companies drive off enemy. After second attack, Col Lownds withdraws defenders to confines of combat base.
22 Jan	ComUSMACV initiates Operation NIAGARA to provide massive air support for Khe Sanh.
	LtCol Mitchell's 1/9 arrives KSCB and takes up positions which encompass rock quarry southwest of combat base.
	E/2/26 is relocated from Hill 558 to prominent ridge-line northeast of 861 as covering force for flank of 2/26; E/2/26 passes to operational control of 3d Battalion. New position is called 861A.
23-28 Jan	Large number of tribesmen and families are evacuated from Khe Sanh area to avoid hostile fire.
27 Jan	37th ARVN Ranger Battalion arrives KSCB and takes up positions in eastern sector of combat base.
30 Jan	Communists launch nation-wide TET Offensive.
5 Feb	NVA battalion attacks E/2/26 on Hill 861A in concert with heavy shelling of KSCB. Enemy gains foothold in northern sector of Company E perimeter but is driven out by savage counterattack; 109 NVA and 7 Marines KIA.
7 Feb	Special Forces camp at Lang Vei overrun by enemy battalion supported by PT-76 Soviet-built tanks; first use of NVA tanks in South Vietnam.
8 Feb	Some 3,000 indigenous personnel, both military and civilian, from Lang Vei move overland to Khe Sanh. After being searched and processed, several hundred refugees are air evacuated.

8 Feb	A/1/9 combat outpost 500 meters west of 1/9 perimeter hit and partially overrun by reinforced NVA battalion. During three-hour battle, reinforcements drive NVA from Marine position and with aid of supporting arms kill 150 North Vietnamese; Col Lownds decides to abandon outpost and units withdraw to 1/9 perimeter.
10 Feb	Marine C-130 of VMGR-152, hit by enemy fire during approach, crashes after landing at Khe Sanh and six are killed.
Feb-Apr	Paradrops, low-altitude extraction systems, and helicopters are primary means of resupplying 26th Marines due to bad weather and heavy enemy fire.
21 Feb	After heavy mortar and artillery barrage, NVA company probes 37th ARVN Ranger lines but withdraws after distant fire fight. It is estimated that 25-30 NVA were killed.
23 Feb	KSCB receives record number of incoming rounds for a single day--1,307. First appearance of enemy trench system around KSCB.
25 Feb	B/1/26 patrol ambushed south of KSCB; 23 Marines KIA.
29 Feb-1 Mar	Estimated NVA regiment maneuvers to attack 37th ARVN Ranger positions but fail to reach defensive wire.
6 Mar	USAF C-123 shot down east of runway; 43 USMC, 4 USAF, and 1 USN personnel killed.
7 Mar	Large groups of refugees begin to filter into the combat base and are evacuated.
8 Mar	ARVN patrols attack enemy trenchline east of runway and kill 26 North Vietnamese.
15 Mar	American intelligence notes withdrawal of major NVA units from Khe Sanh area.
23 Mar	KSCB receives heaviest saturation of enemy rounds for the month of March--1,109.

24 Mar	A/1/9 patrol kills 31 NVA west of 1/9 perimeter.
25 Mar	1/9 CavSqd, 1st ACD begins reconnaissance in force operations east of Khe Sanh in preparation for Operation PEGASUS.
30 Mar	B/1/26 attacks enemy fortified position south of combat base and kills 115 North Vietnamese; 9 Marines are KIA.
	Operation SCOTLAND I terminates with 1,602 confirmed NVA and 205 Marines KIA; estimates place probable enemy dead between 10,000 and 15,000.
	Task Force KILO launches diversionary attack along Gio Linh coastal plain to divert attention away from Ca Lu where 1st ACD, and 1st Marines are staging for Operation PEGASUS.
1 Apr	Operation PEGASUS begins; 2/1 and 2/3 (1st Marines) attack west from Ca Lu along Route 9. Elements of 3d Bde, 1st ACD conduct helo assaults into LZ Mike and Cates. Joint engineer task force begins repair of Route 9 from Ca Lu to Khe Sanh.
3 Apr	2d Bde, 1st ACD assaults LZs Tom and Wharton.
4 Apr	1/5 CavSqd moves northwest from LZ Wharton and attacks enemy units near old French fort; 1st Battalion, 9th Marines moves southeast from rock quarry and assaults Hill 471.
5 Apr	1/9 repulses enemy counterattack on Hill 471 and kills 122 North Vietnamese.
	1st Bde, 1st ACD departs Ca Lu and assaults LZ Snapper.
6 Apr	One company of 3d ARVN Airborne Task Force airlifted to KSCB for the initial link up with defenders.
	Elements of 2d Bde, 1st ACD relieve 1st Battalion, 9th Marines on Hill 471; 1/9 commences sweep to northwest toward Hill 689.

6 Apr	1st Bde, 1st ACD helilifted north of KSCB. 2/26 and 3/26 push north of combat base; Company G, 2/26 engages enemy force and kills 48 NVA.
8 Apr	2/7 CavSqd links up with 26th Marines and conducts official relief of combat base. 1/26 attacks to the west.
	3d ARVN Airborne Task Force air assaults into LZ Snake west of Khe Sanh and kills 78 North Vietnamese.
10 Apr	LtGen Rosson arrives Khe Sanh and directs LtGen Tolson to disengage and prepare for Operation DELAWARE in A Shau Valley.
11 Apr	Engineers complete renovation of Route 9 and road is officially opened.
	Elements of 1st ACD begin withdrawal to Quang Tri City in preparation for Operation DELAWARE; 37th ARVN Ranger Battalion airlifted to Da Nang.
12 Apr	Col Meyers relieves Col Lownds as CO, 26th Marines.
14 Apr	3/26 attacks Hill 881N and kills 106 NVA; 6 Marines are KIA.
15 Apr	Operation PEGASUS terminated; Operation SCOTLAND II begins.
18 Apr	26th Marines withdrawn to Dong Ha and Camp Carroll.
23 May	President Johnson presents the Presidential Unit Citation to 26th Marines and supporting units during White House ceremony.
23 Jun	Although forward fire support bases are maintained in Khe Sanh area, the KSCB is dismantled and abandoned. LZ Stud at Ca Lu is selected as base for air mobile operations in western DMZ area.

APPENDIX D

TASK ORGANIZATION AT KHE SANH, 24 APRIL - 13 MAY 1967

A. 3D MARINES (-) (REIN)   24APR-13MAY67

    HEADQUARTERS COMPANY   24APR-13MAY67

    2D BATTALION (REIN)   26APR-13MAY67
        HEADQUARTERS AND SERVICE COMPANY(-)(REIN)
            DET, HQBN, 3D MARDIV
            DET, HQCO, 3D MAR
            DET, B BTRY (REIN), 1ST BN, 12TH MAR
            DET, 15TH DENTAL CO
            2D CLEARING PLT (REIN), CO B, 3D MED BN
            1ST PLT (-) (REIN), CO A, 3D ENGR BN
            1ST PLT (REIN), CO C, 3D MT BN
            1ST PLT (-) (REIN), CO C, 3D SP BN
            DET, LSU, FLC

        COMPANY E (REIN)
            1ST SEC, 81MM MORTAR PLT
            FAC TEAM
            DET, MED PLT
            DET, INTELLIGENCE SEC
            DET, B BTRY (REIN), 1/12
            1ST SQD, 1ST PLT (REIN), CO A, 3D ENGR BN
            DET, 1ST PLT (REIN), CO C, 3D SP BN

        COMPANY F (REIN)
            DET, H&S CO
            2D SEC, 81MM MORTAR PLT
            FAC TEAM
            DET, MED PLT
            DET, INTELLIGENCE SEC
            DET, B BTRY (REIN), 1/12
            2D SQD, 1ST PLT (REIN), CO A, 3D ENGR BN
            DET, 1ST PLT (REIN), CO C, 3D SP BN

        COMPANY G (REIN)
            DET, H&S CO
            3D SEC, 81MM MORTAR PLT
            DET, MED PLT
            DET, INTELLIGENCE SEC
            DET, B BTRY (REIN), 1/12

        COMPANY H (REIN)
            DET, H&S CO
            4TH SEC, 81MM MORTAR PLT
            FAC TEAM
            DET, MED PLT
            DET, INTELLIGENCE SEC

```
            DET, B BTRY (REIN), 1/12
            3D SQD, 1ST PLT (REIN), CO A, 3D ENGR BN
            DET, 1ST PLT (REIN), CO C, 3D SP BN

        COMPANY A, 1ST BATTALION, 26TH MARINES        11-13MAY67

        COMPANY B, 1ST BATTALION, 26TH MARINES        11-13MAY67

        COMPANY C, 1ST BATTALION, 26TH MARINES        13 MAY 67

        COMPANY D, 1ST BATTALION, 26TH MARINES        11-13MAY67

        COMPANY E, 2D BATTALION, 9TH MARINES          12-13MAY67

        3D PLT (REIN), CO B, 1ST AMTRAC BN

        2D PLT (REIN), CO A, AT BN

        3D PLT, CO B, 3D RECON BN

        2D PLT (REIN), CO A, 3D TANK BN

        106MM RR PLT

3D BATTALION (-) (REIN)
COMMAND GROUP "A"

        COMPANY K                                     25-27APR67
            FO TEAM, BTRY C, 1/12
            DET, H&S CO
            FO TEAM, 81MM MORTAR PLT
            FAC TEAM (-)
            DET, MED PLT

        COMPANY M                                     27APR-1MAY67
            FO TEAM, BRTY C, 1/12
            FO TEAM, 81MM MORTAR PLT
            SCOUT/DOG TEAM
            SCOUT TEAM, 3/3

        COMPANY B, 1ST BATTALION, 9TH MARINES         25-27APR67

        COMPANY K, 3D BATTALION, 9TH MARINES          25APR-13MAY67

        COMPANY M, 3D BATTALION, 9TH MARINES          29APR-13MAY67

        COMPANY F, 2D BATTALION, 3D MARINES           1MAY-3MAY67

        COMPANY C, 1ST BATTALION, 26TH MARINES        5-13MAY67

        COMPANY A, 1ST BATTALION, 26TH MARINES        12-13MAY67
```

BASE DEFENSE/RESERVE

    COMPANY B, 1ST BATTALION, 9TH MARINES   24-27APR67

    COMPANY F, 2D BATTALION, 3D MARINES   27APR-1MAY67

    COMPANY E, 2D BATTALION, 9TH MARINES   1-12MAY67

    COMPANY C, 1ST BATTALION, 26TH MARINES   4-5MAY67

    1ST BATTALION, 26TH MARINES   12-13MAY67

SUPPORTING UNITS

    DIRECT SUPPORT

        BATTERY F (REIN), 2/12   24APR-13MAY67
        BATTERY B, 1/12   27APR-11MAY67
        BATTERY A, 1/12   13MAY

TASK ORGANIZATION AT KHE SANH, 20 JANUARY - 1 APRIL 1968

A. 26TH MARINES

HEADQUARTERS COMPANY	20JAN-31MAR68
1ST BATTALION	20JAN-31MAR68
2D BATTALION	20JAN-31MAR68
3D BATTALION	20JAN-31MAR68

B. ATTACHED AND SUPPORTING UNITS

(1) U. S. MARINE CORPS

1ST BATTALION, 9TH MARINES (LESS CO "C")	22JAN-31MAR68
CO "C", 1ST BATTALION, 9TH MARINES	23JAN-31MAR68
1ST BATTALION, 13TH MARINES	20JAN-31MAR68
1ST PROV, 155MM HOWITZER BTRY	20JAN-31MAR68
DET, 1ST SEARCHLIGHT BTRY 12TH MARINES	20JAN-31MAR68
DET, 3D ENGINEER BATTALION	20JAN-31MAR68
COMPANY "B", 3D RECON BATTALION	20JAN-31MAR68
3D PLATOON, COMPANY "D", 3D RECON BATTALION	20JAN-31MAR68
1ST PLATOON, COMPANY "A", 5TH RECON BATTALION	20JAN-31MAR68
COMPANY "A" (-) 3D ANTITANK BATTALION (REDESIGNATED ANTITANK COMPANY (-), 3D TANK BATTALION)	20JAN-31MAR68
COMPANY "A", 3D SHORE PARTY BATTALION	24JAN-31MAR68
DET, H&S COMPANY, 3D SHORE PARTY BATTALION	24JAN-31MAR68
2D CLEARING PLATOON, COMPANY "C" 3D MED BATTALION	24JAN-31MAR68

OTTER PLATOON, H&S COMPANY
3D MOTOR TRANSPORT BATTALION   20JAN-31MAR68

DET, COMPANY "B", 9TH MOTOR
TRANSPORT BATTALION   20JAN-31MAR68

DET, COMPANY "A", 9TH MOTOR TRANSPORT
BATTALION   20JAN-31MAR68

DET, SU#1, 1ST RADIO BATTALION   20JAN-31MAR68

DET, 3D DENTAL COMPANY   20JAN-31MAR68

DET, HEADQUARTERS COMPANY, HEAD-
QUARTERS BATTALION, 3D MARINE
DIVISION (POSTAL, PHOTO, EXCHANGE,
ISO, AO'S, STAFF AUGMENT)   20JAN-31MAR68

COMBINED ACTION COMPANY "O"
3D COMBINED ACTION GROUP, III MAF   20JAN-31MAR68

DET, COMM CO, HEADQUARTERS BATTALION,
3D MARINE DIVISION   20JAN-31MAR68

DET, 5TH COMM BATTALION   20JAN-31MAR68

DET, 7TH COMM BATTALION   20JAN-31MAR68

DET, FORCE LOGISTICS COMMAND   20JAN-31MAR68

SUB-TEAM #1, 17TH INTERROGATOR-
TRANSLATOR TEAM   20JAN-31MAR68

COMPANY "B", 3D TANK BATTALION, 3D
MARINE DIVISION   20JAN-31MAR68

DET "01", HEADQUARTERS & MAINTENANCE
SQUADRON, MARINE AIRCRAFT GROUP-16   20JAN-31MAR68

DET "01", MARINE OBSERVATION SQUADRON,
MARINE AIRCRAFT GROUP-16   15MAR-31MAR68

DET "2" MARINE AIR SUPPORT SQUADRON
3, MARINE AIR CONTROL GROUP-18   16JAN-31MAR68

DET, HEADQUARTERS & MAINTENANCE
SQUADRON-36, MARINE AIRCRAFT
GROUP-36   20JAN-31MAR68

DET, MARINE AIR TRAFFIC CONTROL UNIT-62,
MARINE AIRCRAFT GROUP-36   20JAN-31MAR68

(2) U. S. NAVY

DET "B", CONSTRUCTION BATTALION,
MOBILE UNIT-301   20JAN-11FEB68

DET, MOBILE CONSTRUCTION BATTALION-10   20JAN-19FEB68

DET, MOBILE CONSTRUCTION BATTALION-53   20JAN-13FEB68

DET, MOBILE CONSTRUCTION BATTALION-5   20JAN-24JAN68

(3) U. S. ARMY

DET. A-101, 5TH SPECIAL FORCES GROUP   20JAN-31MAR68

DET, 44TH ARTILLERY   20JAN-31MAR68

DET, 65TH ARTILLERY   20JAN-31MAR68

DET, 238TH COUNTER-MORTAR RADAR
UNIT, 108TH FIELD ARTILLERY GROUP   22JAN-31MAR68

DET, 1ST PLATOON (SMOKE), 25TH
CHEMICAL COMPANY   9FEB-31MAR68

544TH SIGNAL DET, 37TH SIGNAL
BATTALION   20JAN-31MAR68

(4) U. S. AIR FORCE

DET, (OPERATING LOCATION AJ), 15TH
AERIAL PORT SQUADRON   20JAN-31MAR68

DET, 366TH TRANSPORT SQUADRON, 366TH
COMBAT SUPPORT GROUP   20JAN-31MAR68

DET, 903D AERO MED EVAC SQDN   20JAN-31MAR68

DET "A", 834TH AIR DIVISION   20JAN-31MAR68

ARMY OF THE REPUBLIC OF SOUTH VIETNAM

37TH ARVN RANGER BATTALION   27JAN- 1APR68

APPENDIX E

COMMAND AND STAFF LIST 3D MARINES, 24 APR - 13 MAY 1967
(Period covered during "The Hill Fights")

3D MARINES

Commanding Officer	Col John P. Lanigan (24Apr67-13May67)
Executive Officer	LtCol Jack Westerman (24Apr67-13May67)
S-1	WO Charles M. Christensen (24Apr67-13May67)
S-2	Capt Adolfo Sgambelluri (24Apr67-7May67) Capt James D. McGowan (8May67-13May67)
S-3	Maj Floyd A. Karker (24Apr67-13May67)
S-4	Maj Howard L. Long (24Apr67-13May67)
Communications Officer	Capt Curtis G. Arnold (24Apr67-1May67) Capt George W. Brooks (2May67-13May67)

2D BATTALION, 3D MARINES

Commanding Officer	LtCol Earl R. DeLong (24Apr67-13May67)
Executive Officer	Maj Wendell O. Beard (24Apr67-13May67)
S-1	2dLt Billy L. Heaton (24Apr67-13May67)
S-2	Capt Robert N. Bogard (24Apr67-13May67)
S-3	Capt Douglas W. Lemon (24Apr67-13May67)
S-4	Capt Robert R. Green (24Apr67-13May67)

Commanding Officer
Headquarters and Service Company   Capt Stuart R. Vaughan
                                     (24Apr67-13May67)

Commanding Officer
Company "E"   Capt Alfred E. Lyon
                                     (24Apr67-3May67)
                                     1stLt John F. Adinolfi
                                     (4May67-12May67)
                                     Capt Alfred E. Lyon
                                     (13May67)

Commanding Officer
Company "F"   Capt Martin Sorensen
                                     (24Apr67-9May67)

Commanding Officer
Company "G"   Capt James P. Sheehan
                                     (24Apr67-13May67)

Commanding Officer
Company "H"   Capt Raymond C. Madonna
                                     (24Apr67-13May67)

3D BATTALION, 3D MARINES

Commanding Officer   LtCol Gary Wilder
                                     (24Apr67-13May67)

Executive Officer   Maj Rudolph S. Sutter
                                     (24Apr67-13May67)

S-1   2dLt John C. Ralph
                                     (24Apr67-11May67

S-2   2dLt Evander R. McIver III
                                     (24Apr67-11May67)
                                     2dLt Michael T. Montgomery
                                     (12May67-13May67)

S-3   Capt Thomas A. Stumpf
                                     (24Apr67-13May67)

S-4   SSgt William T. Pope
                                     (24Apr67-30Apr67)
                                     1stLt John H. Admire
                                     (1May67-13May67)

Commanding Officer
Headquarters and Service Company   Capt Robert W. Poolaw
                                        (24Apr67-13May67)

Commanding Officer
Company "I"   Capt Christian L. Harkness
                                        (24Apr67-13May67)

Commanding Officer
Company "K"   Capt Bayliss L. Spivey, Jr.
                                        (24Apr67-13May67)

Commanding Officer
Company "L"   Capt John W. Ripley
                                        (24Apr67-13May67)

Commanding Officer
Company "M"   Capt William R. Griggs
                                        (24Apr67-13May67)

APPENDIX F

COMMAND AND STAFF LIST 26TH MARINES, 20 JAN - 1 APR 1968
(Period covered in Presidential Unit Citation)

26TH MARINES

Commanding Officer

Col David E. Lownds
(12Aug67-1Apr68)

Executive Officer

LtCol Louis A. Rann
(28Sep67-1Apr68)

S-1

1stLt Robert J. Mariz
(29Jan68-29Jan68)(KIA)
Capt Arnold R. Nelson
(30Jan68-8Feb68)
Capt Anthony V. Latorre, Jr.
(9Feb68-1Apr68)

S-2

Capt Harper L. Bohr, Jr.
(1Aug67-7Feb68)
Maj Jerry E. Hudson
(8Feb68-17Mar68)
Capt Thorvald P. E. Holm
(18Mar68-1Apr68)

S-3

Maj Wayne M. Wills
(1Aug67-22Jan68)
LtCol Edward J. A. Castagna
(23Jan68- 1Apr68)

S-4

Maj Aubrey L. Lumpkin
(17Mar68-1Apr68)

Communications Officer

Maj John A. Shepherd
(16Nov67-1Apr68)

1ST BATTALION, 26TH MARINES

Commanding Officer

LtCol James B. Wilkinson
(5Jul67-29Feb68)
LtCol Frederick J. McEwan
(1Mar68-1Apr68)

Executive Officer

Maj Charles E. Davis III
(23Dec67-31Jan68)
Maj Howard J. McCarty
(1Feb68-1Apr68)

S-1	1stLt Stephen A. Fitzgerald (13Dec67-31Jan68)
	1stLt William J. Ferral (1Feb68-1Apr68)
S-2	1stLt Anthony E. Sibley (6Dec67-13Feb68)
	1stLt Ernest E. Spencer (14Feb68-1Apr68)
S-3	Maj Bruce A. Greene (23Dec67-29Jan68)
	Maj Charles E. Davis III (30Jan68-1Apr68)
S-4	Capt Robert C. Onslow (6Nov67-1Apr68)
Commanding Officer Headquarters and Service Company	1stLt Robert A. Brown (20Dec67-16Feb68)
	1stLt Paul G. Lojkovic (17Feb68-20Mar68)
	Capt Lajon R. Hutton (21Mar68-1Apr68)
Commanding Officer Company "A"	Capt Ray G. Snyder (15Dec67-1Apr68)
Commanding Officer Company "B"	Capt Kenneth W. Pipes (20Dec67-1Apr68)
Commanding Officer Company "C"	Capt David L. Ernst (15Jan68-15Feb68)
	2dLt Paul W. Bush (16Feb68-2Mar68)
	Capt Walter J. Egger (3Mar68-22Mar68
	Capt Lawrence E. Seaman, Jr. (23Mar68-1Apr68)
Commanding Officer Company "D"	1stLt Ernest E. Spencer (1Aug67-13Feb68)
	Capt Edward J. Hughes, Jr. (14Feb68-1Apr68)

2D BATTALION, 26TH MARINES

Commanding Officer	LtCol Francis J. Heath, Jr. (Jan68-1Apr68)
Executive Officer	Maj Royce L. Bond (Jan68-1Apr68)
S-1	1stLt Richard J. Gustafson (16Jan-1Apr68)
S-2	1stLt Edwin R. Matthews (Jan68-11Feb68) SSgt Horace E. Roland (12Feb68-9Mar68) 1stLt John C. Wainio (10Mar68-1Apr68)
S-3	Maj Gerald F. Kurth (Jan68-1Apr68)
S-4	Capt Erwin J. Martikke, Jr. (Jan68-18Mar68) Capt Earle G. Breeding, Jr. (19Mar68-1Apr68)
Commanding Officer Headquarters and Service Company	Capt Stanley M. Hartman (Jan68-1Apr68)
Commanding Officer Company "E"	Capt Earle G. Breeding Jr. (Jan68-8Mar68) 1stLt Joseph R. Meeks (9Mar68-1Apr68)
Commanding Officer Company "F"	Capt Charles F. Divelbiss (Jan68-1Apr68)
Commanding Officer Company "G"	Capt Lee R. Overstreet (Jan68-1Apr68)
Commanding Officer Company "H"	Capt Charles O. Broughton (Jan68-1Apr68)

3D BATTALION, 26TH MARINES

Commanding Officer	LtCol Harry L. Alderman (21Aug67-14Mar68)

	LtCol John C. Studt (15Mar68-1Apr68)
Executive Officer	Maj Joseph M. Loughran, Jr. (9Sep67-1Apr68)
S-1	1stLt Edward J. Paurazas Jr. (21Dec67-1Apr68)
S-2	2dLt Jay G. Marks, Jr. (14Jan68-1Apr68)
S-3	Maj Matthew P. Caulfield (24Nov67-1Apr68)
S-4	1stLt Jack A. Brage (16Nov67-1Apr68)
Commanding Officer Headquarters and Service Company	Capt Alfred Lardizabal, Jr. (29Nov67-1Apr68)
Commanding Officer Company "I"	Capt William H. Dabney (24Nov67-1Apr68)
Commanding Officer Company "K"	Capt Norman J. Jasper, Jr. (23Nov67-22Jan68) 1stLt Jerry Saulsbury (23Jan68-27Jan68) Capt Paul L. Snead (28Jan68-1Apr68)
Commanding Officer Company "L"	Capt Richard D. Camp, Jr. (30Jun67-29Jan68) Capt William F. Hurley (30Jan68-1Apr68)
Commanding Officer Company "M"	Capt John J. Gilece, Jr. (29Nov67-31Jan68) 1stLt John T. Esslinger (1Feb68-23Mar68) Capt Walter R. Jenkins (24Mar68-1Apr68)

1ST BATTALION, 9TH MARINES

Commanding Officer	LtCol John F. Mitchell (1Jan68-31Mar68) LtCol John J. H. Cahill (1Apr68)
Executive Officer	Maj Joseph A. Donnelly (1Jan68-1Apr68)
S-1	1stLt Peter A. Woog (1Jan68-1Apr68)
S-2	1stLt Robert J. Arboleda (1Jan68-1Apr68)
S-3	Maj Edward M. Ringley (1Jan68-16Feb68) Capt Charles B. Hartzell (17Feb68-10Mar68) Maj Ted R. Henderson (11Mar68-1Apr68)
S-4	1stLt John M. Georgi (1Jan68-1Apr68)
Commanding Officer Headquarters and Service Company	1stLt Michael J. Walker (9Jan68-13Feb68) Capt John W. Cargile (14Feb68-31Mar68) Capt Edward R. Miller, Jr. (1Apr68)
Commanding Officer Company "A"	Capt Henry J. M. Radcliffe (1Jan68-31Mar68) Capt Henry D. Banks (1Apr68)
Commanding Officer Company "B"	Capt Robert T. Bruner (1Jan68-26Jan68) 1stLt Arthur N. Mangham, Jr. (27Jan68-2Feb68) Capt John R. Williams, Jr. (3Feb68-1Apr68)
Commanding Officer Company "C"	Capt John W. Cargile (9Jan68-13Feb68) Capt Ralph H. Flagler (14Feb68-1Apr68)

| Commanding Officer Company "D" | Capt Don F. Schafer (1Jan68-31Mar68) |
| | Capt John W. Cargile (1Apr68) |

1ST BATTALION, 13TH MARINES

Commanding Officer	LtCol John A. Hennelly (10Dec67-1Apr68)
Executive Officer	Maj Ronald W. Campbell (13Jul67-1Apr68)
S-1	2dLt Daniel W. Kelly (19Nov67-1Apr68)
S-2	1stLt Walter K. Jones (21Dec67-4Mar68)
	1stLt Leslie M. Palm (5Mar68-1Apr68)
S-3	Capt Lawrence R. Salmon (13Jul67-8Mar68)
	Maj Gerald R. Houchin (9Mar68-1Apr68)
S-4	1stLt Harold P. Klunk (1Dec67-20Feb68)
	Capt Tommy J. Hicks (21Feb68-1Apr68)
Commanding Officer Headquarters Battery	1stLt Ralph W. Dunn, Jr. (2Aug67-20Feb68)
	1stLt Walter K. Jones (21Feb68-15Mar68)
	Capt Jerome P. Rogers (16Mar68-21Mar68)
	1stLt Jacob W. Hughes, Jr. (22Mar68-1Apr68)
Commanding Officer Battery "A"	Capt Dennis L. Pardee (Aug67-29Feb68)
	Capt Victor B. Snider (1Mar68-1Apr68)
Commanding Officer Battery "B"	1stLt George G. Wood (21Jan68-29Feb68)
	Capt James C. Uecker (1Mar68-1Apr68)

Commanding Officer
Battery "C"

Capt William J. O'Connor
(28Nov67-1Apr68)

Commanding Officer
Mortar Battery

Capt Michael T. Pierson
(5Jan68-1Apr68)

Commanding Officer
1st Provisional 155
Howitzer Battery, 3/12

Capt Joseph Taylor
(5Jan68-29Feb68)
Capt Stephen J. Hayes
(1Mar68-1Apr68)

ATTACHED UNITS

Commanding Officer
Company "A", 3d AT Battalion

Capt James O. Lea
(20Jan68-1Apr68)

Commanding Officer
Company "B", 3d Tank Battalion

Capt Daniel W. Kent
(-24Jan68)
Capt Claude W. Reinke
(25Jan68-1Apr68)

Commanding Officer
Company "A", 3d Shore Party
Battalion

1stLt Robert L. Singleton
(28Jan68-4Mar68)
Maj Howard W. Wahlfeld
(5Mar68-1Apr68)

UNIT SIZE

● ● ●	PLATOON
I	COMPANY
II	BATTALION
III	REGIMENT
X	BRIGADE

UNIT SYMBOLS

▢ USMC	USMC UNIT (WHEN UNITS OF OTHER SERVICES SHOWN)
⊠	INFANTRY
⊓	ENGINEER / PIONEER
symbol	AIR CAVALRY CP
symbol	AIR CAVALRY

EXAMPLES

3 ⊠ 26 / USMC   3d BATTALION, 26th MARINES

II ⊓ FMF / USMC   11th ENGINEER BATTALION, FLEET MARINE FORCE

3 symbol 1 ACD   3d BRIGADE, 1st AIR CAVALRY DIVISION

1 symbol 7   1st SQUADRON, 7th CAVALRY

APPENDIX G

☆ U.S. GOVERNMENT PRINTING OFFICE : 1977 O—246-661

The device reproduced on the back cover is the oldest military
insignia in continuous use in the United States. It first
appeared, as shown here, on Marine Corps buttons adopted in
1804. With the stars changed to five points, this device has
continued on Marine buttons to the present day.

www.ingramcontent.com/pod-product-compliance
Lightning Source LLC
Chambersburg PA
CBHW080501110426
42742CB00017B/2958

* 9 7 8 1 7 8 0 3 9 6 3 0 9 *